a gun
in my gucci

---

e.c. smith
Special Agent F. B. I. Ret.

Carolyna
& Salso
Good reading,
I hope!

LSI Publishing

ISBN-13: 978-1497347120

ISBN-10: 1497347122

Dedicated to my husband, Tom.
His encouragement, trust and love made my fulfilling career in the FBI possible.

- CONTENTS -

Personal Reflections

For three reasons, it is a genuine privilege to be asked to write the prologue for this splendid telling of a great story about a unique pair of characters, trailblazing FBI Special Agent Elaine Corbitt Smith and mob gambling operator and mob hit survivor Ken Eto.

First, Elaine and her husband T.D. Smith are longtime colleagues and dear family friends. A real-life version of the old TV series "McMillan & Wife," they are a storybook couple. For her part, Elaine is a force of nature. Dedicated, feisty, and an absolute ball of energy, in ever so many ways she turned J. Edgar Hoover's Bureau on its head. This book is reflective of an important job very well done by a beautiful and strong-willed lady who dedicated herself to getting the job done.

Second, Tokyo Joe was a very special person in my 11-year life as an Assistant U.S. Attorney (AUSA). A radio call from the FBI on February 10, 1983, summoned me to join FBI Special Agent in Charge Ed Hegarty at Ken Eto's hospital bedside. A personal bond sealed with drops of Ken's blood on my hands and on my badge began that night at Chicago's Northwest Community Hospital and continued until his death in 2004.

Third, it gives me an opportunity to reflect upon the most important and most successful mission in Elaine's life.

As Elaine recounts, on September 21, 1981, her beloved husband and FBI Principal Firearms Instructor T.D. Smith was critically shot in a training accident at the Bureau's firearms range at the Great Lakes Naval Base. Initially stabilized, T.D. developed a severe infection, and his prognosis for survival was getting bleaker and bleaker. Unwilling to simply sit at her Tommy's bedside and hope for the best, Elaine was Elaine at her finest. Using relationships, connections, and her indomitable fighting spirit, she enlisted the personal attention of one of the nation's most revered surgeons, Dr. George E. Block. Referred to in later years by his University of Chicago

Hospital colleagues as the "General Schwarzkopf of Surgery," Dr. Block agreed to try to save the gravely ill Special Agent Smith. While the doctors and administrators at the Great Lakes Naval Hospital were none too pleased to be second-guessed, it would have taken the intervention of Seal Team Six to keep Elaine from escorting T.D. to the critical care ambulance bound for Dr. Block's OR. Simply put, Elaine and Dr. George E. Block saved T.D.'s life. Elaine's tenacity and drive mark both her personal and her Bureau lives.

Prologue

This book tells a singular story. Two people coming from worlds light years apart — the Chicago Mob and the FBI — see their lives become deeply intertwined. That, one might say, happens with some frequency. Law enforcement officers and former defendants turned witnesses often develop special bonds and close personal relationships. It happened with me and Freddie Mendez, a former FALN member (Fuerzas Armadas de Liberación Nacional Puertorriqueña or Armed Forces of Puerto Rican National Liberation) who I convinced to defect and who ultimately rendered lifesaving service to the multi-agency Chicago Terrorist Task Force (a.k.a. "Wonderful World Police," my beloved organization to which Elaine gives very well-deserved honorable mention).

What is truly unique here, however, is that the protagonists in this story – the FBI's Elaine Smith and the Mob's Tokyo Joe, were mold-breakers in their respective organizations. Far beyond being just another gender-barrier buster, Elaine was positively cyclonic. Beautiful, brash, opinionated, and relentless, Elaine was an agent like no other. I have been driven to many protected witness interviews by FBI agents armed with a Smith & Wesson .357 combat magnum, but never before or since by one in a spotless black Lincoln Town Car wearing a tailored suede jogging suit, a full-length mink coat, and hair, makeup, and nails worthy of the cover of Vogue magazine. One could never be lulled into forgetting the steel that lay beneath the style, however. When Elaine would sternly say to me "OK, Margolis, cut the stories and crap, let's get to work," she meant it. I always said, "OK, Elaine."

Even more of a fish out of water was Tokyo Joe! A Japanese American who lived for years in a (shameful) World War II internment camp becoming a gambling boss specializing in *bolita* for Chicago's Sicilian-dominated Outfit. No one in central casting would ever have imagined the merger of the Mob code of *omertà* and the Japanese warrior code of *Bushido*.

And so truth is really stranger than fiction. Elaine builds a gambling case no one else would touch. The charmed life of the guy called "Joe the Jap" by his Mob cohorts ends with a syndicated gambling conviction. Mob boss Vince Solano foolishly fears that "Joe the Jap" will cut a deal and talk like Joe Valachi, when in fact Eto's ironclad will and adherence to his Japanese warrior code would have had him steadfastly serving his time in stony silence. A Mob assassin (and Cook County Deputy Sheriff) fires three rounds at point-blank range, but fires at exactly the angles that allow for superficial entry and exit flesh wounds with no penetration of the skull. An amazing relationship between two amazing people is about to unfold. There is an often-used phrase for which this story is the paradigm:

"You can't make this s**t up."

Elaine, as a former AUSA, I commend you for your extraordinary service with the Bureau. As your and T.D.'s buddy, I thank you for your many years of true friendship. Finally, as one friend of Tokyo Joe's to another, I'm proud to say to you, "Great job!"

With much respect, admiration, and affection,
Jeremy Margolis

e. c. smith

- CHAPTER ONE -
Dinner and Death

"Hey, Joe. The boss wants to see you tonight." A friendly goombah dinner invitation from the boss is usually welcome. But not when your boss is Chicago crime syndicate capo Vince Solano. And definitely not when his back is against the wall and your ass is on the line. Notwithstanding the deadly implications of the request, Ken Eto, a.k.a. "Tokyo Joe," agreed to meet his boss at a restaurant on the far west side of Chicago. In reality, Solano's invitation was a death warrant. To ensure Eto's attendance at "dinner," he was sending a couple of his boys, John Gattuso and Jasper Campise, to escort Tokyo Joe to the restaurant. They were also the authorized executioners. This termination process was almost ritualistic. The actors all knew their parts in this Mafioso "passion play." While John and Jasper were preparing their weapons and ammunition, the accused was laying out his best suit. Tokyo Joe Eto, the star of this drama, dressed for the part — he knew he was destined to die that cold day in early February 1983. He knew it was a setup. He knew he had screwed up.

Earlier, the Feds had arrested him. The FBI knew the details of his gambling operations. He was destined for prison. Soon they would attempt to break him — offer him a reduced sentence for information. Would he rat on his brothers in crime? Joe knew he would never talk. He would take the heat and do the time. But his boss couldn't trust him. Joe wasn't a "made man." He wasn't even an Italian American. He was a Japanese American and proud of his status as the highest-ranking Asian American in the organization. If he had to die, he would die as a warrior. On his way out of the house, he told his wife where he kept the life insurance policy and then kissed her goodbye. Outside, he sat in his car with the windows open. The cold night air tightened his muscles and helped to focus his mind. The engine remained off. No radio. No sounds other than that of his rapidly beating 64-year-old heart. For 20 minutes, he didn't move. His last day had arrived. He rejected random thoughts of escape. He was an honorable man. He had never dishonored his associates. He would not do so now. Sure, they had trusted him to run his *bolita* rackets, (and multiple other gambling operations that had made the mob millions of dollars over 40 years) but that was something they could control. They watched the money very carefully and Tokyo Joe never tried to screw them. He was loyal to his Outfit bosses, but that meant nothing now. He knew too much. Murder, vice, corruption — the Chicago organized crime syndicate spiderweb of mobsters, gunmen, politicians, cops, lawyers, and judges could not be exposed. Joe had to go. There was nothing else. And Joe knew it. Finally, finding a place of peace in his mind, he turned the key in the ignition and drove to face his executioners. He had accepted his fate.

He was told to pick up two middle-aged mobsters, John Gattuso and Jasper "Jay" Campise, at a "social club" located on the northwest side of Chicago. These "social clubs" were unofficial mob hangouts and were usually storefronts disguised as a VFW Halls or an Italian American Clubs. Joe drove them to the restaurant. Campise sat next to Joe in the front passenger seat; Gattuso sat in the backseat behind Eto — a seating arrangement that was fortuitous for Joe. He didn't participate in the nervous conversation of the killers. They babbled on about the great selection of Italian dishes offered at their upcoming dinner — about Vince Solano having a glass of Chianti waiting for his guests to arrive — about the shitty Chicago winter weather — about the younger generation's lack of respect for the older members of the tribe. It was all small talk bullshit. It passed the time as Joe slowly drove the death car to its destination. He didn't hear their words. He didn't care.

It was early evening when Campise told Joe to turn into a parking lot behind a shuttered movie theater and adjacent to railroad tracks. Darkness had fallen. Campise told Joe to park the car into an isolated parking spot. In front of them, caught in the headlights, icy crosses of barren trees swayed in the whistling wind while sleet tap-danced on the hood like a flurry of frozen maggots. Joe killed the lights and shut off the ignition. Inside, the car was warm and stuffy. It smelled of nervous sweat and stale cigarette smoke. The killers' rapid breathing filled the silence. Joe remained wordless as he had for the entire ride. He sat in a trance, staring at his doorway of death. He had relinquished his body and mind of the illusion of life. He became the cold, moonless night.

Seconds passed. Gattuso fired his gun. Detached, almost as if a spectator, Joe heard and felt the impact of the first shot. He fell forward against the steering wheel. Then he felt the second shot. But he realized he was still alive. He couldn't believe it. He thought he better slide his body to the right down on the seat and get out of the way of another bullet. He heard Campise open his door. Gattuso fired again at point-blank range. Joe took another bullet in his skull. And then he faked his death. He purposely leaned down onto the seat, his hands outstretched and limp. For effect, he intentionally quivered like a dying chicken. The killers exited the car and quickly viewed the execution scene. Blood was spattered all over the driver's seat and windshield. Tokyo Joe's body lay motionless on the front seat. The hit was done. They slammed the car doors and ran away into the night.

Minutes passed. Joe heard their footsteps as they ran away from the car. But he remained still and waited until he sensed it was safe to raise his head. They were gone and he slowly opened his eyes. He could see. His head ached and blood dripped down his forehead. Time held still for the moment. Joe was mystified. Had he moved on to the next world or was he alive? His battered brain debated the situation. And then he summoned every fiber and cell in his body and commanded them to get moving — to get out of the car — to get help — to live. He was alive. Three bullets fired into his head at point-blank range had not killed him. He was a new man, reborn, owing nothing to anyone. They had failed, and he was free. The passion play was over.

He crawled out of the car and stumbled across the frozen parking lot. He fell, righted himself, and moved slowly forward toward the lights. The pain was intense. His legs barely accepted the task of walking. Damaged neurons fired aimlessly within his crippled brain. Stumbling along, he reached the street. A neon sign hanging in the drug store window ironically beckoned: *Terminal Pharmacy.* He banged into the door and summoned all his life force to open it. It sprung free. Inside and now unable to hear because of the noise of the gunshots, he searched for help. An older man wearing a white smock stood behind a counter. A few more steps and he was face to face with the pharmacist. Blood and melting snow dripped off his head onto the floor and the counter.

"Please…please call 911." Eto's voice was ragged. He held his hand to his head and blood filled the spaces between his fingers.

Stunned by the intrusion, the pharmacist studied the wounded man quizzically.

Eto remained steady. "Call 911. Shot in the head…" his voice trailed off. He lowered his head.

Now grasping the situation, the man made the call to 911.

Eto strained to hear the conversation, but he could only see his savior's lips moving.

The operator's voice droned: "What is the nature of your emergency?"

"A man has been shot in the head. He's standing before me. He needs an ambulance. He needs to go to an emergency room." The pharmacist was calm and professional.

"This man. Are you certain he has been shot?" replied the 911 operator.

"Yes. Yes. He's got blood all over him. His head is very bloody."

"Hold on," said the operator. The call went dead.

Twenty seconds later the operator reconnected. "Are you certain he has been shot in the head?"

"Yes. Yes. He's bleeding profusely."

"All right. Is he with you now?"

"Yes."

"Let me talk to him."

The man handed the phone to Eto. Eto gazed at the phone as if it was an unknown object. Slowly he raised it to his head. His world was a madness of ringing sounds and nothing else.

"Hello. When were you shot, sir?" the operator asked flatly. A pause. "Sir. When were you shot?"

Eto heard nothing. "What? Can't hear. Shot in head." Eto waited. "What?"

"Can you hear me?"

Eto remained quiet.

The man grabbed the phone. His face was red. His voice was loud. "Listen. I'm a pharmacist. This man has been shot. Send the damn ambulance."

After a long pause, "All right. We're sending one out now."

The pharmacist slammed the handset into the cradle. "Asshole," he said.

Eto looked at him. "What?"

The man in the white coat simply gave him a thumbs-up.

It took a moment for Eto to recognize the signal. Then he said, "Thank you." His voice was quiet, but clear. It carried the authority of a man who would not die — a survivor — a walking miracle. He was at peace again, but this time in the world of the living. A small knowing smile crept onto Ken "Tokyo Joe" Eto's bloodied face. He waited patiently for his ambulance. It was his turn now.

*　　*　　*

The phone rang, breaking the silence of the night. Deep in sleep and startled, my fingers searched for the handset. I grabbed it and shoved it between my head and the pillow.

"Elaine?"

I floated in the twilight zone between sleep and reality, but I recognized the voice of my FBI boss, Bill Brown. Slowly the words made it out of my mouth, "You know I'm on vacation in Vail…"

The excited voice sputtered, "Ken Eto's been fuckin' shot."

I took a moment to digest the words. I shook my head to clear it. "What happened?"

"Shot in the head. Point blank. Three times. Listen, Elaine. He'll only talk to you — nobody else in the Bureau."

Now I was awake and thinking. If Eto lives, he's going to talk. He's going to talk to me and me alone. This was fantastic.

"Are you there?"

In my excitement, I almost shouted. "I'm flying back tomorrow, Bill. He's all mine!"

"No, Elaine, we'll take care of things for now. Joe is yours when you get back."

I hung up the phone and sunk into the pillow again, thinking about the future and the past. This was the beginning of my new relationship with Ken Eto, the notorious Chicago gangster. No longer adversaries, Mr. Eto and I would be partners now. Destiny and the botched hit had brought us together. We each found our way through life to this nexus — Joe Eto, the unlikely Chicago mobster, and Elaine Smith, the unlikely FBI special agent.

I was not always a crime-fighter. Growing up in Chicago, one would have to have been deaf, dumb, and half-dead not to realize "That Toddling Town" was run by crooked politicians, that cops could be bribed, and that city workers were lazy and in on the scam. In fact, it hasn't much changed, other than the corrupt politicians basically run the city now. When I was a kid, the gasbag pols were all puppets of the Mob, the Outfit, *La Cosa Nostra*, the wise guys — whatever nomenclature one wanted to use, they were all the same.

Chicago in the 1950s and 1960s was a far different place than it is today. The only thing that remains the same today is the horrible, stinking weather. Chicago weather was cold, windy, and always disappointing, no matter what the season. The winters were cloudy, snowy, and never-ending. Just when spring should logically be on its way, a snowstorm would dump 20 inches, even if the date on the calendar was April 1.

The "Windy City" was a city that conventioneers would come to, but really, no one brought their wives. What would the ladies do? Tourism was minimal in those years. Conventioneers gambled, whored around, and spent drunken nights in the clip joints that the Chicago Mob ran. Nevertheless, there were a few nightlife exceptions that offered great entertainment, such as the London House, Chez Paree, and Mister Kelly's. Even though I soon learned they were also controlled by the mob, I still wanted to go to them. These nightclubs had expensive minimum drink rules, sometimes a cover charge, and every weekend, Las Vegas-type headliners like Lena Horne, Nancy Wilson, and the Ramsey Lewis Trio entertained. I loved reading about and seeing the local nightclub area known as Rush Street. As soon as I was old enough to wear a bra, I attempted to get into the bars.

After my junior prom, I went to the London House, and my date, remarkably, was my future husband. The waitress arrived to take drink orders. Obviously I had no drinking expertise, but I wanted to appear knowledgeable. I asked Tom to get me a "sloe gin fizz" as if I knew what that was. Tom bravely told the waitress I wanted a "slow gin fizzy." Mortified by his lack of sophistication and that he had called the drink "fizzy," I thought: We're going to be thrown out of here on our 17-year-old asses.

Little should I have worried, because the London House was located in the 18th Chicago Police District, notorious for its ability to flatly ignore all City of Chicago or State of Illinois laws. A slow gin fizzy costing $20.00 would be served to anyone willing to pay for it. A beat cop working in the 18th District was on a gravy train. It was the home of the Mob's north side crew. They made sure the District Commander got his weekly envelope and instructed him to overlook everything. If the Outfit murdered someone, the Chicago Police in the 18th District would ignore or screw up any evidence pointing to the perpetrator.

When I was a toddler growing up in Chicago, Joe was already working for the Outfit in the same Rush Street area He organized and held card games in which thousands of dollars were floating on the tables. The young punks who provided the muscle for his games grew up to be street bosses, killing their way up the Mob corporate ladder. By the time I was trying to fill out my first bras, Joe was already a debonair, flashy, handsome man. He was something of an exotic — an Asian man who stood out in the company of the Italian thugs. He was much more subtle in the way he spoke, in the way he looked at people, and in the way he carried his muscled, no-fat body. Joe Eto was one smooth gentleman.

Most Chicagoans were unaffected by the corruption of the police department. Fighting vice appeared to be an impossible battle. It was business as usual for "The City That Works" since before Al "Scarface" Capone and prohibition. Then, from 1956 to 1958, Chicago awakened to the kidnappings and murders of young teens. No newspaper carried the headline, "Murders Rob City of Its Innocence," but it happened. Along the way, my innocence was stolen as well.

February 12, 1958, Abraham Lincoln's birthday, was a Monday holiday for Chicago schoolchildren. I was 12 years old. I had been allowed to go to a holiday matinee to see the movie "The Blob." I actually couldn't have cared less what I saw; just going to a movie with my girlfriend Mary Ann was pretty exciting stuff. As city kids, we walked or took the bus or subway everywhere we went. Our mothers didn't drive, and it wouldn't have helped them much if they had because no one owned more than one car, and that one car was how our fathers got to work.

On that day, I walked four blocks to Mary Ann's house and together she and I walked an additional four blocks to the movie theater. We spent the afternoon eating hot buttered popcorn and alternately laughing hysterically at or being terrified by "The Blob," a gooey red substance that relentlessly engulfed one American city after another. Afterward, Mary Ann and I walked home laughing and goofing around. We reached her house, and she ran inside while I continued to walk on to mine.

By then it was about 5 p.m., dark and cold, and I knew I'd better hurry home. I walked past my elementary school. It stood empty and dark on this holiday evening. No one else was walking down the street. I was a 12-year-old girl, alone in the night. I noticed a car that kept driving by very slowly. In my inexperienced, naive way, I knew something didn't feel right. The car circled the block one more time and then pulled next to the curb exactly where I was walking. The driver leaned over and rolled down the passenger side window. "Come here," he said. I was convinced this was danger that I had never seen or experienced before. Panic and fear gripped my mind. I didn't think to scream.

When the man parked, got out, and started jogging around the front of his car toward me, I reacted. I have no recollection of my brain beginning to function with a plan, but I dashed off the sidewalk into the street behind his car, ran across the street, and miraculously found myself steps away from a mom-and-pop grocery store.

I ran into the store. Although all the lights were on, no one was visible. A cotton curtain separated the owner's apartment from the store. I ran to this curtain and called into it, "Please help me. Some man is trying to get me."

The female owner, a large, gypsy-looking woman, drew the curtain aside and said, "Come. Step in here." Peeking from behind the curtain, I saw her waddle to the door, lock it, and come back to me.

"May I use your phone to call my father?"

"Oh, yes," she replied.

I was weak with gratitude and dialed my number, Spring 7-0656.

After a couple of rings I heard my father's voice answer: "Hello."

Still shaking, I sobbed, "Daddy, will you come and get me? Some man just tried to grab me and pull me into his car."

"Where are you?"

By the tone of his voice, I immediately thought, I'll die here in this store if he says he won't come to pick me up. In those days, parents didn't just jump at each and every request their child presented. "I'm at the little store across from school."

"I'll be there," he said as he hung up.

"Thank you so much," I said as I turned to the store owner. "May I stay here until my father comes to get me?"

"Certainly," she said, smiling.

I waited at the front window of the store, hiding behind some signs, straining to catch a glimpse of my father's 1957 four-door Chevy Impala. In less than five minutes he arrived.

The store owner unlocked the door, and I flew out of the store and into the passenger seat. My father didn't look pleased to see me, just a little concerned. I don't remember what I told him, what words I used, or if I cried. I do remember there was no hug, no comforting; he mechanically pulled away from the curb and started to drive home.

In the safety of my dad's car, I looked out the side window. I know we passed the bakery he would go to almost every morning to get us fresh bread and sweet rolls. I also remember exactly what he told me on this ride home. "Your mother is in the hospital recovering from gall bladder surgery."

Oops. In my joy of being able to go to the movie and my fear of almost being abducted, I had forgotten this little detail.

"She doesn't need to worry about this, so we won't tell her or talk about it again." He glanced at me for confirmation, and I nodded.

Years later, I learned that the victims of crimes often think they have done something wrong and try to hide what happened to them. On that school holiday in February 1958, I must have felt ashamed and guilty that this man had tried to grab me. My father asked me to "bury this experience, forget it," and I complied.

As terrified as I had been, I never told my mother. In fact, I never talked about it again until I told my husband. And then I was safely in his arms and he understood my terror. He recalled the caution he took as a youth when walking the streets of Chicago. In 1957, Judith Mae Andersen's 15-year-old body had been cut into pieces, placed in two separate oil drums and set adrift in Lake Michigan's Montrose Harbor. The harbor was just a few miles east of my home. And there were the Schuessler-Peterson murders. Two years before the Andersen girl was found murdered, the brutalized bodies of the Schuessler brothers and their friend had been found in a forest preserve about five miles west of my home.

These murders shocked the citizens of Chicago. They also removed children's sense of freedom as they walked in their neighborhoods, or when they rode buses and subways to go to the beach, shop, or visit relatives. It might have been the murderer of Judith Mae Andersen who tried to grab me that night. If so, I was to be his next victim.

Until college, I never walked in the dark by myself again. As a young teenager, I also arranged my life so that I was never alone while walking. I begged my neighborhood friends to go with me wherever I wanted to go. I asked my father to drive me places and pick me up. I yearned to be old enough to get my driver's license.

Because of my nervousness and fear, I learned to recognize the makes, models, and years of cars. I could memorize license plate numbers in an instant. It was a mental game I played as I walked about Chicago as a youth and into adulthood. Without knowing it, as a young girl, I was, in a way, preparing myself to be an FBI agent. Later, when I had become an agent and while on surveillances, I would astonish my squad mates with my instant recognition of vehicles and recall of license plates.

Like me, youthful circumstances led Joe Eto to his life's work. He was a child of the Great Depression living in California. He hated and rebelled against his father, who was a strong disciplinarian and a religious zealot. At the age of 14, Eto escaped from the confinement of his father's iron hand by "riding the rails" beneath a boxcar of a railroad train heading north. He got a job in the orchards picking fruit. Joe was a rebel and an adventurer. At an early age, he became his own man. Self-taught, he learned the ways of the street to survive and to succeed.

At night, after a long day of backbreaking work, the fruit pickers would play cards and other games of chance for relaxation and the opportunity to win, or lose, some money. More than just a diversion for Joe, he watched the men carefully, and he learned the rules and tricks of the games in order to become a skilled gambler. He watched the players intently, studying their actions and attempting to read their minds. By his mid-teens, he was a good judge of people. And he became a card shark. He traveled along the West Coast, from California to Seattle, gambling for a living. In 1942, he was placed in a government internment camp. Like thousands of other Japanese-American citizens, he had no choice but to spend the war in confinement. But after the war he was freed, and he traveled to Chicago to exploit his talents working within the organized crime community.

Thus, I understood that at early ages, both of us had developed skills useful to our later life's work. Joe went on to work on one side of the mean streets of Chicago, and later I worked on the other. After his vagabond teenage years, he refined his skills as a quick study, an excellent judge of people, an organizer, and someone willing and able to work within a rigid system to succeed — in his case, the Outfit. I, too, became adept at working within a rigid system, organizing, and understanding people. But I chose to work and succeed within the Federal Bureau of Investigation.

- CHAPTER TWO -
A New Career

Some big ideas pop into existence complete and operational like the birth of a baby horse, and others grow slowly over time like an oak tree in a dark forest. For me, the goal to become a special agent evolved slowly. It started as a thought, and then a wish, then moved to a desire, and ultimately became an obsession.

One hot July day in 1977 I played tennis with my friend JoAnn. After the game, we rested on a courtside bench. The sun blazed overhead. I was winded. Sweat poured down my forehead, even soaking through my white terry-cloth visor. I wore a white sleeveless knit top and a short, tightly pleated tennis skirt. Ignoring my beet-red face and my heaving chest, I fit in perfectly at the private lakefront tennis club in the pricey Chicago neighborhood of Lincoln Park.

"Elaine, you are disgustingly out of shape," said JoAnn.

I was shocked. Me, out of shape? I thought. I am thin as a rail and have great legs, and she calls me out of shape! I didn't immediately reply because I began to busy myself extracting a Virginia Slim cigarette out of my tortoise-shell cigarette case. I lit the cigarette with my thin silver lighter and took a drag.

She didn't stop with her comments. "You can't even play two sets of tennis without becoming a worthless wimp shit."

As much as I wanted to fight her comments and say, "Who do you think you are?" I realized she was right. Up until then, I hadn't thought much about whether I was in good condition or not. Shit, I was thin, wasn't that all that mattered?

Reluctantly, and knowing she was right, I grudgingly conceded, "Yeah, I guess you've got a point."

We put our rackets in our bags, went to the court reservation desk and signed out.

During our walk to JoAnn's brownstone apartment, I was a little pissed, but I quickly put it out of my mind as we talked about our children, jobs, husbands, and cool places to eat and shop.

JoAnn had married Marshall, who was a CPA, in addition to being an attorney. He was beginning to make his way into the world of big-money tax shelter deals. It was through JoAnn's exposure to the world of money that I was learning about vacations in St. Maarten, shopping at Neiman Marcus, and dining at all the hot-shit "in" Chicago restaurants and private dining clubs.

Her comment about my lack of physical conditioning gnawed at my brain. My husband Tom could run a six-minute mile. I didn't think I had even *walked* a mile in a very long time. Not wanting to believe it, I was now concerned because of this one critical comment from someone I admired. I set my mind to prove she was wrong. I told Tom what JoAnn had said, and when he didn't tell me she was ridiculous, I knew I was in trouble.

It was the ugly truth. I was out of shape and getting disgustingly more so each day. So, with Tom's eager guidance, I bought a good pair of running shoes (of course, I always had to have the best) and literally started running by going out the front door of our house and down the block. And that was as far as I got. I was able to run one block. So my running routine began. Run one block, walk one block. It took me a year to run one mile.

What I learned, to my dismay, was that I was not a natural runner. Some people can just run gracefully and easily once they have the cardio conditioning. I was not one of those people. My daughter, Kim, was such a person. One day as she ran at Indiana University just for exercise, the women's track coach stopped his car, got out, approached her, and said, "Would you be interested in trying out for the women's track team?"

Indiana University is a Big Ten athletic school. For the track coach to recruit someone who was just running around a campus track for exercise is like a talent scout approaching someone on a Hollywood street for a movie audition.

Although I didn't have speed or excellent form, I became a runner, and I mean a devoted, three-to-four-days-a-week runner. I ran for the next 24 years. That first year, I bought a Sony Walkman and began to lose myself in the euphoria of listening to music, being outdoors, and running. I ran in all kinds of weather because I learned how to layer one ridiculous piece of clothing over another. I didn't care what I looked like running on the streets of my neighborhood; running had become a part of me.

Running gave me the ability to think of myself as being physically equal — don't laugh — to Tom. Also, at that time I realized that perhaps I didn't want to wake up one morning, 50 years old, knowing all I had done in life was to teach elementary and high school students how to read. I wanted something different. How and when the idea of morphing into an FBI agent crept into my psyche, I just don't remember. But over the years, as more women joined the Bureau ranks, Tom kept telling me he thought I'd make great agent. So there I was, one night after dinner, sitting at the table in our little kitchen, pumped up from the pride I felt in my jogging ability, and saying, "What do you think of the idea of me applying to be an agent?"

Tom replied, "I've told you before, I think you would make a great FBI agent. You write well and you find it easy to relate to people, both rich and poor. I think you should try it. I'll bring home an application."

While some children, mostly boys, dream of becoming firemen, there are children (once again, mostly boys) who dream of becoming FBI agents. Call it the Superman syndrome or just wanting to prove you are really remarkable. Becoming an FBI agent is the ultimate in achievement: agents are brainy, have killer fighting skills, and get to use the latest in counter-espionage equipment. Watch out, Agent 007, here I come.

During the Christmas season of 1978, I had but one wish. I didn't want a fur coat or more jewelry. All I wanted, with all of my heart, was to be an FBI special agent. My daughter Kim wanted a pink two-wheel bike, my husband Tom wished for another woodworking tool, and I wanted to go to Quantico, Virginia — the FBI Academy — to be beaten up, sleep deprived, humiliated, and ultimately to carry the credentials and badge that I saw each night as Tom emptied his pockets at the end of the workday. The road to achieving this dream was a long, difficult one and one that seemed as if it could fatefully take a wrong turn at any moment.

A recently published book by Thomas H. Ackerman stated the basic qualifications for becoming an FBI special agent as, "… rigorous and demanding — and sometimes dangerous. Special agents must be mentally and physically fit in order to perform surveillance and undercover work, conduct interviews and interrogations, execute search warrants, make arrests and respond to critical incidents. The position demands alertness, intelligence, and good judgment, whether special agents are involved in fact finding tasks, working with informants, using sophisticated electronic investigative equipment, advising assistant United States Attorneys, or testifying in court. To ensure that the FBI recruits qualified personnel who can face these challenges successfully, special agent applicants must meet the following qualifications to be considered for the position."[1]

I thank the author of this paragraph because I couldn't have said it better. The qualifications he goes on to list include: citizenship, age requirements (minimum of 23 and maximum of 37), education requirements (bachelor's degree from an accredited university), a valid driver's license (no record of many violations allowed), strict eyesight and hearing requirements, passing a medical examination, and displaying a high level of physical fitness.

OK, now all of those required qualifications aren't too bad. It's the application process that you have to go through that will discourage and reject even the most ambitious. The FBI sets certain "critical skills" that ultimately determine whether or not one gets into a new agents' class. The priority of these critical skills changes in a mystical fashion, yet having accounting/finance, computer science/information technology, engineering, foreign language, law, physical science, or intelligence expertise will put you ahead of anyone else. Finally, there is the "catch-all" skill — *diversified*, which means you are part of a minority group underrepresented in the special agent ranks. For me, the fact that I had a master's degree, that I had taught for 11 years, and, most significantly, that I was a woman got me into the FBI. I was diversified (female), qualified, and highly motivated.

When Tom brought home the six-page application form, I immediately started working on it, which was no easy task. I had to list, with exact address and phone number, if appropriate: 1) every place I ever lived; 2) every job I ever held and the name of my supervisors; 3) every school I had attended, starting with kindergarten; 4) the full names all of my immediate relatives; 5) any times I had left the United States, where I had traveled, and the purpose for my travel; and 6) three personal and three professional references. "Gee, these people are compulsively detailed, aren't they?" I remarked to Tom one night as I worked on the application.

Getting the details is the core of the FBI's success as an investigative organization. No one processes evidence the way the FBI does. When we conducted searches, each room we searched was photographed before and after, all items taken as evidence were placed in either a bag or box, and that was labeled with the date, the case number, and location of where the item was found, with the seizing agent's initials. A master log was kept with the times of each seizure, the agent's name, and the number of the photograph taken of the item that corresponded to the number of the frame that captured the photo of that item.

This amazing attention to detail is what brought "bad guys" to their knees when they were charged with a crime in which the FBI had gathered the evidence. This is why I never lost a case in my 22 years as an agent.

Not that I was a genius — I just followed the rules and always listened very carefully to what the federal prosecutors told me they needed to prove the case. In the majority of the federal courts across the United States, 97 percent of the subjects charged by the government plead guilty. [2] Of the approximately 3 percent of those defendants who go to trial, I bet (and here I am just guessing) that only 10 percent of that 3 percent are found not guilty.

The next step in my dream to be an agent was to take the intelligence test. Tom remembered from his own process nine years earlier that large portions of this test consisted of correctly spelling words and matching words to their correct definitions. Somehow the FBI must have thought those two skills indicated intelligence — go figure. I know there is a correlation between intelligence and vocabulary, but I do not think spelling has a damn thing to do with how smart you are. Not wanting to blow this dream on my first step, and always thinking I am much dumber than perhaps I am, I studied vocabulary development for graduate students. I actually was a terrible speller. But fortunately I found a workbook for people entering the legal profession on how to improve spelling skills. For several months, after teaching school all day, making dinner, and getting Kim ready for bed, I studied and did workbook exercises at night. The preparation process became an obsession.

In the end, I passed the intelligence test. I should also mention the required psychological test. I had been warned not to be too extreme in my answers, and apparently I scored in a manner that didn't indicate I was a nut ball. Later however, I met many agents who left me wondering how they ever passed even the crudest of psychological screening tests. One of my FBI Academy classmates passed the psych test, but years later was arrested for exposing himself to little schoolchildren. He also beat his wife. He was able to hide this outrageous behavior throughout training school and for four years while functioning as a special agent.

The last and final step in the testing phase was the interview conducted by a panel of three agents. Since Tom was an agent in Chicago, I had to have my interview conducted in a field office located elsewhere. This was done so there couldn't be any undue favorable or negative influence in how the panel scored my responses to their scripted questions.

We selected Denver. I could have gone to Springfield, Illinois, or some other Midwestern location, but since we had planned a skiing trip to Vail around the same time they wanted to schedule an interview, we decided to mix business with pleasure. Off went the Smith family for a ski vacation in February 1979, with a quick stop to stay with agent friends for one night so I could attend my interview the next day. Following that interview, we would be on our way up to the mountains.

Even after more than 25 years, I will never forget the day of my interview. I dressed in my best professional outfit, and Tom drove me to the downtown Denver FBI office. We had left Kim at our friends' home to play with their daughter, whom she already knew well. On the ride into Denver I kept thinking about the total eclipse of the sun that was to occur a few minutes after the interview was to begin at 11:00 a.m. This had to be a sign of something, didn't it?

I entered the interview room and met the three agents. Everyone took a seat and I spoke first, "You know, there's a total eclipse of the sun occurring outside that window right now. That eclipse is a sign that it is my destiny to become an FBI agent."

The three uptight agents just looked at me with quizzical expressions on their faces and none of them made any comment. I suspected they didn't think my comment was funny or a clever way to break the ice.

I can now understand that it was an astonishing thing to say, and the interviewing agents had to wonder, Who is this weirdo we have to interview today? Is she some sort of tarot card reader or astrology nut? In any event, my attempt to break the ice and develop rapport went right over their heads. Recognizing this, for the balance of the interview I controlled any inventive or humorous interjections in answering their questions. I must have demonstrated I was a serious, well-educated, informed, and driven woman. Later I found out my interviewers had scored my answers in the top range. This was enough to get me placed on the A-list of diversified candidates to initiate my background investigation, schedule my physical examination, and place me into a class at Quantico. My desire, dream, and obsession to become an FBI agent began to look real.

The FBI's concern for detail and thoroughness is evident in its examination of the backgrounds of every employee hired. Neighbors for the past 20 years would be interviewed. Schools attended would be contacted and records obtained. Relatives (of both the candidate and spouse) would be checked for criminal histories and credit ratings. The FBI did not want deadbeats or anyone with a history that might be used to blackmail or threaten an agent. Former President of the United States Richard Nixon applied to be an FBI agent and was rejected. How strange is it that a person can be President of the United States but not an FBI agent? Then again, FBI agents aren't voted into office — but they are fully vetted by the Bureau.

I received regular reports of the background investigation activity from neighbors, friends, and references. They all said the nondescript agents who questioned them seemed very robotic and their questions somewhat simplistic. Some of the questions asked were: "Was I loyal to my country?" "Was I financially responsible?" "Did I abuse liquor or drugs?" and, weirdly, "Did they think I could shoot someone?" All of my references, I am sure answered, perhaps too eagerly, that I would be able to shoot someone in an instant, since I had been shooting off my mouth all my life. I never did find out if they asked that question about the male candidates for their background checks.

The last and final step before receiving one's appointment as an FBI special agent in training was to take the medical examination given by the doctors at the Great Lakes Naval Base north of Chicago. I was hoping these government doctors might be prone to miss any defect or abnormality I might have. After being examined by a series of seemingly disinterested medical doctors performing examinations for almost an entire day, their evaluation of me read "Fit for Duty." Yes, sir! Thank you, sir! At the moment, I was elated with the doctors' perfunctory evaluation. Three years later, I would be devastated by the "life saving" efforts of other Great Lakes doctors who nearly killed my Tom. But that's another story.

After I was formally accepted into the FBI Academy and ready to begin my training as a member of the New Agents Class (NAC) of 6/79, I prepared to formally change my career and my life. One of the most intimidating aspects of making a commitment to the FBI is that you have to quit your job and tell everyone that you are about to begin a new, glamorous, and exciting career. But a few weeks or months after your grand announcement, you may fail to make it and be sent home to eat humble pie, begging to get your old job back. I remember the excitement of my departure from the world of teaching. At my going-away party, my colleagues cajoled me into doing 20 men's push-ups on the floor of the teacher's lounge. I performed this "manly act" for them. In amazement and delight they cheered and congratulated me — Mrs. Smith, the reading teacher — as I headed out into the unknown and macho world of this adventurous undertaking. With an air of confidence masking my nervous anticipation, I accepted their best wishes, all the while wondering about the future.

The training academy had a reputation for firing candidates with little or no concern for the sacrifices made, responsibilities abandoned, and financial and personal risks taken to pursue this dream. The instructors at Quantico thought new agents in training were expendable because thousands of others waited in line for the chance to replace the failures. None of the instructors thought of the time and expense the FBI had invested in putting together a class of new agents. In 1979, it cost more than $10,000 to test, interview, and conduct a background investigation and physical examination for each member of my class. Most importantly to me, none of them thought about what each new agent had given up to be at Quantico.

In my class, 35 hopefuls were sworn in on June 23, 1979, at the J. Edgar Hoover Building in Washington, D.C. When we graduated on September 13, 1979, there were only 29. What happened to the six who were asked to leave, I do not know. I do know that one woman, Paula, went back to the police department that she had left and, within 10 years, was appointed the Chief of Police and held that position for 20 years. That proves that if you flunk out of the FBI Academy you aren't a loser for life. Go Paula!

Tom flew first-class to Washington, D.C., when he went to training school on January 2, 1970. It was the only flight we could get. But nine years later, Tom and I drove from Chicago to Washington, D.C., in our Honda Civic. We shared the driving chores while our daughter Kim rode in the backseat. Sunday night we stayed at a motel that was directly under the takeoff and landing pattern of Washington National Airport. Planes were restricted from taking off or landing after 10:00 p.m. but they started taking off again at 5:00 a.m. Who was sleeping anyway? Well, Kim did, but both Tom and I were nervous wrecks. Would I be strong enough to make it through Quantico and realize my dream? Or would I come home without a gun, badge, and credentials?

For the tenth time I responded to Tom's drilling, "I won't quit, Tom. I know I won't. I'll stay in and make them fire me." Tom knew that women had a more difficult time at Quantico, and if necessary, he wanted to leave open the option of a small legal chance to prove discrimination. If I quit, that case would be more difficult to prove: Did the disparity of treatment drive me out, or was it my own weakness? All I can say now is, I was prepared for the worst, but I found it to be as equitable a system as was possible in 1979. It was still a miserable four months, and much of the pain I endured *was* because I was female, but not because I was being targeted as a woman.

At 8:30 a.m. Tom, Kim, and I drove up to the Hoover Building. I kissed and hugged them as if I were walking to the gallows. How I would miss the comfort and love they provided to me in their own special way. Although my desire to have this opportunity with the FBI had become a driving force in my life, the raw emotion of leaving the only man I had ever loved and the daily contact with my beautiful young daughter was the most challenging emotional struggle I had ever faced in my 34 years.

That same day, Tom drove 12 hours back to Chicago. He said Kim was relaxed and easy, with her feet up on the dashboard, playing some game, reading a book, eating, and dozing all the way back. Years later when I asked Kim about dropping her mom off in Washington, D.C., to be gone for four months, she recalled, "I don't remember driving to Washington, D.C. Nor do I remember being scared that you were going. I thought it would be fun to be with Dad, to eat cereal for dinner and be able to wear whatever clothes I picked out. I'm sure I missed you, but I never thought your going was a permanent thing, so I wasn't filled with desperately sad emotion."

J. Edgar Hoover was the Director of the Federal Bureau of Investigation from his appointment in May 1924 until his death in May 1972. He was an egocentric and obsessive-compulsive man who molded the national investigative agency into a very personal, very powerful crime-fighting machine. The jurisdictional powers of the FBI trumped all state laws. And his special agents were chosen from the most highly educated men in America. With these two aces in Hoover' pocket, coupled with his intense and dominating personality, he established the premier law enforcement agency in the world. Becoming an FBI special agent was the dream career of thousands of men in America. After 1973, Hoover's death, and intense recruiting, it became the aspiration of many women as well — of which I was now one.

My roommate at Quantico, Linda, shared her impression of me on our first day: "Yikes — that is one very sophisticated woman." She went on to say, "But, much to my relief, I realized that you could joke about yourself when you admitted that you had used your visitor's pass, instead of the gold FBI badge, to hold in your left hand while you raised your right hand to swear allegiance to the United States and to conduct yourself according to the standards set by the President of the United States."

I had a premonition of having to room with a dyke who could do one-armed push-ups. But just the opposite occurred. Linda was a soft Southern woman, extra bright and very witty. In the women's locker room, Linda and I changed from our "business attire" (uncomfortable pantyhose, teamed with either a conservative suit or dress) into our "gym attire" (masculine, blue cotton shorts and light blue T-shirts). Linda leaned over to me and whispered, "I saw the boxing gloves out on the table."

A shiver of cold ran through my veins. "Ah, shit, no," was all I could say. There were countless other training activities that were painful, but boxing was the worst. Both Linda and I dreaded the thought of "entering the ring."

Boxing came at the end of physical training, a class we had each day in new agents' school. What appeared to be practical training at the time later seemed sort of ludicrous once I started my investigative career as an FBI special agent. Each day we would practice our push-ups, pull-ups, and sit-ups. This was done ad nauseam, or until my muscles started to quiver and I couldn't do one more "up" if my life depended on it. Then we'd move on to handcuffing practice.

"You don't just slap the handcuffs any old way on an arrestee of the FBI!" screamed my instructor. Then he related the proper technique.

You bladed your body toward the person and ordered him to turn away from you and place his hands behind his back, palms up. Then, after holstering your weapon, you carefully would sidestep nearer, but always maintaining a safe distance from the bad guy. While you did your thing, your partner kept his weapon trained on the "K 5 or kill zone" of the arrestee. Now you could close in to cuff the person. You'd make sure his palms were facing up, and then you'd place the loose steel ring around the left wrist and almost simultaneously slip the other ring on the right wrist. A final clicking flourish of the cuffs locked them together, and you had your man cuffed.

Over and over we paired up with a partner as the bad guy and faced every permutation of how the bad guy could position himself or not cooperate. Such practice continued until the last 15 minutes of class. Then we were directed across the gym to a table filled with boxing gloves.

Linda walked next to me and said, "I'm getting instant diarrhea."

I knew this wasn't far from the truth because my bowels were also feeling a little loose.

We were shown how to properly put on our gloves, and then, standing in a big group, we watched Coach Archie, our practical training instructor, spar with one of our classmates. The coach was a black guy, around 6 feet 2 inches tall, all muscle, and in top shape. He had been a college track star and later the head track coach at Ball State University in Indiana. He was fierce looking. However, I learned he was a kind man; he could have humiliated most of my male classmates, but he never did. Archie showed all the various techniques of how to protect your face and deflect an opponent's punches. He then lectured and demonstrated how to throw a punch — of course, we were supposed to replicate his movements. But I was overcome with fear. I couldn't concentrate. I had never been punched, and the thought of taking a punch terrified me.

Boxing class taught me many lessons. First, we were never allowed to box one of the other four women in our class because that would have been "too easy." Second, once I got out on the street, I knew I could never get into a boxing match because I would lose. Third, it hurt like no other pain I had encountered, even childbirth, to get punched in the face, on the side of your head, or on either ear. It hurt like hell. Fourth, I learned from being hit hard that saying, "your teeth rattle," "there is a ringing in your ears," and "you see stars" were based in truth. Finally, it taught me that if I didn't box like my life depended on it while at the FBI Academy, later I would experience the pain of failure.

That first day of learning the art of boxing, I was paired up with another Smith, Mark Smith. A muscular man of about six feet tall, he was a kind, friendly guy who had graduated from the United States Naval Academy and had been a practicing attorney after law school. Initially, he was gentle. I was even able to deflect some of his blows and get a punch that landed on his mouth. But Coach Archie saw that Mark was pulling his punches against his 108-pound female opponent.

"Smith!" he shouted at my boxing mate. "Do you think you're playing here? Let's get fighting like you mean it!"

At that moment, I guessed that Mark Smith didn't want to prove his boxing ability by beating me up, but the gentleness had to stop. That was when I first experienced rattling teeth and ringing ears.

"Change partners!" Archie called.

I thought, This is going to go on until I am killed. Should I just walk out of this torture chamber before I am carried out on a stretcher? I knew walking out would deal a deadly blow to my dream of becoming an FBI agent, so I moved over to the next mat and stood in front of another alphabetically close classmate, Orin. Whenever you talked to Orin, he almost knocked you out with his bad breath. All he had to do was blow on me and I would have gone down.

But Orin had something to prove, and he wasn't going to get called on the carpet for going easy on one of the girls. His attitude toward the female trainees was, "If they want this job, they'll have to fight for it just like the men."

I tried to avoid Orin's onslaught by holding my gloves in front of my face and by hopping around on the mat to avoid his punches as they collided again and again with my face, ears, and forehead. My head snapped back and forth. I was a rag doll. Desperately, I searched the recesses of my mind for a way to get a punch into his ugly-ass face, but it seemed impossible. He pummeled me. My teeth rattled, my ears rang, my forehead ached, and I had started to see stars — pretty little twinkling things that jumped around in my vision of Orin's pock-marked face.

The whistle blew. Coach Archie yelled, "Everyone to the showers. Put your gloves on the table as you leave the gym."

I turned to leave the gym, but before I could lower my head as I walked out, Coach Archie saw my face. Tears spilled down my cheeks.

"Smith, come over here," he demanded.

I obediently stood next him, head down, averting my eyes from his, those of the other physical trainers who mingled around him, and, most importantly, those of my classmates.

"Smith, what are you thinking right now?"

Out popped words I never would have expected: "I am going to have my husband beat the shit out of Orin." Coach Archie never mentioned to me that he knew my husband personally. I don't think he did. What he did know, though, was Tom's reputation. He knew Tom could have polished off Orin with one hand tied behind his back.

"Come on back to my office, Smith."

I didn't know what to expect, but I was happy not to go into the women's locker room with my face still wet with tears. We walked into his office. A framed photo hung on the wall: the image of my husband Tom boxing with another agent. Although their boxing garb was dated and their haircuts very short, it was evident the photo had been taken for public relations purposes to demonstrate to the public that men like Tom

Smith were ideal FBI specimens — the embodiment of all the physical toughness that the job required. I knew of this photo, but I was shocked to find it framed in my instructor's office.

"See this photo?" Archie asked.

"Well, yes, it's my husband Tom boxing." My inner voice said, *how ironic.*

Archie continued, "Smith, I want you to remember this picture, because by the time we are finished training you, you are going to be as tough as your husband, and you will beat the shit out of whomever you fight."

I swallowed and uttered a speculative, "Yes?"

"Yes is right," Archie replied. "I am going to make you a fighter. You're going to *want* to beat the shit out of your opponent. Now, go take your shower so you're not late to your next class."

As I walked out of the gym office, around the corner, and into the women's locker room, I only remember thinking, what was that? Me, a physical fighter? No, I'm not buying that. I'm still going to tell Tommy about this Orin guy and have him take care of it.

Thereafter, whenever Archie thought I was not boxing or wrestling in an aggressive, wild-cat manner, he would make me get down on the floor, do 10 push-ups — and these are men's push-ups, not those punk-ass ladies' push-ups with your knees on the ground — and go into another fight. What I learned was that in each physical confrontation, I had to put every drop of my strength and energy into winning the fight, or I'd be in for more punishment. I never did win a fight, but the men in the class understood that when they were paired up with me, they'd be facing this crazy, try-to-win-at-all-costs opponent.

Early in my training I realized that my physical conditioning would help, but if the chips were down to life or death, I would always opt to shoot a male suspect rather than fight him. My winning record in fighting was a big fat zero. And for the record, Tom never beat the shit out of Orin . He just blew off my request as the ravings of a maniac.

The combination of returning to a college-like dormitory with no personal touches; attending hours of lectures in the classroom daily; being physically tormented each day by wrestling, boxing, and running in sweltering heat; and shooting weapons a minimum of four hours every other day made for a difficult life.

Unfortunately, our classroom lectures were rarely enlightening. In my view, they didn't provide proper training in investigative techniques. I kept thinking that there had to be a curriculum that made sense and allowed the staff to prepare new agents for the tasks of their future careers. Teach them well enough so they could productively hit the street as soon as they checked into their assigned divisions — that was my hope. I am sorry to say, there is little I remember learning in those four long months that translated into real-life preparation for a federal crime investigator — except for being trained to wrestle, box, and handcuff an arrestee in 10 seconds flat and becoming one of the best trained marksmen this side of U.S. Marine Corps.

Well, OK, I will take back some of that bad talk about what we learned in about four to six hours a day for 120 workdays. We did learn some very useful skills, such as taking and lifting fingerprints accurately. When most police take the fingerprints of an arrestee, they inadvertently smear the fingerprint card — they don't use enough ink to put down a good impression, they use too much ink and make all the lines and ridges of a fingerprint blur together, or they don't roll the finger so the entire surface of the finger is captured. And those are just the most obvious mistakes that can happen when taking fingerprints. When these mistakes happen, they make the prints indecipherable and, therefore, impossible to match to any known or unknown suspects. Nowadays the task is done electronically, making this previously vital learning experience obsolete.

We also learned how to process a crime or search a scene in a planned, photographed, meticulously detailed, and recorded manner. And we were taught how to effectively conduct an interview. When done properly, one can develop a short-term relationship with the interviewee, and the agent, if properly prepared, can cover all of the areas of questioning that are essential to prove or disprove the violation of a federal law. The interview is a waste of time if the report is confusingly written or missing any of the key elements that were discussed. Most FBI interviews are comprehensively written and follow a fairly prescribed format. They are rarely challenged in federal courts. Interviews of witnesses are worthless if they cannot stand up to the review of a federal prosecutor, a defense attorney, or a federal judge. These are all are anal-retentive, professionally arrogant, and demanding people.

Once, while I was on the stand testifying in New York federal court, the defense attorney for a Genovese (New York family) mobster — jumped on a mistake I had made in an interview report. During cross-examination he attacked me with continued, humiliating questioning about the report. I realized that I had omitted the word "not" in a certain sentence. The sentence that I screwed up went something like this: "Jack Wringer's girlfriend, Alexia, did (not) provide her signature on all of the account records." You can see the difference that my mistake made. Did stockbroker Jack forge Alexia's signatures on all these fake accounts he had opened in her name, or not? [3] Be careful, little FBI agents, when writing your reports. There is a big, bad defense attorney just waiting to slap you around in court.

Relentlessly, my training continued. Firearms instruction was comprehensive. We were required to meet the shooting standards for a Smith and Wesson .38 special 2 1/2-inch barrel handgun, a pump-action shotgun, a rifle, and an M-16, the semiautomatic weapon made famous in Vietnam.

All of our firearms training was done outdoors. The intense sun and oppressive humidity of a Virginia summer made the long afternoons on the range torturous. After firing hundreds of rounds in the standing, sitting, and prone positions, we were taught how to disassemble, clean, and reassemble each weapon. Good God, who would have ever thought I could have done that?

Quantico, Virginia, is a densely forested area that housed basic and advance training for the U.S. Marines. It also was the location of the FBI Academy, a maze of buildings connected by enclosed walkways. Located in the middle of a Marine base, and with access to it tighter than Fort Knox, the seclusion and quiet was unnerving for me — I was accustomed to the action and noise of the city. As trainees, we saw no one but FBI instructors, police officers who attended a special school offered to them, FBI agents returning for additional training, and the maintenance staff and cafeteria workers. We were not allowed to leave Quantico until the end of the third week. By then I had become so brainwashed that just going to a shopping mall not far from the Academy on Saturday afternoon almost blew my mind. I recall walking in the mall — the lights and sounds were so bright and loud they left me a little awestruck. Then I saw fat people! There were no fat, unfit people at Quantico. Unlike the outside world, my new training environment was isolated, restricted, totally controlled, and highly disciplined.

The weeks dragged on with new challenges — intense study and testing — legal tests; rules and procedure tests; tests on interview techniques, report writing, and evidence recovery; processing tests; and others I can't even remember. A score under 75 on any test was failing. Since I had just completed the comprehensive examination for my master's degree, studying was not a foreign activity. I prepared for the tests by over studying. I am proud to say I never got a score less than 95 on any FBI test. Several of my classmates were not that fortunate and were asked to leave because they failed a particular test.

What was so unsettling about a classmate flunking out was their immediate disappearance. The poor victim learned of his failure, packed his bags, and was gone before the next day of class. At 8:00 a.m. the morning after a test, we entered our classroom and frantically looked around for any missing person. We never said good-bye to any of our fellow trainees who left Quantico. When you walked by their rooms, their names had been removed from the little slots next to the doors and poof, those people with whom you had shared wrestling sweat or stood next to while shooting hundreds of rounds of bullets were gone. None of us cried and mourned that we couldn't see those people again; we were just thankful that it hadn't been us. At that time in our lives, we were so preoccupied with saving our own butts that we didn't have the energy to dwell on those people's feelings of loss, or for that matter, the loss to the FBI of another "dreamer." The shame of rejection was of such magnitude that they only wanted to quietly slip away into the night.

Slipping away into the night was not for me. By the twelfth week of training school, I had passed all of my tests. I passed my firearms qualifications. I qualified in performing 35 men's push-ups, 45 women's pull-ups, and running a two-mile obstacle course, all within the prescribed time limits. The next four weeks were devoted to more of the same, but without the pressure of physical and firearms qualifications.

Tom and Kim came to visit the twelfth weekend. It was wonderful to see them and share what I had been doing. Recently, Kim, my now adult daughter, wrote to me about that moment:

> *"I remember visiting you once while you were in*
>
> *training. I thought the uniforms they made you all wear*
>
> *were silly because you were all adults. I remember eating*
>
> *something in the cafeteria and thinking that the FBI*
>
> *training school was a lot like going to school — you had to*

eat, play, and be with other people your own age —some of whom you liked and others whom you did not. I immediately really liked Linda. She is the only other person I remember meeting at Quantico.

During this one visit, I remember it being insanely hot. We were taking a walk around the grounds where you would run. There was a plague-like invasion of cicadas and I remember the sound they made being almost deafening. I was wearing open-toed sandals that day. As we were walking, a cicada popped onto the front tip of my sandal sole. As I lifted my foot to flick it off, it slid under my toes. I still remember the feeling of it struggling and being really terrified. I think you guys just laughed. As we walked on, Dad continued to flick the dead cicada carcass shells at me — which infuriated me.

I was not impressed by the physical things you had to do, nor was I scared about the firearms training — mostly because I believe I was so used to physically exerting myself and it was a pretty dominant family culture trait of ours to be fit and excel in sports even against boys. Also, because Dad was so physically fit, I think I assumed everyone's family was like ours. I had become familiar with guns and firearms with Dad at the range, where I had shot a gun and watched other guys practice. I think if you had been the first FBI agent in the family, the experience would have been different, but because Dad never made a big deal of you being there, I didn't either.

My other vivid memory was attending your graduation. I remember the room being small, dark, and red and sitting in a chair. Everyone was dressed up and smelled good. I do remember Dad giving you your credentials, but I figured, 'Who else would do that?' Not realizing that it was a special kind of thing. I know now this was the first time a spouse had awarded FBI credentials in the history of the Bureau. I was kind of bored because I remember just having to sit and listen for a while and being too shy to talk to other people. Linda came and talked to me — that made me feel better."

Tell you what, Kim, your mom felt much better when she graduated, as did your dad, who put his reputation on the line by encouraging his wife to be an FBI agent.

My ambition had been realized and now I was going home to my husband, family, friends, and dearest daughter. When I looked into a mirror, the woman to whom Tom had awarded her FBI credentials looked harder and tougher than I had ever looked. I was mentally and physically prepared to tackle the career of a lifetime. After listening to a lecture about the evil enterprise called "organized crime" in Chicago, I decided investigating these criminals was my goal. I was on my way back to Chicago to take on "the Outfit."

- CHAPTER THREE -
Assignment: Organized Crime

Tom and I rode home from work in his FBI company car, also known as a "Bucar" (short for bureau car). "They're going to have to pay me a lot more to work these kinds of cases," I muttered. "I don't want to do background investigations. All the questions asked are just the same." I had been reviewing the backgrounds of federal judicial candidates or federal prosecutors recruited from Yale, Harvard, or other prestigious law schools. But rarely was there even a scent of taint or corruption.

"That work is important," said Tom. "Maybe it's boring but..."

"Yeah, I understand how important it is to the integrity of the federal system," I responded, parroting the company line. I knew such background investigations were needed, but I was working at the bottom of the investigative food chain. Even though I was just a rookie with less than four months as an agent, I was anxious to work the big ones. I just didn't like doing what was considered grunt work in the Bureau. I was determined to do something challenging. I wanted recognition as a kick-ass agent. Could I change the Bureau's attitude that female agents just couldn't cut it? I was going to try.

In my four short months in the Chicago office, I observed the male agents interact with the few female agents they met. Generally, they thought a female agent was "fresh meat" if she wasn't married. At that time, most female agents were unmarried. If you were married, you were then invisible as a sexual object, thank God, and, married or not, you were still seen as worthless when it came to being someone who might actually solve a crime. The male agents were always waiting for a woman to fail, and then, like vultures, they would swoop in with an "I told you so." It was part jealousy, part turf protection, and a good deal of insecurity.

Imagine…if women could actually do investigations, why would they even need men?

I also observed that many of these "hot shot" agents weren't all that smart, good-looking, or accomplished. I was emboldened. "Screw their attitude. I can do this job. I just want the chance to do it."

Every day, parading around the office in front of my eyes were the agents at the top of the prestige ladder — those who worked bank robberies and fugitives, the tough guys like Tommy. Also at the top of the heap were the organized crime fighters. Now I say "fighters" in a sarcastic manner, because from what I could discern, there wasn't much bad happening to the organized crime guys — at least what the FBI was doing.

But these dudes sure did look good and had copped some mega attitude. Some of them had undercover roles to play and informants they met, which meant they had to fit in with the bad guys. During that era, agents tried to blend into the environment of organized crime. So they would dress like John Travolta in the movie "Saturday Night Fever" — tight pants, shirts opened at least three buttons, and gold chains around their necks.

These costumes clearly missed the reality of "mobster chic." During the summer of 1980, I watched Outfit guys walk in and out of a gambling joint called Oldsters for Youngsters. These dudes could have been the inhabitants of a home for the aged and they dressed that way. The north side crew boss, Caesar DiVarco, wore polyester pants with no waistband, and if it was chilly, a short waist-length zippered jacket.

Organized crime agents watched too much TV and spent too many nights at the movies, or maybe they were just scamming their FBI bosses. They had discovered how to get out of wearing the FBI dress code, which was an ensemble made up of a conservative suit, a white or light-blue shirt, a tie, and wingtip shoes.

Also, they didn't drive normal Bucars. They all had leased Cadillacs, Lincoln Town Cars, or Buick Rivieras. These beauties could be seen illegally parked all around the Federal Building. They couldn't park them in the FBI garage because they would then be identifiable as FBI cars. God forbid! I am sure these clever guys had convinced our bosses that the Mob had 24-hour surveillance on the Federal Building using crooked Chicago cops as eyes and ears.

Whether the whole façade the agents presented was a hoax or not, I didn't know, but I wanted in that clique. I wanted to act like they did. And I wanted to investigate the top-echelon criminals, the Chicago Mob.

How was I going to do that? Knowing that there were several organized crime squads, I began observing the supervisors of each. I sought out the friendliest and most approachable of the lot. I made discrete inquires to a few trusted people about which manager they thought might be the most amenable to a female on his squad. Taking their advice, and considering my observations, I decided to approach a white-haired, middle-aged manager named Ray Shyrock. I knew Ray fancied himself a ladies' man, and it was this predilection I decided to utilize. For a week I worked to build up my courage, and one morning, not bold enough to just enter, I knocked on the doorjamb of his open door.

"Come on in," he said. "You're Elaine Smith, aren't you?"

Demurely I answered while shaking his hand, "Yes, I am."

"Mr. Shyrock, I was just wondering if I might be able to take you to breakfast one morning this week. I'd like to talk to you about something."

"Oh!" he said, a little startled. "Sure."

"How about tomorrow?" I quickly asked.

"Great," he replied.

"Does 8 a.m. work?"

"That sounds good," he slowly responded.

Before anything else could be said, I backed out of the doorway and called, "I'll be down here at that time, Ray. Thanks!"

Ah ha! I had him. My first step had gone according to plan. Get the old coot out of the office, eating on my tab, relaxing, but very curious about what I have to say and then — bingo — in an earnest, sincere way, I'll ask him for the honor of working for him.

Ray was obviously smitten, but he said he would have to defer to the agents on his squad to see if they would agree to it. What? Since when did the FBI become a democracy? Maybe old Ray is not as stupid as he looks. He is going back to his boys to see if they know anything derogatory about me before committing. Then if he denies me, he'll slip out of the blame and transfer it to the boys.

In my four short months of employment, there had been an incident that could have been interpreted by the other agents as derogatory. My squad was divided between fraud-by-wire agents (investment scams, basically) and background investigation agents. Two of my agents, Ernie and Brian, created the potential problem. It was a late afternoon. Nearby, I overheard the two men as they talked about an arrest they had scheduled for the next morning. I vaguely remember them alluding to me, saying, "Maybe the new agent would like to go on this caper." I distinctly do not remember anyone asking me for help on the arrest, or them giving me any indication they were inviting me to this party — a party I was just dying to attend, where I could utilize those awesome skills I had been honing for the entire past summer.

The next day I was called down to see the new agent training co-coordinator, which was a joke of a position, because in four months I had never even met Lou. He told me, in a heavy Texas accent, "Uh, Elaine, it is unacceptable in the FBI for an agent to refuse to participate in an arrest."

"What?" I was shocked.

"Well, Ernie and Brian asked you to go on an arrest with them and you blew off that request."

I was upset that I had missed my first chance to go on an arrest, but more astonished that Ernie and Brian thought they had asked me to go. On top of that, rather than talk to me about why I didn't want to go on the arrest, they snitched me out.

"I wasn't asked to go on their arrest," I said. "I could overhear their conversation and I thought they were messing with me. 'Oh, does the new little agent want to go on our big bad arrest?' And me, not wanting to be too forward or pushy, I didn't walk over to their desks and say, 'Are you guys asking me to participate in the arrest tomorrow morning?'"

Lou seemed to understand, and afterward he told Ernie and Brian my explanation. They also got it. From this experience I realized that at least some of my male co-workers were unsure and nervous when it came to treating female agents as their equals and asking them for help. I forgot about the incident, but Tom still carried resentment. He was certain they tried to hurt me.

Much to my amazement, this little incident didn't get blown out of proportion, and the agents on Ray's squad must have thought I wouldn't be that offensive. Ray called my supervisor and asked if I could be transferred to his squad to work beginning January 1980. I was going to work on the organized crime crew! Damn, let me at 'em. Another one of my dreams had come true.

But before I fast-forward to meeting the man who made my organized crime dreams come true, I have to tell the story about when I finally got to make my first arrest as an FBI agent — or, well, ever.

It was Halloween night. Now, most parents enjoy being home and going trick-or-treating with their children, but late that afternoon, Chad, another agent on my squad, had invited me to help on an arrest. I called Tom, who assured me he would be home to make sure Kim had an enjoyable Halloween. Relieved, I joined the pre-raid meeting.

Chad gathered me and five other agents together around his desk in the squad area and briefed us with the general description of the subject, who was wanted for bank fraud. He told us that we would leave the office at 5 p.m. and as a conga line of Bucars, drive up to the house, exit our vehicles, knock on the door, and arrest the dude. Easy, huh? I was amazed at the casual nature of this arrest plan. At Quantico, arrests were planned as if we were redoing the invasion of Normandy.

Feeling sorry for me, or perhaps wanting to keep an eye on me, Chad asked if I would drive him. Sure, I'd be proud to — sort of like being the driver for the general. Two other cars pulled out of the garage at the same time that we did, carrying the four other agents that made up the arrest team.

Since I knew the city, Chad and I quickly discussed what route to take to the South Side slum where the subject lived. As we drove out onto the streets, it was apparent that this was going to be a long night. It was pouring rain and traffic was at its rush-hour worst. It took forever to go a few blocks.

My heart was beating fast, my head was spinning with all the precautions we should have talked about, and as I crept my way through the downtown Chicago streets, I glanced over at Chad and he was asleep!

Training school hadn't prepared me for this. Here I was with my heart rate near maximum, and this Chad guy had fallen asleep on the way to the arrest. Either the instructors at Quantico were delusional about what really goes on in the field, or Chad was one cool agent.

All three Bureau cars converged in the empty lot of a defunct gas station. The radio call from one of the other cars awakened my sleeping partner. *"Hey, Chad, we're parked here at the corner of Loomis and 73rd on the southeast corner. It's a deserted gas station."* They were waiting at the rendezvous. We arrived a few minutes later.

Traffic conditions had improved now. There were few cars moving in this bombed-out neighborhood because few people owned vehicles that ran, but the weather conditions had deteriorated. It was raining harder and big puddles had formed in the pockmarked streets and sidewalks.

Chad, not wanting to get wet, repeated the address of the subject's house over the radio. *"We will be going to 1401 73rd Place. Ernie, you and Brian pull out and lead the way."* Ernie and Brian's car swung out of the deserted gas station, followed by the next car, with me at the wheel of Chad's car bringing up the rear.

Ernie and Brian drove directly to 73rd Place, turned left and crept down the street in order to read the numbers on the houses. The rain fell in sheets now. As the three cars moved snail-like down the street, groups of costumed children clumped together on the sidewalk, going trick-or-treating house to house. I wondered what we would do if some of these kids were walking up to the front door as we were storming the house making the arrest. I had visions of a gun battle erupting with innocent trick-or-treating children shot in the crossfire.

Before I could say anything, the first car abruptly pulled over to the side of the street and stopped. Ernie and Brian flew out, drawing their guns as they jogged across the lawn. The agents in the second car did the same thing. As I pulled over to the curb behind them, even before I had the car stopped, the sleepy Chad was already out of the car and leading the gang of agents up to the front door. Brian and Ernie signaled they would cover the back door.

I parked the car, killed the engine, and jumped out into the pouring rain. As I ran in the dark up to the dilapidated house, I heard a vicious dog barking from some unknown yet close location. I took a back-up position at the bottom of the rotten wooden front door; my hand was on my gun, but it was not drawn. I was not going to be accused of shooting one of those trick-or-treaters who might want to join in all the excitement.

Chad banged loudly on the front door, yelling, "Open up! FBI!" Someone finally opened the door. I couldn't hear the conversation between Chad and an unknown person. Brian, who was behind the house, called out, "What the hell is going on up there? We've got a dog back here."

Chad motioned to me that I should bring Brian and Ernie up to the front of the house, and I quickly ran to the side of the house and waved at Brian and Ernie to come up front. While doing so, I walked in mud up to the top of my new black leather pumps. Damn the pumps, and damn the squishy cold mud, and where was that dog?

By the time Brian, Ernie, and I got back to the front of the house, Chad and the other two agents were waiting for us on the sidewalk.

"This is the wrong house. It's 73rd Street, not 73rd Place. It's just one street over. Let's go," Chad said.

I wanted to scream, "You mean we have to do this over again, you dumb shit?"

We all quickly walked back to our cars and drove off, following in the same positions. Brian and Ernie eyeballed the correct address again, but this time on 73rd Street. The whole takedown took place exactly how we had practiced it just one block over, except this time, a suspect was arrested. Chad then selected Ernie and Brian to assist him in transporting the prisoner to the federal lock-up. One of the other agents was asked if she could drive me home.

That other agent was Marlene, who had become a friend of mine. I couldn't wait to get into the car to see what she had to say about the whole experience, but I never did tell her or anyone else about Chad falling asleep. Years later it became public knowledge that Chad had narcolepsy. We did protect our own.

*   *   *

In January 1980, I took a new assignment with Squad 6C, Organized Crime – North Side Crew. I reported for my new assignment one Monday morning carrying all of my Bureau possessions. I asked the squad secretary which desk I could take. She informed me that desk assignments were very hierarchal and required the approval of those agents with surrounding desks. No joke. Had she known I was coming, she would have canvassed the boys on Friday and asked, "Now where are we going to put the new agent on Monday when she arrives?" Later I determined that she answered all of the squad phone calls, took care of the time and attendance records for the agents (like in school), took dictation from the supervisor, ordered supplies, and was the all-around "den mother" to the boys. The addition of a female agent to the squad often meant that the squad secretary, no longer the "queen," developed a negative attitude toward the female agent. However, the squad secretary of 6C, Judy, was a sweet, naive woman and was exceptionally helpful to me while I learned the rules and procedures of the FBI at warp speed in that first year. She had worked for the FBI for 10 years already and knew all of the paperwork cold. If there was anything that could get you in trouble in the FBI, it was not doing the paperwork properly — J. Edger Hoover was a compulsive nut.

Judy showed me my desk, where supplies were, and where my mail folder would be, and then went into Ray's office to tell him I had reported to the squad. As I was putting my meager Bureau and personal supplies and papers in the big desk, Ray came out of his office, smiling his wide, yellow-toothed grin, "Welcome to Squad 6C!"

"Well, thank you very much," I replied. I told him I was happy to be there, and I meant every word of it.

"Come into my office."

Oh, boy, now the important stuff. I grabbed a notepad and followed him in. I have always thought it disrespectful to the meeting host to join a meeting without bringing along a notepad and pen. I wonder if such people are so arrogant as to think they can exactly remember exactly the details of the discussion and the action list without writing it down — not me, I was ready pen in hand.

I sat on the edge of the visitor's chair in Ray's office as he spoke. "We have started a Title III on this squad. I was able to get you transferred over here because I need people to monitor it. The agents that have been doing it have to get back to their cases, so I needed new bodies. You will work an 8 to 6 shift Monday through Friday and on Saturday if the target comes into his office. You will have an undercover car and will not come into the office unless you need to do something administratively necessary. Jerry is the case agent and he'll tell you all about it, okay?" Ray gave me a big, wide, yellow-toothed grin again as he got up from his chair.

I thanked Ray and walked back to my desk and looked at my notes: *Jerry, 8–6, Title 3.* What was a Title III? How did you monitor a Title III? Were these people speaking a foreign language? Undercover car? Hot shit. I had now arrived in the big leagues.

I scanned around the squad area and looked at all of the impressive black and gold name plaques on each of the agents' desks in an attempt to find this Jerry dude. FBI agents all sat together at desks in big squad areas, and two agents shared one phone. But each agent sat in an executive swivel armchair and had one of those fancy-looking name plaques, as if they were generals. There is a caste system in the FBI, and the agents know it, as does everyone else. If you are not a special agent, you are not worthy.

As I was thinking about how happy I was that I was on the top of the pecking order, even if I didn't have a pecker, I spied the name "Gerald" on a nameplate. There was Gerry. He was sitting at his desk, in the back of the office, talking on his phone. Nice, preppy-looking blonde guy. I discretely eyeballed him until he got off his phone and then I walked over and introduced myself.

He looked at me with little recognition of what significance I would play in his life and as if he was so distracted he could barely concentrate on anything.

"Ray said I was to begin monitoring for you tomorrow," I said in hopes of helping this poor, good-looking young guy along. Ah. Then a glimmer of understanding showed in his eyes.

"Yes. I'm going over there in about an hour. I'll take you with me. Lynne Hunt will explain everything to you. Here is a copy of the affidavit. Read that in the meantime. Oh, here are your car keys. It should be parked on the sixth floor of the garage. The license plate number is written on the tag there. It's a gray Pontiac Grand Prix."

Gerry picked up something else to read. I assumed I had been dismissed. Well, so much for the relaxed getting to know each other and "welcome aboard" attitude, and so much for the team spirit of working together on bringing down organized crime in Chicago, and so much for even explaining a single thing so that someone might be able to understand what these people were talking about.

I sat down at my desk to read the "Affidavit in Application for Title III Interception." I didn't even quite remember what that was as a legal document. I felt as isolated as I had been my first day when I raised my right hand and held my visitor's badge in my left to be sworn in as an FBI agent. They hadn't even told me to look through the folder on the desk to find the badge that was in there.

There was no camaraderie at the Bureau. At least none in which I had been included. There had been no one to guide me, to talk to me as an experienced friend, to make me feel included. This had not happened in training school, nor was it happening out here in the field. Like on Halloween night, when I was cold, soaking wet, and being led by an arresting agent I knew was just "wrong." Certainly, there was no one I could tell about how alarming it had been. There was no whining allowed. Just tough it out. So tough it out I did, in many ways to prove myself, and to prove that a woman could kick ass in making organized crime cases — the top echelon of criminal work in the FBI.

One also had to contend with the tough Chicago winters. As Gerry and I walked through the dry, filth-littered downtown streets, the wind cut right through my coat onto my bare skin. I was miserably cold and vowed I had to get a new coat — a fur coat — no joke.

The "off-site" was located in an office building designed by the world-famous architect Louis Sullivan in the 1880s. It was, and had been for at least 50 years, occupied by jewelry trade businesses. Many years before

Tom brought me there to select the diamond for my engagement ring, and later to size a magnificent 18-carat aquamarine ring (gem quality, thank you) that he had given me for our 10th wedding anniversary. All in all it was an interesting location for our work.

The FBI had rented an office in the building so that we could drop wires from video and sound receivers located in the target's office and connect them to the image and sound recorders in our surreptitious office below. Pretty damn cool. My mood immediately turned upward.

At work, I saw why Gerry was such a distracted mess. This Title III stuff was a nightmare of legal paperwork and hoopla. To do our job, it was necessary to prove that law enforcement had no other way to obtain evidence against someone known to be committing illegal acts (try to figure that one out) except by violating the privacy of the criminals by taping their phone calls and videotaping their actions. This seemed to fly in the face of all the rights our Constitution had promised, but what did I know?

So there I sat in an office for my first three months as an organized crime agent, watching George. George was the jewelry fence for Anthony "The Ant" Spilotro, the Chicago Outfit's representative in Las Vegas. The Ant was the main character in the movie "Casino." He was also a big-time asshole. His fence, George, wasn't so big-time, but he ran with the right crowd, and the theory was that you should pick them off one at a time, working your way up the food chain.

Unfortunately, George died of a heart attack before he could be indicted. Lynne Hunt, my monitoring partner, who became my dearest friend, knew he would die that way, from watching him eight to ten hours a day, five to six days a week. George was at least 60 pounds overweight, had a wicked cough, and was angry from sunup to sundown. The only exercise he ever got was getting up from behind his desk, putting a porno video in the player, taking off his pants, sitting down behind his desk again, and masturbating.

On a daily basis, George played host to a cast of organized crime characters who were the dumbest, most prejudiced, most opinionated, least educated, and most flawed individuals one could ever imagine. One afternoon, fat Herbie Blitzstein, a 300-pound lieutenant of Tony Spilotro, and George got into a conversation about Jacqueline Kennedy. They kept referring to her as a "cunt." Lynne and I controlled our impulses. We would have liked to run up the stairs to George's office, burst in, and strangle the two of them. We looked forward to George's eventual arrest, and we begged Gerry to let us be the two "cunts" who would put the handcuffs on him.

Blitzstein was part of Spilotro's gang. They were jewelry thieves and murderers. A few years down the road, I would learn firsthand from my friend Joe that organized crime's influence was at the highest levels in the Chicago Police Department. This gave Spilotro's crews the freedom to commit scores that were poorly planned, unsophisticated, and clumsy. If they got caught, they just had their friends in the C.P.D. mess up the case to such a degree that no prosecutor, judge, or jury could find them guilty.

But back to our friend George the jeweler. A thief is only as good as his fence. A fence is only as good as he is able to move gold and stones. Used jewelry is not exactly something Daddy can wrap up in a box and give to Mommy for Christmas. What usually happens is that a piece of jewelry gets cut down and melted for its gold content. The stones are removed and sold to jewelers who make them into new pieces.

Lynne and I watched George faithfully show up at his office day in and day out for three months, and we never saw him sell one piece of jewelry. What was he doing? I honestly can't exactly say what he did all day. All I remember is that he didn't make jewelry, sell jewelry, appraise jewelry, or buy jewelry. He was very friendly with everyone in the building, particularly the newcomers to the trade, the Hispanics. Perhaps, after hours, and somewhere else, our boy George did his real work by passing off the hot shit from Tony Spilotro to the jewelry "chop shops."

It was easy to become dulled into a sense of complacency while working on cases against "The Chicago Outfit," "Chicago Syndicate," or the "Chicago Mob."[4] Evidence gathering moved at glacial speed. I was too anxious, too much of a rookie to sit back and wait for some old fart to talk while we listened and watched as he and his dim-witted friends discussed politics or how they could screw someone out of something. They truly were the cheapest sons of bitches I had ever heard. They were also the most ruthless.

I later realized that the surveillance of George was a very good use of our time, even if we felt bored and our youthful energies were underutilized in this effort to get to Tony Spilotro through George. Spilotro was an evil man, and the men who worked with him had to be just as vile. He had "made his bones" way back in 1962. Making your bones is accomplished when you kill someone on behalf of the bosses and don't get caught by the police. The unlucky victims who unwittingly helped Tony make his bones were two guys who committed a robbery in Melrose Park, a notorious Mob-laden suburban Chicago bedroom community. These guys were not part of the Outfit, and nobody pulled jobs in the Chicago Outfit's backyard.

But Tony had a problem. He was told to find these two bastards, but when he went out looking for them, he couldn't corner both at the same time. One day he located one of the robbers, Billy McCarthy. But not Jimmy Miraglia. So, the genius he was, he grabbed Billy and brought him to Outfit boss Sam "Mad Sam" DeStefano's home. In Sam's garage they put Billy's head in a vise. These were desperate times and desperate measures had to be used.

Billy struggled, but Sam held his head in the vise as Tony twisted the handle and continued to twist and tighten the vise. "Where the fuck is Jimmy?" demanded Tony. Spit, blood, and screaming mixed together in that horrific scene that was done methodically to torture Billy into telling them where Jimmy was. Billy screamed in pain and withheld the information until his left eye popped out of its socket. Bleeding profusely, with his eye squished on the floor, Billy freaked out. In what must have been excruciating pain, between crying and drawling, he blabbered Jimmy's whereabouts. Tony then thanked him, and with some help from "Mad Sam" to position Billy's body, he slit his throat. Then he went out to find Jimmy. The other robber was a luckier man than Billy. He wasn't tortured. But his throat was slit from ear to ear. [5] I think that's a quick way to die — sort of like slowly chopping your head off?

There can be no doubt that organized crime is an evil menace to society. It controls the sale of vices — prostitution, gambling, juice loans, profits from thefts, burglaries, and scams; it enforces its terror by torture and murder; and it guarantees its continued existence by the bribery of law enforcement, including judges and politicians.

In a press release upon the indictment of 14 defendants for alleged organized crime activities, alleging 18 mob murders, United States Attorney Pat Fitzgerald said, "After so many years it lifts the veil of secrecy and exposes the violent underworld of organized crime." Fitzgerald, who went to Harvard University on a full academic scholarship, did not use the mythological inference of "underworld" casually. The mythological underworld is a place where one is condemned to spend his life in a state of continued torture and wretched suffering. So is the life of an organized crime member or his victims.

– CHAPTER FOUR –
The Old Dog Barks

"Why are you giving me this case, Lynne?" I asked incredulously as Lynne leaned her tall, thin body over my desk, placing a file folder in front of me.

"Well, it's this way," she sighed. "I'm resigning from the Bureau to go back to California and help my dad."

"What? Why?" I shot back in a sharp voice. I didn't mean to sound like that, but suddenly it was like I was back in fourth grade and my best friend was telling me she was moving, and I would once again be doomed to standing alone on the playground, feeling like the outsider again. Lynne understood this fear in me.

She pulled a chair over next to my desk and sat down. "My dad is dying of brain cancer. He wants me to come back and run the business."

"Oh, I'm so sorry, Lynne," I mumbled.

"Yeah," she quietly replied.

"Is there any hope? Any treatment?"

"No. My mom has taken him to the best specialists in California. It's just a matter of time."

Instinctively, I reached out and held her very cold hand. After three months of eight- to ten-hour days, sitting together listening and watching George, bit by bit we learned each other's life story. I knew how much she loved and admired her father. He was a World War II fighter pilot who later became a very successful businessman. Together with Lynne's also amazing mother, these talented people worked long hours to build a small retail empire. Now they were asking their princess give up her dream career as an FBI agent and take on the burden of running the multimillion-dollar corporation at the same time her father was dying.

Had her father really asked her to do that? Or had she volunteered? I never asked Lynne. My thought today is that she felt it her responsibility to return home and provide some peace of mind to her dying father and grieving mother.

Everything about Lynne's life would not have predicted her strength of character and resolve. She grew up in Southern California, born after her parents had made it. She attended private schools, lived in a large, sprawling California ranch home, hung out at the family's second home in Palm Springs, spent summers surfing at the beach house they rented, and, to top it all off, dressed like a model. At 5 feet 10 inches tall and perennially tan, she turned heads whenever she walked into the office.

After law school and passing the California Bar on the first try, she took the job of being a public defender for a short period of time in San Diego County. She said she wanted to put her clients in jail, rather than keep them out, so she realized a career as an FBI agent might be more suited to her philosophical temperament.

Since she was the ideal Southern California girl, was an excellent long-distance runner, knew how to surf, had family money, was an attorney, and on top of all that was smart, she was most any man's dream. Not to mention that of an FBI recruiter. When Lynne walked into the San Diego office and met the recruiter, he — and it was a he; remember this was 1978 — jumped at the chance to put Lynne through the series of tests, knowing full well she would pass.

Now, my first friend — besides my roommate Linda at Quantico — was leaving and giving me this "Old Dog" case these organized crime guys had assigned to her when she was transferred to the squad just a couple months before me. In Bureau jargon an Old Dog case was one that had gone unsolved for years and had been transferred from agent to agent in futile attempts to find a solution or close it.

"Now, I think there might be some potential here, Elaine," she said to me.

"Great," I said without conviction. I suspected this case was just something given to her to occupy her time. "Why are you quitting?" I asked. "Can't you take a leave of absence?"

Lynne didn't answer me. I was getting pushy and couldn't stop myself.

"Don't you see that this is what all the men think we will do when we take this job? Haven't you heard them talk about how we take up spaces at training school that men with families and careers could have just for us to satisfy some whim we have to prove ourselves?"

Her eyes started to tear over.

"Oh, I don't want to hurt your feelings, Lynnie. You are so talented and so cool. I need you. I don't want you to go. I need you to fight both of these battles. Bad guys and here at the office. These guys are willing to have their token female agents. Bimbos or ugly and incompetent. But not women like you. You scare the shit out of them."

She didn't have a comeback for me because she already had made up her mind and had committed to her father and mother. She picked up the file folder. "This case has some potential because the Chicago Police just arrested Eto. He's running the business of *bolita* and you can work that angle by seeing what the cops have. At least you're starting with someone who's verifiably active."

"Oh, my," I sighed deeply, giving in. "Okay, Lynne, I'll pay attention and listen."

Lynne's comment on verifiable criminal activity didn't really sink in that day, but in retrospect it sure does. Organized crime members went years without the interference of law enforcement. Did you know that is true? "Made" members of the Chicago Outfit went without arrests or investigations for 10, 15, or 20 years. Talk about having the fix in.[6] Sure, the Chicago cops would occasionally pick up the "boys" in a gambling raid, but the judges were always "fixed" and the defendants went nowhere but home.

The Internal Revenue Service (IRS) did a great job of harassing mobsters, but it took years to make a case, and by then the slick tax attorneys had weaseled the criminal tax case down to a tax liability, which was "pay a fine" and "don't go to jail."

But these men were evil. They were torturers, killers, corruptors, and purveyors of every type of vice, and they were the puppet masters of every crew that pulled a major cartage or jewelry heist in Chicago since the 1920s. They owned the city of Chicago. They did what they wanted, to whom they wanted, when they wanted, and no law enforcement agency had taken them down.

So on March 18, 1980, in the pages of a thin FBI file, I first met Ken "Joe" Eto. It was a fortuitous day for me. I was given the case by my friend from Southern California, who had no idea about the Chicago Mob, but she recognized it as a potential jewel. Everybody else who worked organized crime saw it as a case involving a minor, not even an Italian mobster, as something to keep the "little ladies" busy in between the tasks they saw to give us. These broads were not going to be making major cases, so why give them one?

Eto's FBI file was about 30 pages thick, and it was composed of his latest rap sheet[7] and notes called "correlation information," which was a compilation of all the references found about "Ken Eto" in all of the FBI files in which his name was mentioned. This information characterized Eto as having 14 different aliases. Most of them were ridiculous and were not devised by Eto to confuse or confound law enforcement. Perhaps he had willingly called himself "Montana Joe," "Joe Eto," and "Joe Nakamura," but I cannot imagine he gave himself the names "Tokyo Joe," "Kenneth Ito," "The Jap," "The Chinaman," or "Joe the Jap." After listening to hundreds of hours of Outfit boys' conversations through Title III wiretaps, I can see how, in their perverse, discriminatory way, they would have stupidly and rudely called Ken Eto all of these different names. The same goes for any of the Chicago policemen who might have arrested him. They certainly were not exactly a politically or ethnically sensitive group.

The FBI clerk who put together the file noted that Ken Eto had a brother who lived on Chicago's north side and whose name was Joseph. Why Ken Eto took his brother's name, Joe, was never explained. It was evident that the FBI had known of Eto's Mob association since 1970, and since that time there had been four previous "go-nowhere" investigations attempted on my slippery Mob target.

From unidentified FBI sources, some of Eto's associates were Sam Salvador Sarcinelli, Phil Caliendo, Arnold Kimmes, and Charlie Miyoshi. Then the file presented some of the FBI's best work in the organized crime area, reading the newspaper. It quoted an article, "Mob Generation Gap Endangers Tony Accardo and His Pals," from the Sunday, May 1, 1977, "Chicago Tribune."[8] It noted that Vincent Solano, 57, former chauffeur for the late Ross Prio and President of Local 1 of the Laborers' Union, was the north side boss and his lieutenants were Joseph DiVarco, Michael Glitta, Ken Eto, Marshall Caifano, and Leonard Patrick. The clerk summarized all the information about Eto as:

KEN ETO, Sr.
Date of Birth: October 19, 1919
Place of Birth: Stockton, California
Address: 5451 North East River Road, Chicago, Illinois
Description: Male/Jap, 5'5", 155 lbs., black hair, brown eyes
Convictions: "Eto has been arrest (sic) at least six times since 1942 that have included Conspiracy and Syndicate gambling. He is a convicted felon having been sentenced to years in Idaho State prison in 1950 for Obtaining Money Under False Pretenses."
Status: Subordinate – North Area
Function: Street Man

Remarks: Top Oriental in Bolita and Policy Rackets and is also involved in narcotics.

When I got the nerve to chat with some of the other agents on the squad, who had slowly begun to recognize that I was a human being, I ran the names by them. Eto's associates were verified as being maybe the likely lineup, but no one could definitively say yes or no, because no one had a snitch placed high enough, or who was reliable enough, to validate even the newspaper information.

Each day I keenly tuned in to the constant conversations that bounced between the agents in our open squad area, while pretending to be silently working on my own matters. There was an incessant flow of Mob gossip, but it did surprise me that these agents didn't spend all that much time out on the street among it all. Many of my squad mates were buried under mountains of paperwork. When preparing for or finishing Title III wiretaps, everybody came up with little bits and pieces of information that they shared, argued over, or bragged about, and I overheard all of it.

I also began to overhear strategic problems they were having with their investigations and started quietly going over to their desks and volunteering to help them. The first time was for an agent named Jim Dietz. Additionally, I started to answer everyone's telephone when they were not there and Judy, our secretary, couldn't get to it. I took meticulous telephone messages for each agent. I already looked like I thought I was too good for them, but I wanted to try to prove that I really didn't think that (at least not all the time). Actually, I was willing to do anything to be accepted and to learn.

Unexpectedly, I did learn that many of these bright men with multiple college degrees just didn't use their imaginations very much. Totally wrapped up in their worlds of "spook stuff," they spooked themselves into inaction. They were gun-shy of making cold calls or accidentally revealing too much to the wrong person. Agents are often required to make "pretext" calls to get information — you pretend to be someone you are not, or introduce a phony situation that is designed to make the person on the other end of the call reveal something or otherwise assist in your investigation. In a way, it involves playacting, and it takes a degree of confidence, skill, and finesse to successfully make such calls. One had to be a little bold to instantly come up with a believable and non-suspicious reason to be asking questions of a stranger. Perhaps I felt I could come up with a lie easier than others could, since I always had a devious streak that I needed to suppress. This pretext call business was an art, and over time I found that I was a natural cold call artist.

To solve one of Jim Dietz's problems regarding Caesar DiVarco, who was, coincidentally, Ken Eto's Mob under boss, I found an off-site lookout. I just walked into the perfectly situated office building and asked to speak to the manager. I told him I was interested in renting an office suite with a certain view, nothing else, just the view. Within a few short hours we had a lookout that faced the Rush Street hangout of the north side crew. The tenant who rented the space cleared out an office suite, gave us our own key and said, "Oh, now, we don't even want to know why you need to be there. We know what the FBI does is top secret." This job was a great boost for my ego. What a trip for a woman to be armed not only with a gun, but also with all the power those three letters, "FBI," brought.

On Jim's case, I also volunteered to handle the fixed surveillance work. By doing so, I learned that Jim was interested in determining the make, license, and description of the north side Outfit vehicles. I got to know each of the crew members' physical descriptions, recognize their faces, and categorize the type of clothing they usually wore. Within my range of view, I saw who they met on the street, the way they walked, and where they went.

I was privately tutored onsite by George, the clerk and office photographer. He taught me how to set up a tripod, properly position the camera, insert and remove film, read a light meter, select the f-stop, and keep a detailed, trial-validated photo log — talk about priceless investigative skills. When I finally got to Eto and took his picture doing something illegal, he wouldn't know he had been shot, but he would be dead in court.

So as the winter of 1980 turned into the spring, I learned about the north side crew, but I never saw Eto. At the time he lived on Chestnut, just around the corner from my "perch." It was a miracle he escaped my camera. I had spent so much time looking out my window that I could tell Mike Glitta, the porno king, from behind, two blocks away. Caesar DiVarco, the street boss, was an instant spot, because he was such a short little fart, and he ambled as if he had no destination, a very unlikely way for someone in a big city to walk. Eyeballing Joe Arnold, the juice loan man, was also effortless. He was 6 feet 3 inches tall and had the world's worst posture. He must have spent too much time bending over to try to catch all of the orders little Caesar whispered to him in his raspy voice.

No one would believe "d'ese guys," walking up and down Rush Street, could run a criminal empire. The north side crew did not get the same amount of newspaper ink as the other crews, but they were just as violent as Joey Lombardo and the punk Tony Spilotro. And they were into the same shit as everyone else — corruption, prostitution, pornography, gambling, extortion, juice, theft, and murder.

But the north side crew was special in that they were sitting on the so-called "honey pot" of Chicago. This area was home to some of the wealthiest Chicagoans and most expensive lakeside real estate. This was also where everyone came to play: glamorous nightclubs, smoky jazz bars, the Playboy mansion, go-go clubs, gambling dens that hosted games in which thousands of dollars changed hands, and prostitutes — not your stand-on-the-street whores — but call girls. This was the location of the city's best hotels and finest French restaurants. Also, any business in this geographical area that was involved in vice paid the Outfit.

If you wanted a liquor license, you had to grease the palm of the local alderman. From there, the payments started. From the alderman and the infamously corrupt policemen at the 18th District to the Outfit's muscle that was sent in to shake you down, if you did business in the Rush Street area, there were no "ifs, ands, or buts," no "I'm not interested," no "talk to my lawyer." There was no way to avoid paying the Outfit. You paid. It was the price of doing business and everyone knew it.

According to my skinny FBI file and the squad hearsay, Eto was described as a syndicate gambling kingpin and top muscleman for the Italian mob. I thought, "Was there something wrong here?" That question kept me thinking that the case was a cheap hand-off just to keep me out of the big-time work. What's a Japanese guy doing in the mob? Screw them, I thought. I'll make this Eto thing and move on up the ladder to bigger fish — like the Italians.

The file also indicated that Eto allegedly controlled *bolita* for the Chicago *La Costra Nostra* (LCN). What the hell is *bolita?* The term kingpin probably meant he made a lot of money and ran the operation. That's good — more money meant more time in jail. I looked up the federal statute and found I needed to prove that a gambling kingpin took in more than $2,000 a day in wagers.[9]

A top muscleman was easy to figure out. I guessed he was a killer, like "squish your head in a vise" Tony Spilotro. But what was this *bolita*? Is there a dictionary of gambling terms? One day, as I was trying to figure it out, my supervisor approached me and said, "Smith, I'm going to call my friend Jules Gallett. He's the Commander in Vice Control at the Chicago Police Department. You'll ride along with some of his guys that work *bolita*."

"That sounds like a great idea, Ray. Just let me know when and where."

Actually, I thought, I'm not just stroking Ray, that does sound exciting. A little scary, but exciting, and certainly it will be a learning experience. If I survived. There was never a loving relationship between the Chicago Police Department and the FBI and, depending upon whom I was put with, it could be a little dicey.

While Ray made those arrangements, I continued to do research in old newspaper files and Chicago Police files to try to find out why Eto was called "muscle." One day in my mail folder I found the results of a search I had asked Ruthie to perform. She was one of our clerks assigned to the Chicago Police "dead file" room. The documents were yellowed with age and had been typed on an old Olivetti typewriter, one of those big black things you've seen in old gangster movies that were used by crime reporters. I knew them because in 1961 I had learned how to type on one of those relics. The heading on the report read:

Detective Division   *February 2, 1958*
From: Chief of Detectives
To: Commissioner of Police
Subject: "Supplementary Report Re- Fatal Cutting of the body of Santiago Rosa Gonzalez, male, Puerto Rican, 3631 N. Pine Grove Avenue, found fatally cut in vacant lot at 1814 W. Washburne Ave. at 6:30 a.m. this date. Homicide file #58.
Report of: Dets. F. Sloan, G. Damice, Car 68, Homicide Section, D.B.
Dets. J. Mahoney, J. Loftus, Car 69, Homicide Section, D.B.

The detective's report detailed the interviews and observations done by the Chicago Police after Amus Morris, a 12-year-old newspaper boy, walked out onto the front porch of his home at 6:30 a.m. on a frigid cold February 2, 1958 morning, looked over at the vacant lot next door to his house and saw the body of Santiago Gonzalez. Santiago was lying on his back, at an angle. He had been thrown between the rear bumper of a 1955 Buick and an empty, rusted 50-gallon drum. Amus went running back into the house to tell his mother, who then called the police.

Police stomped into the trash-strewn vacant lot in response to Amus' mother's call and found Santiago's fully clothed body. He would have looked pretty dapper in his blue overcoat, brown suit, white shirt and tie, and brown dress shoes, if his stomach hadn't been cut open and his intestines pulled out.

The area beat-coppers identified the victim by utilizing the age-old investigative technique of riffling through his pockets to locate his wallet. They then went back to their squad car, where it was a hell of a lot warmer, called the station, and reported what they had found. They told the station to get the homicide "dicks" over to the 23rd District because they had another case. The 23rd District dispatcher notified the Homicide Section at Chicago Police Headquarters and the Crime Lab, which immediately sent photographers to the dump scene.

Now the lowly beat cops had had their much anticipated breakfast plans screwed up. There was no way they'd have their part of this thing cleaned up before their stomachs started growling with hunger. All this topped off another long, freeze-your-ass-off night in Chicago.

I soon learned the mindset of Chicago coppers, and I can guarantee you, they were none too upset about finding a disemboweled Puerto Rican, even a nicely dressed one, lying in a vacant lot. The district coppers just had to make sure no one messed with the body until the Crime Lab guys got there. The paddy wagon boys would transport the body to the Cook County Morgue.

Once the Crime Lab guys started taking their pictures of the victim, people in the neighborhood had to be pushed away from the gruesome scene, although everyone had come to the conclusion that Santiago had not been killed there. When you gut someone, there is a lot of blood. There wasn't a lot of blood on the frozen, snow-dusted dirt of this lot.

"Come on. Let's get this one out of here before we're stiffer than he is," yelled one of the cops.

Mrs. Ramona Gonzalez was wild with fear. Her mind kept going back to when she woke up last night, alone in her bed, and thinking she had heard someone calling out, "Help! Help! No!" and screaming. Now she was sitting at the local police station in a hard wooden chair, barely dressed after being rushed out of the house and to the County Morgue to identify the body of her darling. She was shivering, afraid, and thinking her dearest, handsome Chave was dead. It was his voice she had heard.

Several men approached her. These men were different because they wore suits. "Mrs. Gonzalez, we would like to take you home to talk some more and see if there is anything there that might lead us to whomever might have done this to your husband."

"Oh, *si*," she sighed.

One of the detectives wrote in his report that once Mrs. Gonzalez was home, she became more relaxed. Almost before she could take off her coat after walking in the door of her apartment, she told the homicide detectives, "I believe the gambling syndicate murdered my husband. It is headed by a Chinese man named Joe, and he owns a restaurant on Chestnut and Clark Street, but I have never seen him."

Ramona continued, now sobbing and beginning to shiver again, "In 1957, when I was in Gary, Indiana, with our daughter, my husband came after me. He was black and blue all over his body. I was shocked and right away wanted to know how this had happened to him. He told me he had been beaten with a tire iron by some hoodlums on Clark Street in Chicago. He said he didn't know why."

Quieting down a little now and realizing that her husband probably had not been very candid with her, Ramona went on. "At the end of last year, Americo Delgado told me that my husband was fighting the gambling syndicate and was going to be killed. Detectives, these are the people that dragged my husband out of our vestibule last night. I heard his screams! I heard his screams! These are the people that killed my Chave."

Breaking the silent sobbing that was racking Ramona's body and the stoic silence of the detectives, the phone began to ring in the tiny apartment. A detective tapped Ramona's shoulder and motioned for her to answer the phone; as he did that, another detective tiptoed to the bedroom and picked up the extension. It was Gabe, Santiago's best friend, calling. He was calling to let Ramona know that he had found out about Chave's slaying: "Yes, the guys had been pointing the finger at him."

Although I was reading the police report with rapt attention and the black-and-white photographs of Santiago's body were horrific, I did not really understand how this had anything to do with Ken Eto. That is, until I got to the interview of Ken Eto on February 3, 1958, at Chicago Police Headquarters. An interview personally conducted by none other than the Commander of Homicide, Lieutenant James McMahon. Now I realized that the Chinese man was a Japanese man. His real name was Ken, but his street name was Joe. His gambling empire was *bolita* and Chave was Puerto Rican and only Puerto Ricans played *bolita*.

I read the interview of Joe "The Chinaman" Eto. It went something like this: "Hello. I am Lt. James McMahon, Commander of Homicide for the Chicago Police Department. How are you today? We are going to conduct an interview that will look like it is an interview into the brutal murder, actually the medieval method of murder, the disembowelment of Santiago Gonzalez. But don't worry; this is just a pretend interview. This interview won't make you sweat or even make your tummy get a little gassy. It will be over in about three minutes. At the bottom of one typed page you will need to sign your name. Okay? Does that sound fair to you?"

"Yes, after I read it," replied Eto.

Well, I knew at that point that Ken Eto had never been charged with the murder of Santiago Gonzalez and neither had anyone else. One thing I knew for sure was that when the word "muscle" was used with Eto's name I always visualized Chave's body in that vacant lot on that cold February morning in 1958. Now I wanted some handcuffs on Eto's wrists.

Summer takes a long time coming to Chicago, and even in April and May Chicagoans search for some signs of warmth and new beginnings. Mine came in the form of a scraggly Italian auto body repairman named Frank. I had never even met an auto body repairman. This one soon became a best friend.

One surprisingly warm May afternoon, the other organized squad supervisor, Sergeant York — that was the name everyone called Jim York, came strolling over to my boss Ray. "I just had a guy call in wanting to give information about Ken Eto and Sam Sarcinelli. I thought I'd go out to meet him on my way home tonight."

"Damn if you will!" shouted Ray.

Since my desk was just outside Ray's office and I had a ringside seat, I almost fell off my chair. I didn't know Ray could raise his voice.

He continued in a loud voice, "The Ken Eto case is on my squad, and if anyone meets an informant on Ken Eto, it will be my agent."

Sarge then interjected in his whinny New Jersey accent, "Well, I thought since Sarcinelli was a south side guy..."

Ray cut him off at the knees. "York, that's why you came slinking over here to tell me about it. You knew it was wrong, so give me the guy's name and number. We'll handle it."

I wanted to jump up and say, "This is my case," but I controlled every fiber of my body and remained in my chair to watch "The Sarge" hand over a piece of paper to Ray and walk back to his squad area. Mind you, I was watching all of this while pretending to do something of presidential importance at my desk. In fact, the office is where all FBI agents learn their best surveillance techniques.

Ray strolled over to me and handed me the name of Frank Aster and a phone number. He said, "Call this guy. He may have some information on Ken Eto." Then he walked away. No advice. No "I'll send someone with you." Nothing.

I picked up the phone and called the number. Someone answered, "Blah, Blah, Auto Body Shop."

I wasn't able to understand the name of the auto body shop, but I went ahead and said, "May I speak to Frank Guliata ?"

"This is Frank."

Thank God, I thought.

We had a sort of cryptic conversation that ended with us agreeing to meet that evening at 5:30 p.m. at a coffee shop somewhere on 1st Avenue in Melrose Park — the same Melrose Park where all the mobsters lived and the same turf that was violated by those hapless robbers Billy and Jimmy resulting in their brutal extermination. I was less than a year out of the FBI Academy and still didn't have the courage to meet an informant on my own, especially one that could be as critical as this one. So I did what was natural; I turned to Tom. I called him at his office all of about 100 feet away and asked if he would go with me to meet this new informant. I'm sure he heard the excitement in my voice. Without hesitation, he agreed. He would call Grandma to let her know that we would be home a little late that evening. Success, this night, and overall in my career as a FBI special agent, was only possible because of the support of my husband Tom, who stepped in to help me when I asked him, and a mother-in-law who cared for our daughter with devotion and love. Without either of them, I never would have been able to spend the long hours away from home that I did or endure the mental stress of achieving my goals.

Frank turned out to be an Italian grease monkey who thought he was a ladies' man, so he basically ignored Tom and talked to me. I took over and focused on how I could get him to forget about the $10,000 he wanted for the information about "Joe the Jap" he was willing to sell us. Even as a rookie, I knew the Bureau was not going to give $10,000 to anyone for any information. I continued talking, really schmoozing him now, and was able to learn that his information did pertain to *bolita*. He kept going back to this Sarcinelli guy, though, and how he had lots of cocaine.

I didn't care about cocaine. I wanted Eto. Our meeting ended with me saying we'd meet in a day or two, and I'd talk to my bosses about the $10,000. I smiled warmly and shook his hand like I had been thrilled to have been in his company. Tom shook his hand stiffly.

That night I decided having another agent along on these informant meetings was wrong. If you met in a public place and you wore your gun, it was safe. Then the informant had only one personality to deal with — mine. I wanted my personality, my warmth, my smile, my goals, and my words to win them over and keep them on track. On that evening in May 1980, I began to hone my technique of being a criminal recruiter for the FBI. Assistant Director William McGarity once told me he thought I had been one of the best informant developers in the Bureau. That's great, but it did take an emotional toll.

As Tom and I got in his Bureau car for the long drive home in rush-hour traffic, pumped up with excitement, I said, "I don't even think he understood that you're my husband." I had been worried the informant would have thought it lame that the FBI agent for the Ken Eto case had to bring her husband along on the meeting. Truth be told, I didn't feel comfortable enough to ask anyone on my squad to go with me. No other agent had ever asked me to join one of their informant meetings. Besides the fact that I was an outsider, asking someone do an interview at 5:30 p.m. was inconvenient. Most agents would be on their commute home at that time and uninterested in meeting some potential damn source. But I had a personality that forced me to strike when I had the opportunity. I can thank my husband, Special Agent Thomas Daniel Smith, for providing me the flexibility to take advantage of these opportunities.

- CHAPTER FIVE -
Hill Street Blues

On the way home from meeting Frankie in Melrose Park, Tom gave me a quick lesson in the operation of informants — FBI style. Working with informants can be a complicated and risky business. The process is fraught with legal complications. The special agent working with an informant walks the very thin line of wanting to use his information in legal documents, but runs the risk of having to disclose the informant's identity if the court orders it.

Believing or not believing an informant's information is also tricky. Informants are usually self-interested, wily bastards. They can easily manipulate some well-educated agents who may have law or accounting degrees but who are not street-savvy. They will inundate the agent with a confusing barrage of half-truths, lies, and street talk. Trouble arrives when that agent puts this information into an affidavit and swears to its veracity before a federal judge. If it is found out to be a lie, that special agent has lost his credibility forever and he becomes worthless as an agent — bye-bye.

On top of the legal issues, there are Bureau rules and regulations devised to make an agent's life miserable. Pages and pages of forms must be filled out. These forms are found in a locked room and are available only during hours designated according to the whims of a person called the "informant coordinator."

Some of these forms are necessary to sign up an informant. Once executed, all of them have to be reviewed and approved by your supervisor. At least that part, the review of Frankie's paperwork by my supervisor "Ray, out to lunch," would be no problem. Other issues would be trickier.

I had to deal with the expectations of my new informant, the Italian stallion Frankie, a.k.a. "grease monkey." He was banking on me bringing the first payment for his services to our next meeting, and knowing the typical FBI informant deal that I had to sell him, I anticipated his reaction. "You're telling me that the fuckin' cheap FBI won't give me $10,000 and I gotta live by these goddamned Attorney General Guidelines that tell me I'm a useless fuck? And you'll never back me up on anything I do or say? And if I do get paid a few pennies for my information, I gotta declare it on my fucking income tax return? You gotta be kiddin'. That's the deal?" Facing this anticipated hurdle, I wondered how I was ever going to get any information to hang Ken Eto. I knew that if Frankie turned out to really know the workings of the north side crew, my case would be doable.

When I walked into work the next morning, hungover from a sleepless night, I was resolute that I would solve my problems by conquering the FBI's informant system. I was greeted warmly by Jack Hunt, an agent who had been unusually nice to me ever since my friend Lynnie had resigned from the Bureau and gone back to California. I decided to utilize this new friendship.

"Hey, Jack, can you show me the manual that explains how to operate an informant?" I knew Jack was the second guy in charge of the squad when Ray wasn't there and thought he should know.

"Sure. Come on in Ray's office. We keep it in the safe," he drawled.

I had always stayed several yards away from Hunt. He was a former Arkansas Razorbacks football star who had "redneck" tattooed all over him. Jack was a defensive back for Arkansas, but he looked like he could have played defensive backfield.

The safe combination was conspicuously written on Ray's desk blotter — so much for the extra security. Hunt spun the dial of the big, gray, industrial-looking safe, opened one of the file drawers, pulled out a manual, and handed it to me.

Still concerned about security, he said, "Don't leave it on your desk. It has to be in your hands or under lock at all times."

Well, I thought, I better do this task right away. After saying hello to Judy, the secretary, and agent Jim Dietz, who I now called "Dietzie," and without even hanging up my coat, I sat down at my desk and started to study and take notes. Operating this Frankie guy was going to be my ticket to Ken Eto.

By 10 a.m. I had filled out the forms for the FBI and Judy had typed them. For my use, I made a list of the "Absolutely No You Cannot Dos" and the "You Immediately Must Dos." I went in to see if Ray was in his office. "Mr. Razorback" sat with his feet up on Ray's desk, talking on the phone like he belonged there. I tried to back out, but he cackled into the poor person's ear on the other end, "Guess who just walked in? Special Agent Elaine Corbitt Smith," emphasizing my middle name as a screaming affectation of a "liberated woman." He paused while the other person said something. Then he smiled and said, "Right. Talk to you later."

He hung up the phone, looked up, and gave me a shit-eating grin. "Hey, Elaine, what I can do *to* you? Oh, I mean — *for* you?"

I wanted to say, "You big hick. So which one of your little buddies were you talking to as I walked into the office? And what's the big joke? Incidentally, it's inappropriate for someone pretending to be management to say, 'What can I do *to* you?'" While all of these thoughts were spinning in my head, I actually said, "Jack, could you look over my paperwork? And if it's okay, approve it in Ray's absence? And I could use a little guidance on my problem with this dude wanting a $10,000 payment for his information?"

He laughed. "That's a good one, Smith. $10,000." He chuckled some more. Then he settled down to review my paperwork. Perhaps this brute could even read. I looked out the window at the rainy Chicago day and thought about nothing. It felt good.

Jack scribbled his signature on the bottom of the forms like he was some sort of Arkansas John Hancock, threw his pen on the desk, leaned back in the sumptuous executive chair, put his hands behind his head, and said in his most professorial manner, "Well, you just have to string this guy along. Never let him think you won't try to get him that $10,000." Pointing a finger at me now, he added, "You just can't say for sure you'll get it for him. Tell him you'll try to get him as much as you can. And maybe that $10,000 will have to be in small increments, like $200, $400, $500 at a time. But only if and when he brings you the information. In the FBI, we pay on a COD basis — Cash on Delivery. Also, none of these papers have to be signed by your source until 90 days have passed. So you can see him for the next three months before you have to show him these Attorney General Guidelines. When he sees them, he might squawk about reporting payments to the IRS and all that other stuff."

Well put, Jack; my thoughts exactly.

He collected the papers he had signed and haphazardly thrown all over the desk, handed them to me, and got up from Ray's chair. As he walked out of the office past me, he smiled and winked.

Great advice, I thought, but what an asshole.

That afternoon I met Frankie again in Melrose Park. This time for lunch at a hot dog stand. I went alone. I bought hot dogs and fries for both of us and watched him eat and talk with his mouth full of food. The food that didn't make it into his mouth spilled onto his grease-covered gray work pants and shirt. Anyone who says being an FBI agent is a glamorous job just doesn't know the reality.

I was still nervous about easing Frankie into his role as an informant and his expectations about getting paid big bucks for his services. So I turned the conversation to the topic of growing up in Chicago — where we went to high school and that he was a "greaser" and I was a "preppie" — the two distinct classes of students in the Chicago Public Schools in those years. Greasers were kids who were destined to go no further than high school, if they made it that far. Usually from blue-collar families, they would look forward to becoming laborers or tradesmen, if lucky. Greasers took "Basic" English, science, and shop classes, while preppies were tracked into college preparatory classes of "Reserved" English, science, math, and foreign languages. Although we had very different experiences in high school, Frankie now seemed relaxed, enjoying our conversation and the hot dog cuisine. After we ate, I brought up Jack Hunt's "dribble" plan for Frankie's $10,000 payment.

To my surprise, he said, "Ah, I knew you couldn't give me no $10,000. I was just testin' ya to see what ya'd say."

I frowned. "Oh," I replied a little sadly and disappointedly, like I had been tricked.

Frank immediately interjected, "I didn't mean to hurt your feelings or nothin'."

"No, it's not that, Frank. You see, I'm new at this. I figure I am going to believe everything you say to me, because if I don't, I'll go crazy trying to second-guess you. We have to be partners and trust each other. My only rule is, if you lie to me, our partnership is over. I'll walk away and never come back because I cannot deal in lies. Not one. Not a half of one. I do not have time for liars or game boys."

Where the hell was all of this coming from? I didn't know then and I still don't know. I never planned to say it, but out it came, and it was the truth. In terms of our relationship, I was telling Frank what I needed and where we stood. Our time spent together was not for relaxation or enjoyment. It wasn't to develop a new friendship or play a game. My goal was to bring Ken Eto to justice. Frankie had to know where he stood with me — at my side, but not too close.

Frankie's reply to my impassioned plea was, "Yeah, yeah, I know where you're comin' from. I won't play no more games with you. In fact, I'll talk to Wally (meaning Walter Micus, who also worked for Eto) and see if he'll let me 'help' him a little bit. He's a lazy bastard. He'll probably go for it. That way I'll get to know exactly what he's doin' for Joe the Jap."

"Great, Frank, that is exactly what I need, and as we get details from you, I'll be able to request payment for your information. Little by little, we may be able to put a case together. What do you think?"

"Yeah! Dat's the ticket," Frank exclaimed, like some retard.

What a goofball, I thought. But then again, I guess I'm just a snob.

On my drive through midday traffic, I thought about how little I actually knew about Ken Eto. I knew I had to get a better handle on him before I could think about trying to build a case against him. I needed to flesh out his background. He had been described as the Mob's gambling kingpin and muscle. At first glance, in my rookie opinion, he appeared to be a misfit in the Mob. Ethnic groups of all types participated in illegal activity in Chicago. Jews often played the role of bookies and jewelry fences for the Outfit. Weekly pay rollers, such as the crooked Irish cops, judges, and politicians, kept the Outfit's illegal businesses from any serious prosecution by the law. Actual membership in the *La Costra Nostra* (translated as "our thing") was reserved only for Italians from Sicily. But how did this Japanese guy, born in Stockton, California, fit into the inner circle of the Chicago Mob? How did he even find his way there?

I fell back on my natural habits, which were grounded in my many lonely days as a bookworm. Not exactly announcing where I was going to wander that afternoon, off I went to the dusty old Chicago Public Library, located in the business district of Chicago. The main library was the source of all reference material and the knowledge fountain from which all the neighborhood libraries drank.

The Chicago Public Libraries were known for their helpful, young, and cheerful staff. This, of course, is a sarcastic statement. The employees were generally old women who appeared to bathe infrequently, wore sensible shoes, and were lost in their own myopic worlds. If you even slowed as you passed their desks, which displayed the signs "Information" or "Resource Assistance," they looked daggers at you. If you ignored those looks and asked a question, they might pretend to be deaf. Research in this library would be a do-it-yourself project. One must remember that this was in the pre-Google days.

I scanned the directory, just inside the impressive front doors of the very large gothic building. I was glad to have spent enough time in libraries to know my way around their compulsively standardized organizational system. The information I searched for today wasn't graduate-level research. It was more like elementary school social studies, but necessary.

Where the hell was Stockton, California? Why was Eto born there and not in Chicago? I found my answers quickly. Stockton, California, is a town just east of the Oakland/San Francisco area. This was not a Southern California town with sandy beaches, surfing dudes, and Beverly Hills shopping, but rather a working-class town. Anyway, in 1919, when Eto was born, California was a different, quieter, and less sophisticated place. I wondered why Eto's family emigrated from Japan to Stockton.

Quickly I determined it was easier and closer for Asian immigrants to enter the United States in California. No surprise — geographically, it's the closest state, and it offered ready employment. Stockton was smack in the middle of California's agricultural fruit basket, the San Joaquin Valley. According to census records, at the turn of the century, American companies recruited Japanese immigrants to work for California railroads, canneries, and in the farmlands of the central valley. Their labor was cheap, and the Japanese were soon recognized as being particularly talented and knowledgeable about horticulture. They became important contributors to the success and rapid growth of California's agricultural industry. This fruit production dominated America's markets from the early 1900s until the Great Depression began in 1929.

Wow, now that I thought about my target, he was 60 years old. I was 35. He was old enough to be my father, and he probably experienced the same sorts of things that my own father had. I now looked at Eto differently.

My dad was born in 1907, so he was 12 years older than Eto, but they had both lived through the Great Depression, which changed every American in deep and lasting ways. Eto was in his teen years in the 1930s when the citizens of the United States struggled to feed their families. It couldn't have been an easy existence for the Eto family, new immigrants and, from what I could find through my research, most likely agricultural workers, who were poorly paid to begin with. Add to that the pervasive discrimination against the Japanese that existed at that time, and it must have been a very difficult childhood for Ken Eto.

My mom and dad, never victims of discrimination, were unable to erase the financial scars the Depression left on them. My dad, who had been trained as an electrician, was unable to secure a job working as one during the Depression. Finally, with the increased demand for skilled workers created by World War II, he took a well-paying job at Douglas Aircraft and become a member of the all-powerful and very restricted International Brotherhood of Electrical Workers. He spent the war years installing the electrical systems for planes that rolled off the assembly lines to be used in the bombings and dog fights in the war against Japan and Germany.

And Ken Eto — where was he during the war against Japan and Germany? As an American-born man of Japanese descent, he went from the Great Depression right into the Japanese internment camps of World War II.

This Eto story was becoming a lesson in the U.S. history of hard knocks. I had only a vague idea about the compulsory internment of Japanese Americans after the bombing of Pearl Harbor. I had no idea how and why we had rounded up all the Japanese living in the U.S. and put them in camps. Why weren't German Americans and Italian Americans put into camps? Was it because they were not as easy to visually identify and thus more difficult to discriminate against? Or was it just racial discrimination plain and simple?

Lost in my reading and discovery, I detected a nearby stench that snapped my head up from the long communal desk at which I was sitting. Damn. Some homeless man who smelled like pee and all the old garbage smells I could conjure from my stench memory bank had just slid in next to me to take a nap. Gathering up my books, notes, coat, and purse, all the while trying to hold my nose, I fled to another room to find a table not occupied by a stink bomb.

Finding a more suitable spot, my research took me to the effective date of the establishment of the various Japanese internment camps. On March 18, 1942, the War Relocation Authority was created. But even before that date, I found the U.S. had taken some pretty drastic steps against Japanese immigrants. First it denied them the right to work as contract laborers, which was probably the original incentive for the Etos and most of the Japanese residents to come to the San Joaquin Valley. On November 13, 1922, a racially based law went into effect prohibiting Japanese from becoming naturalized citizens. In 1924, President Calvin Coolidge signed a bill that effectively ended Japanese immigration to the U.S. And on July 25, 1941, months before the December 7 Japanese bombing of Pearl Harbor, President Franklin Delano Roosevelt froze all Japanese assets in the U.S. [10]

In early 1941, up and down the West Coast of America, Japanese families, neighborhood by neighborhood, were rounded up and put into "assembly centers" and then into "relocation centers," which housed Japanese Americans during the war years. Throughout 1942, these relocation centers were opened in God-awful, sparsely populated places. There was a reason these areas lacked residents. These lands were arid, far from other population centers, had extreme shifts in temperature, and lacked any agricultural potential or natural beauty. Internment camps, although not like the concentration camps of the Nazis, sure didn't sound like something the U.S. had any reason to be proud about or emphasize in any public educational curriculum.[11] Perhaps that was why someone like me, who had been educated in the '50s and '60s, knew little about this shameful event in American history.

Enough history for this afternoon — I needed to return to the office before I started sympathizing with my enemy, Ken Eto. But now I knew what a miserable childhood he must have endured.

When I got back into the office, I found a note from Ray: *Call Commander Jules Gallett, CPD. Plan on working 4–12 starting tomorrow.* This was notice of my upcoming on-the-job training with the infamous Vice Control Division (VCD) of the Chicago Police Department, located in an old police station on Chicago's west side. It was actually the building shown on the opening segment of "Hill Street Blues," the supposedly realistic cop show. I was going to learn about Eto's game, *bolita*. In typical fashion, the FBI provided suitable preparation for a new assignment — like "none". After the fact, I found out that, legally, a federal law enforcement agent has no jurisdictional right to go on a local search warrant or arrest. It would have been nice to know that before I began working that first night with the Chicago cops.

Since I was now on the 4–12 shift, I wasn't exactly overloaded with other professional commitments. I made sure Tom and Grandma had Kim covered. And then I contemplated my wardrobe for the nights on the streets of Chicago working with the vice police. I had to look professional, but not too stuffy; classy, but not too Saks Fifth Avenue; and on top of it all, I had to be comfortable and able to wear a gun. This was not an easy outfit to construct.

I arrived in my Bucar at Hill Street,[12] the location of the Vice Control Division, at exactly 4 p.m. The VCD was in a burned-out, war-torn west side neighborhood. Many of the houses had been victims of arson and had been torn down or were abandoned, hollowed-out shells. Empty lots were filled with debris and vermin. In the middle of all of this stood the police station, a red brick building more than 100 years old and looking every day of its age, but somehow still impressive. Most of the property was owned or soon to be owned by the University of Illinois for future development, and it is today a thriving part of the city.

Patrol cars and unmarked police cars were haphazardly parked on the streets and vacant lots surroundings the old building. It was shift change, so everyone was at the station. Even though my FBI car was a beater, almost as bad as the cop cars, it troubled me to leave it parked in this neighborhood. It was the only car available to me now since I had given up my fancy car when I stopped working the wiretap. At least it wouldn't attract attention.

As I walked up the old, well-worn stone stairs into the station, I wondered about all the different people who climbed this way over the past century — either frightened out of their minds or confident their "fix" was in. That must have been how Ken Eto felt when these jokers arrested him not too long ago. Did they even bring him here? Where had they booked him? He would have been a big catch, and a prize like Eto would have been paraded through the station, even if they knew it was just for show. Or were the arresting cops on the up and up, only trying to do their jobs?

At the top of the stairs, the double-door entry was hung with enormous, heavy, shiny green doors. I figured each time a coat of paint dulled, another one had been slapped on — too much trouble to remove the old paint. Now the paint probably weighed more than the doors. Beyond the foyer the space was filled with furniture, cardboard boxes, and human congestion. For lack of space, file cabinets had been illegally placed on emergency stair landings. Tucked into an alcove, a tired old fingerprinting desk waited for customers. Beyond this mess stood another set of double doors, held open by a chair, which exposed a room about the size of a school classroom. Beat-up, spartan metal desks and chairs filled the workspace. File boxes were stacked high adjacent to the desks and along the walls. Business was booming at Hill Street. Behind each desk sat uniformed or plainclothes cops. Women — I assumed by their dress, hookers — were handcuffed to chairs at the police desks.

Pervading the scene was the odor of cigarette smoke and unclean bodies. The big casement windows along one wall were thrown open, and enormous fans in the corners of the room created a background din, but did little to eliminate the stench or the heat. At best, the fans provided white noise.

As I entered the room, not one person looked up from their desk, interrupted their conversation, stopped typing, or in any way made note of me. That was fine with me. I really didn't want to make a big splash here at VCD. I looked around for someone to ask for directions. After standing there for a moment, I stopped some old, fat, balding dick as he walked by me with, "Excuse me, I'm here to see Commander Gallett. Could you direct me to his office?"

"Oh, yeah, sure," he said to me in perfect Chicago factory lingo. "Come this way."

I quickly followed after him through the labyrinth of desks and boxes. We made our way to a wall of tall file cabinets, and I peeked through a slit between them — a tiny office was visible beyond. The old fart peeled off and left me on my own as I knocked on the doorframe of Commander Gallett's office door. Inside sat two men conversing — shooting the bull would be more like it.

"I'm sorry to interrupt, but I didn't know where else to go. I'm Elaine Smith. My boss, Ray Shyrock, sent me over to learn something."

"Elaine Smith! Come on in."

As I walked into Commander Gallett's cubbyhole of an office, the other dude slithered out the door, immediately forgotten by Gallett.

"Please sit down."

Jules Gallett seemed out of place at the CPD. He was dressed impeccably, every hair was in place as if he'd had a recent haircut, and he was as tan as if he'd been in Florida the last two weeks. He appeared to have OCD (obsessive-compulsive disorder) about his office, which was an oasis of neatness and organization in a vast terrain of mess and disorder. Tom told me that Jules was so compulsive that he sewed his front pants pockets shut so he couldn't put anything in them to mess up the look of his slacks. Above all else, Tom told me Jules Gallett was a good cop.

I sat down and adjusted my navy blue linen blazer so that my weapon would be neatly concealed — an FBI protocol type of thing. Never display your weapon. That was considered "hot dog." We are gentlemen, investigators, intellectuals, and men of the law, not gunslingers.

"So you want to catch Ken Eto?" Gallett asked me.

"Well, I do have a case on him. I want to learn about *bolita*, and gambling in general, and how it is operated from the street on up the food chain." Really meaning the organized crime bosses, but these coppers never went there. "I would like to find out how VCD approaches the crime of gambling and develops their cases." Oh, my God, what a liar I was becoming. What I really wanted to ask was: What do you guys have on Eto? Can I use it to jump-start my case?

"Good, good," Gallett replied.

I don't even think he listened to the line I had just run by him.

"I've teamed you up with the two guys who recently pinched Eto and work *bolita* in the city, Frank Garza and Clifford Berti. I think they're out with some of their informants working up information to conduct a raid tonight. They asked that you wait here for them. They'll be back soon."

He escorted me out of his tiny, neat office and pulled up a chair next to a desk piled high with boxes filled with junk in the land of the great mess. I faced the entire room and could view the zoo-like activity to my heart's content. What the hell? I've got to wait around for these idiots? And wait around is what I did — for over an hour. A parade of prostitutes

— white and black, and handcuffed — waltzed past. Various black guys sat handcuffed being questioned by cops about crimes unknown to me. I could identify the cops by the swagger with which they walked and the loud banter they exchanged with their fellow officers in arms. Speaking of arms, they all wore their guns on their hips, flapping in the breeze, available for anyone with enough balls to grab and go on a killing spree or just escape. Just sitting in here was dangerous.[13]

Finally, two guys rushed up to me. The prematurely bald guy declared, "We're sorry we're late. We were out getting probable cause for a search warrant we want to execute on a *bolita* collection point tonight."

"Oh, that's okay," I replied. "I've been watching the entertainment here."

It really wasn't okay, though. If I was to learn anything about *bolita*, I needed to find out how they obtained their probable cause to get a search warrant. Why did they leave me here while they did that?

"Probable cause" are the facts and circumstances within one's knowledge to warrant that a reasonable person would think a search/arrest had was justified. The evidence leads you to believe a crime had been committed, or that certain property was subject to seizure because it was used during the commission of a crime. The first and most important step of my job, to arrest and convict Ken Eto, would be to get probable cause to search his tabulating room and prove he was operating an interstate gambling operation.

I had been cut out of that learning experience, but who knows if I would have learned anything. Later that night, I read the one-page affidavit that was written in support of the search warrant. It looked like no federal search warrant affidavit I had ever read. I would be going for the ride only to see what I could learn from the street, not how the law dictated what these boys could practice.

Finally, Berti, the prematurely bald guy, who was the more talkative of the two, said we needed to do some neighborhood work, and we left the station. As we approached their unmarked car, Berti said, "Our usual vehicle is being used by one of the commanders whose car is being repaired, so we have to drive this one. I'm sorry." He then opened the back door of a 1974 four-door beige Chevrolet that was covered with dents and missing its hubcaps. It also had no back bumper.

The backseat, which I came to know very well, was clad in beige plastic, and the springs in the seat had long since ceased to function. It was like an old mattress that sagged to the floor of the car. There were no seat belts. The windows were locked closed. There were no door handles. I sure hoped Berti and Garza were gentlemen, because other than climbing over the front seat, there was no way out for me. The other thing that bothered me was imagining the bodily fluids and remnants of contraband that were lurking on and under the seat.

According to them, we were headed for a Puerto Rican neighborhood to talk to a few people they knew and see what was going on. Well, now, that was logical since this was a game of chance played by Puerto Ricans and today was Tuesday, the day that, at midnight, three numbers would be drawn to determine the winners.

On our way to the "hood" in the backseat of the unmarked cop car, I felt as if I was flying through the streets of Chicago. These dudes had no consideration for the traffic laws or for the fact that I was sliding from one side to the other on the slippery plastic seat like a 110-pound rag doll. It was virtually impossible to talk because Berti and Garza's windows were open and the wind came rushing in along with all the big city street noise: buses stopping and starting, cars honking, sirens blaring, and music blasting from ghetto cars, to name just a few. I don't think Berti and Garza ever intended to talk to me, because once we pulled away from the Hill Street station, they never looked back at me.

At this point, since I certainly wasn't going to be involved in any conversation with them, I decided to really concentrate on the neighborhood and observe the action. Not that I expected to see signs that said *Bolita Tickets Sold Here*, but where were the logical places? The grocery stores, one on every corner, and the taverns, one on every block, were strong candidates. It is somewhat ironic that the *bolita* odds are in reality much better than our state-sponsored lotto scheme, but all the profits there go toward education.

Suddenly Garza said to Berti, "Stop — stop here." Berti slammed on the brakes, throwing me forward into the front seat. Garza jumped out of the car and walked quickly over to some guy coming out of an apartment building entranceway that was squeezed between two storefront businesses.

Berti remained in the car with me. I thought that Garza must have been assigned to *bolita* because he spoke Spanish, which was what he was doing with this guy on the street. On the other hand, Berti, a *gringo* in his late 30s, was probably assigned to investigate *bolita* because he pissed off someone, somewhere, and they wanted to get even with him. Berti turned his body toward me and leaned over the seat, "So you want to get Eto?"

"I have the case on him," I replied for the second time that night. "Do you have any ideas how I can do that?"

Berti shrugged his shoulders as if to say: Who, little old me? "No," he said. Then he couldn't help himself and went on to say, "Guess you have to get a snitch in his tabulating room. I hear he has all Orientals and they keep their mouths shut. Not like the Puerto Ricans who talk, talk, talk, but it's all lies."

Garza jumped back into the car. "Poncho is collecting and will be at Molina's tonight."

"Fuckin' great!" Berti exclaimed, then turned back to me and said, "Oh, excuse me."

I replied, "I am shocked and amazed that you would say that word around an FBI agent!"

We all laughed, and then Berti, who couldn't contain himself, said, "Looks like you might see a little action tonight, Agent Smith."

I smiled but thought, "Oh shit."

From there, we then drove to the infamous 18th District police station in the Rush Street area. We walked up to the second-floor detectives' room. God only knows where everyone was, because it was completely empty. This was one of the highest-crime areas in the city, and there was not one detective to be seen. This was just weird.

Berti, apparently the brains of the team, and who felt right at home, got busy and typed a one-page affidavit for a search warrant. On this page he attested to two informants telling him the address where *bolita* wagers were going to be collected that evening and that this was a violation of the gambling laws of the State of Illinois. He gave the first names of the men who were going to be collecting the wagers, but no other identifying information. He supplied the address of the drop-off location, but not which apartment.

Berti then faxed his masterpiece to the Assistant State's Attorney who was on duty for reviewing such matters. Then he turned to me and said, "Let's have something to eat."

I was starving because somehow dinner had not been included in my time yet. It took no convincing for me to jump on that idea. We had a few hours until 11 p.m., the witching hour to have the *bolita* wagers into the tabulating room.

Off we went in the rattletrap police car to the *barrio* to eat. I knew of a hundred or so decent-to-wonderful restaurants in the vicinity of the 18th District, but apparently Berti and Garza had already decided where we were going to dine. It turned out to be a joint in the same Puerto Rican neighborhood in which we were going to conduct the raid.

The owner knew them and greeted them warmly. *"Amigos, venga aqui. Quien es una chica, uh?"* They all laughed. I did know some Spanish since I minored in it in college, but this Puerto Rican Spanish was very different from the language they taught us at the University of Illinois. Still, I did understand the implied sexual innuendo, as ridiculous as it was considering how I was dressed and how I carried myself. Mentally, I cut the owner some slack. I knew there were fewer Chicago policewomen in 1980 than even female FBI agents. He couldn't guess I was part of the team. To him I was a *chica*. So be it.

We ate. Garza and Berti filled their tummies with enormous amounts of Caribbean chow. Prudently, I ate like a bird, knowing ahead of me lay another bouncing ride in their car and that I was feeling some tension about the upcoming raid. But as they wolfed down their food, they relaxed and taught me the details of *bolita*.

It was a weekly lottery based in Puerto Rico, since the U.S. did not have legalized gambling as of yet. The players could bet as little as 25 cents on a three-number combination. The guys that took these bets were ordinarily the local merchants, who made a little cut of the winnings if any of the merchant's customers bet a winning number.

There were the runners, who gathered all the bets from the stores as they closed or around 10 p.m. on Tuesday nights; there were the collectors, who the runners delivered the bets to; and then there were the tabulators, who waited until midnight to hear the winning number announced in Puerto Rico and who stayed up all night going through thousands of numbers to see who won and then figuring out their winnings based on the size of their bets. Computerization hadn't been perfected to assist in the labor-intensive process of manually going through the numbers.

I was exhausted just contemplating all the math and all the work for such a stupid thing. I had no affinity for gambling or for math, at that, and saw no realization of a dream in trying to win something so statistically improbable. Berti assured me that the man who controlled the game or was the banker made big money on all the losers and that his profit ratio was immense.

Using the pay phone at the restaurant, Berti had called the Assistant State's Attorney, who told him his search warrant had been approved and he would fax the signed document to Hill Street that evening. Berti returned and announced, "We're a 'go ahead' for the raid."

They stood up even though we hadn't paid, and I said, "We haven't gotten our bill."

Berti replied, "He's our friend. Not to worry."

How typical, I thought. Chicago cops, always on the take. On the table, I left what I thought my portion of the bill should have been. They didn't comment, but I knew they saw my action.

Jumping back into the car, which of course was parked illegally, almost on the sidewalk in front of the restaurant, we cruised the neighborhood until about 11:30 p.m. Berti and Garza thought this was the optimal time for the runners to drop off their numbers. Once again my heart was beating faster than I thought was healthy. I had heard these Puerto Rican dudes were dangerous. As we drove around the neighborhood, we heard the police radio chatter: "*Shooting at 2316 Fullerton,*" "*Man found with knife wound in alley behind 1516 Logan Square,*" and so on.

Finally, Berti said to Garza, "I think it's time." He stepped on the accelerator and the car shot like a cannon through the red light we were stopped at, with me gasping for breath by his sudden decision.

Now why did he have to do that? I knew what was on his mind: Let's show this Miss Fancy Pants FBI Agent how to shit in her pants. After traveling at close to light speed on a two-lane potholed city street, Berti flew up to the curb in front of an apartment building, put the car in park, and turned it off. He and Garza jumped out.

Quickly, as if a second thought as he left the car, Berti turned to me and said, "You better stay here in the car." Sweeter words had never been spoken to me.

- CHAPTER SIX -
Frankie Comes Through

"You wouldn't have shot me, would you?" rasped the stocky, middle-aged Colombian. As Tom struggled to fingerprint his gnarled fingers, I stood by, guarding his every move.

I looked at this dark, sleazy man, who had just purchased $250,000 worth of stolen bonds from an undercover FBI agent, and said with solid conviction, "Oh, yes, I would have." And that was the truth.

He stared at me with his pinpoint dark eyes that telegraphed the disappointment of my answer. It was as if I had erased every good, soft, caring quality he associated with women. I gazed back at him, restraining the impulse to tell him I wouldn't risk the life of my husband or anyone else. I would shoot him if necessary. He was just another crook.

I shocked the Columbian when I walked up to his booth at the International House of Pancakes, pointed my Smith & Wesson 357 revolver at him, and said, "Slowly raise your hands above the table. You are under arrest by the FBI." At gunpoint, he was astonished but immediately complied with all my instructions. Slowly, he looked away from me and sized up the situation. Tommy was behind him, and two other agents also aimed their guns at him. If shooting erupted, only he would be hit, as everyone was careful not to be in the others' line of fire.

As we traveled from the far south side of Chicago to the downtown FBI office, the Colombian sat silent in the backseat of our car, his hands uncomfortably cuffed behind his back. I guess he just had to get the question off his chest. And now he knew and I knew. With that question, and with that answer, I had articulated my personal philosophy of justified murder, in this case also known as self-defense. I would kill someone to save my ass, the ass of a fellow agent, or the ass of an innocent bystander — no hesitation, no equivocation. At my swearing-in ceremony as I took the oath, I believed I would do my job, but until I was faced with the reality of life-and-death situations, I didn't know for sure. Now I did know, and this increased my confidence and authority.

After the arrest of this Colombian, I knew that I was finally and completely accepted by the other agents. When I was asked to help, I was thrilled. It was a badge of honor. The male case agent for this stolen bond caper worked on another organized crime squad. But he realized the practicality of bringing in a female agent. Undercover "buys" such as this take time — a whole sequence of "you show me yours and I'll show you mine" has to take place. There may be long pauses while the "shows" are retrieved from other locations. And the participants are always jumpy — ready to bolt at the slightest hint of danger. Two male diners occupying a table for an extended period of time might raise suspicions. But on this day, the nice couple sitting at a nearby table looked harmless and hungry. We ate a pancake lunch, drank about 10 cups of coffee, and conversed like a normal twosome. I was the female half of this nondescript couple, and after drinking all that coffee, my nerves were so jittery I might have shot my own mother. But everything went as planned. Ultimately, it was a very successful arrest or "collar," as the police would call it. Another bad guy bit the dust.

After I calmed down and dictated the detailed log each agent must make after an arrest, I decided to talk to Ray about the Chicago Vice Control Division ride-along program. I sure hadn't seen much of Ray lately, and I wanted him to know what I had worked out with his friends over at Hill Street. We met in his office. I brought him up to date.

"Those two detectives assigned to me think that I should ride along with them again on Tuesday night. They want to hit another collection station. Other than that, they don't think they can do anything else, unless they nab someone in the Fto ring who would cooperate with the FBI." My expression revealed that this was an unlikely possibility.

"Okay. Then you haven't found them very helpful?"

"Well, yes and no, Ray. These boys are working on the street level of *bolita*. Everything flows up to the controller or banker. That's Eto. But they have no idea how to get to him. Personally, I think my time would be best spent developing Frankie — my new informant. I'd like to get him inside. Take over Walter Micus' position. Micus is tabulating for Eto now and he's not exactly a go-getter. I'm thinking Frankie can exploit Micus' lazy characteristics. Maybe he can slowly weasel his way into working hand-in-hand with the boss man. Then we'll have someone on the inside."

Ray smiled. "Right. I think you've got something there!" He pounded on his desk with both of his hands and continued, "That sounds like a good plan. Go ahead then and see what you can do." He smiled one of his big yellow-toothed smiles and looked toward the door. I knew once again, I had stretched his attention span to its limit.

"Okay, I'll try it that way. Thanks for your help, Ray."

I was pleased. One more night of flying around in the backseat of that deathtrap car and staying out way past my bedtime. And just one more night of putting up with the bullshit that Berti and Garza were trying to feed me. Sure, they had explained how *bolita* worked, but they didn't work *bolita*. I wasn't sure what they were up to, but they weren't smashing gambling activity in the Puerto Rican community. The night they "raided" the house they thought was the wager collection point, I sat in the car waiting for almost an hour. Then they returned empty-handed. They said someone must have changed the drop-off or that all the wagers had already removed from the tabulating room. I knew their informants were stroking them or they were stroking me, and I didn't know how much longer I could play the game without telling them that.

I sat down at my desk and started to put all my stuff away. The Bureau had a strict policy that every desk had to be completely cleared off at the end of the day. Nothing could be on your desk. Not a note. Not a phone number. Nothing but your ink-blotter pad, your phone, and your big-ass nameplate.

Night clerks came through the office and inspected the desktops and checked to see if the desk drawers and all storeroom doors were locked. There were spies everywhere looking to get you in trouble. Reports were written on anyone who left any investigative paperwork on his or her desk or any locks unlocked. A violation of these security rules would be cause for a reprimand. There was unspoken institutional pressure that each agent was responsible for the integrity for the secrets of our Bureau. A bit repressive and anal, but after a while, it all became second nature.

Everyone has a personal life — even me. While this week had been a stressful one, now I was going home for a weekend of fun. Joe Eto was always on my mind, but right now I looked forward to spending time with my wonderful family and to a lineup of social activities that took me far away from the Mob. As I turned down the street on which our little red brick English Tudor home was situated, I saw Kim riding her pink bike with her friend Chrisy and Grandma Smith sitting on the front step smoking a Parliament menthol cigarette. She was a dear person. Her devotion to Kim was deep, and without her help, I would have been much less able to be so engrossed in my work. At the time, there weren't any Chicago-based female agents with children, except me. Much later, other female special agents would also face the difficult task of combining their careers with the work and responsibility of motherhood. Thankfully, I had help in that department.

"Hi, Grams," I said as I walked up to the house and bent over to give her a hug and a kiss. "What's going on?"

"Oh, same old, same old, you know." She rose with a groan, and I could see that her arthritis was really killing her today.

Kim flew up the walkway to the house and screeched to a stop. "Hi, Mommy."

"Hi, my sweetie pie. Want to have pizza and play Pac-Man tonight?"

"Sure."

With that she started to turn her bike to leave, but I said, "Wait. Wait a minute here. I need a kiss."

She stopped where she was, still straddled, balancing on her bike, and I walked over to her. I kissed her soft, warm forehead, cheeks, and lips and hugged her head to my chest. I was taking not one kiss, but many. No matter how old she became, Kim always let me kiss and hug her, and each time it was an incredible delight.

"Ride back and forth in front of the house until your dad gets home. He's right behind me." As I walked inside the house, it smelled clean, and all the furniture and floors were shining. Thank God for my Polish cleaning lady, also. A girl sure did need a back-up crew to have a neat, clean house and not go crazy trying to keep it that way.

Grandma was getting her things together, and I waited until she had her car keys in hand and light spring coat on.

"Thanks, Grams. I do so appreciate you. Talk to you tomorrow." Then I hugged her again. Slowly she walked out the front door so she could say good-bye to Kim and drive the short way to her widow's apartment.

The weekends were a time to let my mind drift. The intensity of the workweek gave way to a more leisurely pace at home. I'm a firm believer that solving problems requires both brainstorming with others and solitary "mental wandering time." Since I had become an avid jogger, I had even run into parked cars while lost in thought. Often people would ask, "Hey, you want to run together?" I'd always decline because I was a very slow runner, and also I needed time alone with my thoughts to plan and think. By Sunday night, I was always anxious to return to work. Call me crazy, but I called myself lucky. Work wasn't drudgery for me; it was my creative outlet.

Monday morning I always refocused. Back in the office, I rolled over a typical Monday morning refrain: Elaine, you've wasted enough time — now get on with it. The first thing I did was telephone Frankie. I imagined him hard at work banging out dents this early morning

"Oh, have I got news for you, babe," he said.

I wanted to say, "Don't call me 'babe.' It sends chills of revulsion up and down my spine," but I didn't. Instead I suggested a lunch meeting. "How about hot dogs at 12:30, Frank?"

"Sure," he replied.

I had some research to do on Ken Eto's personal life. I called the clerk who had contact with the telephone companies. I needed Eto's phone records. It had been a while since I requested them.

"You know," said the clerk, "if we request the record in the middle of the customer's billing cycle, they wait until the next one. Maybe that's what happened. I'll check for you today." I thanked her profusely with gratitude for the thankless job she did, day in and day out. Then I ordered up any marriage, divorce, and birth records recorded in Cook County with Eto's name associated with them. With them I would be able to determine whom he had married and if he had any children. Right now he was at the age at which he could be a grandfather. Don't these Mob guys ever retire?

Later I caught up with my informant. "Okay, Frankie. Micus is going to let you ride along with him on Tuesday night when he picks up the bets, right?"

"Yeah," he said, exposing a mouthful of fries. "I didn't want to get too pushy, ya know? So I've been kinda plantin' the idea that da Puerto Rican guys are none too trustworthy. So I thought I'd ride along, sort of as his protection. He bought the idea, hook, line, and sinker."

"That's great! You tell me where he goes and next time I'll set up and document everything." I knew we needed evidence of interstate gambling activity. "You did say he went to Indiana, didn't you?"

"Yeah, that's what he says," he replied.

"Here's the $250 for the information that you have given me so far."

"That's a long way from $10,000, Elaine," Frank whined.

"Come on, Frank. You know I told you I could only pay you as you provided information. The more valuable the information, the bigger the amount of money you will receive. What you find out tomorrow night will be worth a lot more when we can corroborate it with our surveillance."

"Okay, okay. I'm just teasin' ya."

"I hope so. Just know I will not cheat you. I'll fight for the most money I can get for you. We're going to be stars when we take this Eto guy down."

"Ah, you can leave me out. That guy's a killer and I don't want no part of him." He looked frightened.

"I understand. Then I'll be the star and you can know you made me one. And you get some dough to boot."

Back at the office, I found my desk loaded with a month's worth of phone records for Eto — calls made to and from his high-rise pad at 21 East Chestnut — and a series of marriage, divorce, and birth records.

Oh, goody, goody, I thought. It may sound weird to get excited about records, but that was part of the job too — the details were all important. But before I could get into those phone and vital records, as they are called in Cook County, my sense of "first things first" made me reread Eto's arrest report. I wanted to understand his criminal history.

His first arrest was on April 12, 1942, in Tacoma, Washington for "violation of the curfew law." He spent 12 days in jail for that "crime;" since he was 23 years old at the time, I doubted they had busted him for a juvenile offense. He was a Japanese American and Pearl Harbor was fresh in everyone's mind. So they slapped him in jail for 12 days for a minor infraction — a sign of those turbulent and phobic times.

I read down, and from what I could decipher from the cryptic rap sheet abbreviations, on March 6, 1950, the sheriff in Pocatello, Idaho,[14] issued a fugitive warrant for Eto, charging him with "obtaining money under false pretenses."

There was then another entry on March 15, 1950, so I figured they must have caught and arrested him. The next entry was on October 13, 1950, and all it read was, "Boise, Idaho – St. Penn #8092. O.M.F.P. 14 yrs." Idaho had sentenced Eto to 14 years in the state penitentiary.[15] Yikes! They threw the book at him.

I needed to summarize Eto's life for myself. He was born to Japanese immigrants in Stockton, California, in 1919. From the time he was 10 years old and until the outbreak of World War II in 1941, he lived during the worst economic times known in the United States. Bingo! When World War II was declared, he happened to be of the race and nationality most targeted for war hatred, and in fact he was rounded up and put into internment camps until the fall of 1945. Eto was a free man for five years and then was arrested for "obtaining money under false pretenses" and given a 14-year sentence in the Idaho state penitentiary.

What the hell? This sounds like the worst life one could imagine. It just didn't fit my stereotypical concept of the life of a son of Japanese Americans. Ken Eto was becoming a more puzzling enigma.

Then I saw that he was paroled to Chicago on September 12, 1951. He must have gotten out on an appeal or something. I doubt the fix was in, all the way in Pocatello, Idaho, because I wasn't sure if Eto moved to Chicago after being released from the internment camp in Idaho in 1945. I would have to look into that. Ken Eto's next encounter with law enforcement came on November 19, 1951, with our friends at the Chicago Police Department. This was for "investigation" and it had been conducted by "Officer Mullen & Co.," 36th District. What was that "& Company"? There was no report number indicated on the rap sheet, nor an arrest number, so I knew there would be no official report of this encounter between Mr. Eto and the Chicago Police. I also could not find a District 36. Maybe the Chicago Police had renumbered the districts since 1951, or "Officer Mullen & Co." just made it up? More outrageous things have been done. The phone on my desk rang and snapped me out of research mode.

"Hello, this is Elaine Smith." (I never answered the phone, "Hello, this is Special Agent Elaine Smith," for fear that I would get the typical reply, "Oh, what's so special about you?" To which I always wanted come back with, "Well, you'll never find out.")

"Hey, Elaine. It's me, Frankie."

"Hi, Frankie; how are you doing?" I replied smoothly and warmly.

"I got some good news," Frankie said, drawing out the words "good news" slowly and with a little giggle in his voice. My heart started to beat a little faster and I quickly grabbed a pad of paper, placed the day's date at the top, and got ready.

"Well, ya see, Micus, he's so fuckin' dumb and lazy. He's bought this story of me riding along to keep him company when he picks up the Jap's bets. And I was askin' him if I needed to bring a baseball bat or somethin' to keep us company. He says, 'Oh, no. He didn't think so, because we was in and out of the places so fast.' So, now, here's the best part," he continued on, more excited. "He told me where he went."

"No shit, Frankie?" I said, trying not to scream, "Tell me, tell me, and tell me now."

"Yeah," Frankie replied, and then he just stopped.

I groaned back into the phone. "Frank, you aren't going to play games with me now, are you?"

He whimpered back, "Well, how much do you think you'll be able to get me for this information?"

"Frank, you know I can't get you anything," I said, lowering and softening my voice, "until I can verify what you've told me. I know you aren't going to lie, but my boss would laugh me out of his office if I asked for a payment without verifying the information first."

There was a pause on the other end of the line. Finally, Frank said, "You got it. So, here's what he told me. First, he picks up from some

Puerto Rican on the corner of Chicago and State around 10:30 at the Burger King. Then he drives all the way to East Chicago, Indiana — he hates this part — to a place called Brother's Restaurant and picks up from a guy named Flowers around 11:00." He paused. "He gets real nervous because it's hard to make it from Chicago and State to East Chicago, Indiana, in a half-hour. You know, driving with those gamblin' tickets in the car makes him twice as nervous. I told him I'd take the rap on the gamblin' stuff. I didn't care."

"Wait a minute, Frank," I said in a firm voice. "You are not taking the rap for anyone. You are going to have to keep your yap shut."

"Okay, okay. I will just wait for beautiful you to come down and bond me out."

Frank was fantasizing again. "No, Frank, that isn't going to happen because that will blow the whole thing out of the water, right?"

"Yeah, but you wouldn't let me rot in jail, would you?"

"No, Frank. I would never let you rot in jail. So, review the whole routine again. I just have to make sure I have it right. And what car does Micus drive? What's the license plate? And are you going to go with him next Tuesday?"

When I got off the phone with Frank, I could have danced like a go-go dancer all around the squad room from the top of one desk to the next. This was too exciting to be true. Joe Eto was one baby step closer to meeting his law enforcement challenger. But this one was different. She played by the rules, and because of that, the rules stuck when they should and couldn't be begged, bought, or stolen.

Then the reality of what I had to do took grip of me as I started to plan my next steps. I was so hyped up with the excitement of knowing the drop-off locations and times of the *bolita* tickets, I was unable to concentrate. After pushing papers around on my desk and doing some stupid organizing activity, I reverted to doing what I had learned to do in the past few years when nervous or frustrated — either run or vacuum the floor. Since most people at the office would have considered me a lunatic if I had gone to the janitor's closet and gotten out the industrial vacuum cleaner and had begun vacuuming the squad area, I picked up my gym bag and went to the gym.

All through my 22 years as an FBI agent, I ran three to four times a week, either before work or during the day. Running kept my weight well below the required standards and was a great mental release. When I ran before work, I applied my makeup as I would each morning. After a run during the day, I would shower, put on clean underwear and the same clothes, fix my hair the best I could without blowing it dry, and return to work. I made no attempt to reapply my makeup and never wore lipstick. Remember, I did say that, "Being a FBI agent was not about glamour and primping."

I enjoyed running outside whenever I could. It was ridiculously windy down by the lake, but that was my choice that day. With a head wind of about 30 knots, the run was horrific and I thought of nothing but wanting to stop and walk. Heading back to the gym with the wind at my back was sensational. I imagined myself running like a real runner, not jogging at a pitiful pace.

On my return, I was probably looking pretty rough when I walked into the specialty squad supervisor's office, creatively named "Surveillance Squad." During the wind-at-my-back jogging segment, I realized I needed to put together some agents to follow Micus as he made his *bolita* pick-ups in Chicago and then in Indiana. I had never even been on surveillance myself. How the hell was I going to organize and run one?

Before entering, I asked Dick, the supervisor, "Can I come in are you busy?" Dick said, "Sure, you can come in. We are planning our schedule for next week. Do you need some help with a case?" I knew Dick and his crew had been trying to drum up some business because many agents were not sold on the concept of a specialty squad for surveillance. Most of them wanted to do their own surveillance work, see their targets commit their crimes, and make the arrest. Anyway, on the day I walked into Dick's office, he was all smiles and pleasantries. He knew I was on an organized crime squad and that was the big time.

"Well, Dick, what I would like to do is ride along with one of your teams for a week, or if that would be too long, just a day or two. I just want to learn what it is like to do surveillance. I am a new agent and have a great opportunity to witness the drop off of gambling wagers, and I have never even been on surveillance."

As I was speaking these words, though, I could see a profound metamorphosis taking place in this man. The pencil that he was holding in his hand started to twitch. His full Irish face was quickly changing from ruddy to bright red. His body began to squirm in his chair. As these small but noticeable changes were occurring, I must have found them unsettling, because I began, very slowly, to take backward steps toward the door.

When I had finished speaking, Dick bellowed at the top of his voice, "You mean you want to ride along with one of my handpicked teams? Do you think you can learn how they utilize the most sophisticated and advanced surveillance techniques known in law enforcement today in a week, in a day, or in two days? Are you fucking crazy? My teams are just that — teams. It will be a cold day in hell before any woman is a member of my squad. Now get the fuck out of my office!" Even though that "cold day in hell" eventually came, as women are now an asset to investigations and especially to surveillance operations, it still shocked me.

As I left, I meekly said, "Thank you." I wandered to my squad area and sat down in a daze. Something was wrong here. What was it? It didn't feel very good. I was asking for help and was told to get out of Dick's office. I was told no woman would ever be on this man's squad. I had just been the victim of sexual discrimination and I didn't even know what to call it. I just knew it didn't feel good and it wasn't right. I also knew that when his parents named him Dick, they sure were right on target. He was one.

- CHAPTER SEVEN -
The Great Surveillance

Now I had a problem. I had to organize and direct surveillance of Joe Eto, but I had never done one. I needed help, and I needed it fast. One screw-up and it would be very difficult to get another opportunity to observe this wily bastard.

I telephoned my new friend, the photography clerk, George. "Hey, George, how are you?"

"Tired," he replied, which seemed like a less than enthusiastic response. I guessed he was accustomed to being stroked and used by agents and thought that was what I was about. I continued, undeterred by his icy reply. "I have some big-deal moving surveillances to do on Ken Eto. I was hoping you might be able to give me some guidance on getting the photographic evidence I need to convict him."

"Well, Elaine, you caught me in the darkroom. Right in the middle of developing some photos. My timer says I won't be finished for a while. Can we make an appointment for sometime tomorrow morning?"

I checked my watch — almost 6 p.m. No wonder there wasn't anyone else in the squad room, my stomach was starting to grumble, and George was tired. "Sure, George. Sorry to have interrupted you. I'll call you when I get in tomorrow. Thanks."

As I cleared my desk for the evening, I realized that typically I was the last one on the squad to leave at night — I would turn off the lights and check to see if everyone had cleared their desks and locked the storage rooms. Why was I still at work? For one, I lived in the city of Chicago, while most other agents resided in far out suburbs. These agents bought large suburban tract homes and were assured of better schools for their children, but they dealt with an agonizing 60- to 90-minute commute to and from work. Mine was 20 to 30 minutes. Anyway, Tom and I were city rats. We had grown up in the city, taken public transportation all our lives, loved the ethnic bakeries and sausage shops, and were aware of the safe middle-class locations to raise families.

There was another reason I stayed late. I was driven to prove I could do this job as well as anyone else. I was always had an attitude of determination, but now I understood that to really investigate a case and catch a mobster, one had to be a little obsessed. When I was 12 years old, my mother took me to a "chubby girls" store to purchase a party dress. I was humiliated. I can still see myself in the mirror — chubby. But when I walked out of that store, I vowed to never to return. Immediately I put myself on a diet of 1,000 calories a day. A year later, when I was 13, we went to buy a graduation dress. The new me wore a size 2 and weighed 89 pounds.

For me, graduation from elementary school to high school signaled entry into the big time. I was determined to claim my place in the world. I was tired of being the girl the boys pushed into the bushes, but otherwise paid no attention. I had goals to achieve, places to go, and things to do. Even though I entered a big city high school of 4,600 students, I vowed not to be just a number. I wanted to be top dog. I was elected Freshman Queen. I made the varsity cheerleading squad in the second semester of my freshman year and remained a cheerleader for three and a half years. In my senior year, I was captain of the cheerleaders, crowned Homecoming Queen, and president of the most prestigious service club.

In my junior year of high school, I went steady with the captain and quarterback of the football team. Then I met Tom, who had just been elected captain of the football team for our senior year. I broke up with the old captain and began to twist Tom around my little finger. Adolescent psychologists might have called me a "bitch in training." My drive to compete to win what I wanted ruled my waking moments. In the 1960s, being a cheerleader and a beauty queen and having the high school All-

American football player as my devoted boyfriend were considered major levels of accomplishment for a young woman.

I entered the University of Illinois with Tom at my side, or so I thought — then my world was turned upside down. He told me he didn't know if he loved me anymore. In so many words, he implied I had become a bitch. Although he didn't use that word because Tom didn't, and still doesn't, swear like I do. He dropped me cold. My heart actually ached. I carried a hollow feeling in my stomach. Privately, for months, I sobbed over my loss. After my first three months at the University of Illinois, I stopped menstruating and I came down with strep throat. I begged my parents to come and take me home. They came and I went home for a week. My mother nursed me back to physical health. But I was thrown into physiological shock — humbled, lonely, and sick. I lost the young man who I loved for all the right reasons, not because he was a football star. I was in mourning without a clue how to heal myself or turn things around.

When I started at the University of Illinois, I pledged one of the most prestigious sororities. For once I took my older sister's advice. She said, "Join the sorority with people you like, not for the prestige." Damn, I didn't even know what sorority was the most the notable. But I pledged the sorority that felt most comfortable to me. The one I selected happened to be considered a top choice. My sorority was ranked each year as one of the top three sororities — those with the highest grades and the most beauty queens.

I was assigned a pledge mother, and shortly thereafter she was elected the University of Illinois' Homecoming Queen. Quite an impressive accomplishment considering there were 40,000 undergraduate students. My first pledge semester I began to think this sorority was grooming me for the type of recognition I had received in high school.

When my sorority sisters began to push me to compete in the areas in which I had been so successful in high school, I rebelled. I told them in no uncertain terms where they could shove it; although we sorority women didn't talk like that. Shockingly, they understood. They allowed me, in an environment of respect, to seek whatever accomplishments I decided to attain.

In that first semester of college, with the loss of Tom's love and the intensive demands of a large university that typically flunked out 20 percent of its freshman class, my psychological and physical torment caused me to struggle academically and my grades were indicative of that. My second semester with my pride challenged, I decided I had to improve my grades and find a new way to fulfill myself.

My new friends, with whom I developed lasting and strong relationships, stood by my side. Rather than trying to realize the fictional dreams of American pop culture as it was in the 1960s, I developed new goals that would give me a sense of satisfaction and achievement. I realized I was no longer "queen bitch" but someone that valued more that the trappings of success.

Happily, Tom and I continued to see each other and there was no commitment on his behalf, he saw the change in me saw, and I once again became the person he had originally loved. We were engaged in our sophomore year of college when Tom gave me a diamond engagement ring that was the largest in the house, but I had already learned a lasting lesson in life. Love and consideration of others is the most important. But all of my snotty arrogance had not been erased. Forgive me, but I wasn't going to marry some cheap son-of-a-bitch who gave me a tiny chip of a diamond.

After staring out the window next to my desk and mentally wandering, I realized that except for a skeleton crew of clerical personnel and at least one agent who was on duty during the night and early morning hours, the office was empty. I was alone at my desk in the dark. It was time to go home to the man I loved. Otherwise Tom just might eat everything Grandma prepared for dinner, leaving me to a meal of cold cereal. I was done chasing mobsters for the night.

The next morning I sat at my desk still concerned about my surveillance deficiency and how to avoid looking like a total moron. Not long ago, and out of the blue, all of the agents working north side crew targets, including me, were moved from the eighth floor to the ninth and were assigned to a new boss: Supervisory Special Agent William I. Brown. In this new location, I now sat next to a window and my new boss was Bill Brown, who knew all about Ken Eto and was very excited about my case. I got to know my new secretary and some new agents on the squad. Fortunately, these guys seemed to have a slightly better attitude toward women in the FBI.

Gene, one of the new agents, joined me for chitchat. He half-sat on the edge of my desk smoking, smiling, and being sort of silly. He frequently had this "shit eating half grin on his face." I saw an opportunity. I would invite him into my world. Abruptly, I asked him, "Will you help me do a surveillances on Eto when he has his *bolita* lists picked up?"

He let out a long drag of smoke, aimed at the ceiling, looked down at me without that silly smile, and said seriously. "So, what do you exactly have to witness?

I explained that there would be two *bolita* drop-off locations and that my informant was going to be riding along with Eto's guy. We needed to witness these events.

"Yeah, yeah," he said with a little Detroit factory accent thrown in, "I understand what you have to prove." He took another drag from his cigarette and blew out the smoke as he gathered his thoughts. "You need a minimum of four cars. People will have to work a 4-to-12 shift. Select someone to keep the log. Pick a radio channel. Decide where we'll meet. Get permission to go into the Indiana territory. Lastly talk to the informant constantly. How does that sound?"

I took notes. But he talked so fast that I barely got the first point down by the time he was done. He pulled up from his perch on my desk and seemed as if he were going to leave.

"Wait, Gene," I said, almost grabbing at him. "Will you help me?"

"When is it again?"

"Next Tuesday night."

"I guess so." And I saw his eyes twinkle, as if with all his casualness he had just been pulling my leg. "Ask me for help anytime; it's not like I've got a lot to do around here anyway — and get Bill to assign two other guys to join the surveillance team. That way you don't have to go beggin' these assholes."

So that was how Gene and I began our partnership. He was a happy-go-lucky guy, smart as a whip, funny as a comedian, and, unknown to me at the time, an alcoholic. I was flying high with the kindness of this one person when I really needed the help. I was running hot. I felt like touching my rear and saying, "Tss! Tss! Tss!" But, for the sake of office decorum, I restrained myself.

Next on the agenda was surveillance photography. The FBI trusted no outsiders to do repair work on our vehicles or radio systems, make or duplicate our recordings, or take or develop our photographs. At headquarters in Washington D.C., a staff of special agents who were qualified experts would be called to testify worldwide about the FBI's photographs. These agents had graduate-level degrees in the chemistry of photography. That was why every field office, including ours, had a fully equipped and sophisticated photography studio.

George was in charge of our studio, and I needed his help on the choice of camera for night work and how to shoot photos for a moving surveillance. When I explained my plan, George selected the camera, film, and light meter and showed me how to get it set up. He placed everything into a black camera bag as large as I was. He was so methodical, I almost wanted to scream. But this was his business, and he knew what he was doing. I wondered if he could be even more helpful.

"George, why don't you come on these surveillances with me? You've certainly had more training in photography than I have. I know you're not an agent but…"

He looked at me with utter astonishment. "Generally agents like to take their own photos, Elaine."

"Well, George, that's just stupid, isn't it, when you're the one with the most training in photography."

He shrugged his shoulders. "I guess there isn't anything preventing me from doing that. You request me, and I'll get approval from my supervisor. Then I can do it," he replied like a robotic clerical government employee.

"Great, George. That's just wonderful. Now I don't have to worry about ruining my one big chance. You can do that."

George turned bright red, and I tapped him lightly on his shoulder and said, "George, I know you'll do a much better job than anyone else in this office. I trust you completely. I'm so grateful to have you help me."

Now George turned even redder, but he straightened with pride. I knew he was pleased that he would be used effectively and completely to the full extent of his skills and talents. The only hitch in this plan was that the first Tuesday of surveillance, he couldn't join the team. Nevertheless, he said he could loan me his surveillance van. He assured me I would never be "made" by Eto in that vehicle.

Although my focus was on Ken Eto, the Chicago Mob in general was a constant source of rumor and discussion for my new squad. Office banter was a major activity — the male agents bragged and told war stories daily. It was considered poor form to ever interrupt their usually loud and animated informational exchanges. I was beginning to get the feel of the social structure of this very male and macho environment. Soon I might even be comfortable joining in. But for now, I just listened carefully for useful information.

In May of that year, down in Miami, of all places, Marshall Caifano, 68 years old, a known Chicago Rush Street associate of Eto's and a syndicate hit man, was sentenced to 20 years in prison. He was a co-conspirator in the sale of General Electric stock certificates valued at $4 million stolen in 1968 from an O'Hare International Airport cargo area.

Why hadn't this case been investigated and prosecuted in Chicago? Why weren't we now down in Miami in his jail cell offering him some more comfortable accommodations if he just talked a little bit about his organized crime buddies on the north side? Here he was, 68 years old, looking at 20 years in prison. He was going to die there. Sixty-eight years old plus 20 years equals 88 years old, which equals death.

No one said a thing. No one questioned why the case had been brought in Miami, not Chicago. No one said, "Boss, let me get on a plane and go down there and see if I can push the right buttons with the guy. I mean, give this aging mobster some time to settle into the horrible reality of prison life. Then let me have a chance at him." The FBI did not take advantage of the opportunities that jumped into its lap.

A few months before that, a Mob gofer named Bobby Urban shot Big Joe Arnold in the stomach. Arnold was street racketeer, Caesar DiVarco's right-hand man. Urban confessed to the shooting and said he did it because Arnold had slapped him around in front of his girlfriend. My squad friend Dietzie was all over that incident because DiVarco was his target, but it seemed that Dietzie had his hands tied. He wanted to spirit Urban away from Chicago. He knew he could get him to flip on everything he had witnessed Big Joe Arnold do in the years he served as a Mob lackey. There was no way the Bureau would let him do it. Another opportunity for an earful of useful information was lost.

And, to add more fuel to my fire of outrage, according to the papers, Tony Accardo was spending the winter months in Palm Springs. His source of income was reported to be his social security pension. What the hell was that? You mean to tell me that the cost of living is so cheap that when I retire, I, too, can live in Palm Springs on my social security and play golf every day? Where was the IRS?

That was another thing I had to do. I had to get Ken Eto's IRS information. I wondered what his income was attributed to. I was all juiced up again. Should I go running or vacuum? I better go on surveillance.

From the end of June 1980 until August 20, 1980, my life was filled with nothing else but spinning a web that would entrap Ken Eto in an interstate gambling case. I was going to gather evidence and execute a search warrant to grab all of his gambling records. Then I would have him indicted and arrested. After that I would flip him and he would reveal all the details of his Mob associates. Finally, I'd put him in jail.

The plan sounded magnificent. If I had known how grueling, nerve-wracking, and difficult it was going to be, I might have thought more seriously about doing it in such a short time. But I was obsessed. I had no thoughts of giving up. My overriding worry was that my web was very delicate — a strong wind would blow it down. I would have to trap my prey when the opportunity presented itself, and that opportunity was Frankie. There was no fight in him. Now he was my partner 24/7, and he didn't even ask about that $10,000 anymore.

Our first surveillance on June 17, 1980, was the template for the seven that followed. Except for a few variations in the vehicles the targets used, it stayed consistently the same. Thank God crooks just can't take change. It is human nature to have a routine. That is why it is so easy to grab or kidnap someone. Day after day, a person conforms to the same pattern of activities known to be successful. He displays the same behaviors and handles tasks in the same manner. The only exception to this rule would be the erratic behavior of a stone-cold junkie.

Day one of surveillance, Frankie told me that he had everything planned. He was going to be picked up by Micus at 10 p.m. Tuesday night. The two would drive to the corner of Chicago and State in Chicago and wait in Micus' car until 10:30 p.m. Then Micus would enter the Burger King and wait casually for the Puerto Rican dude to show up with the brown paper bag full of *bolita* slips and money.

My FBI surveillance team was to assemble at that same location at 10:15 p.m. Each person knew the exact description of Micus' car, a gray AMC Hornet bearing Illinois license plate JJ 8435. It was a small, weirdly shaped car. Only the most extreme losers, like Micus, would have purchased one, and I was teased unmercifully about the type of vehicle we were following.

Everyone had been briefed on the radio channel we would use. There was one main channel everyone used ordinarily. But in this case, we selected another frequency that was used exclusively by our team. In case there was an emergency, it was still monitored by the radio room in the office. Each person had a description of Micus, Frankie, the informant, and where they were going to go after the Burger King pick-up. Gene, my newest sidekick, was chosen to hang out inside Burger King to observe the actual bag drop. It was up to Ivan, Bill, and me to make sure that once the drop took place we would witness Micus get into his car with the bag and begin driving toward East Chicago, Indiana. Frankie said the Indiana pick-up had been scheduled for 11:30 p.m. at a greasy spoon called Brother's Restaurant.

We were not going to try to follow Micus 15 miles to East Chicago through Chicago traffic, even at 10 o'clock at night. It is just too easy to be made. Following someone for miles can be nerve-wracking, and not wanting to lose the subject, the tail is tempted to "lock bumpers" with the target car to ease the tension. This opens up the likelihood that the tailing car will be made and the meeting aborted. Since we knew where they were going and Frankie was riding along with our pigeon, we felt comfortable lying back rather than getting burned. "Burned" in FBI lingo meant the target has identified your car as someone who is following them. A burned car is useless and will be taken out of surveillance. Then we would be down one car, and that would reduce the chance of success. In doing any surveillance, intelligence like Frankie was giving us made it much easier to follow the pigeon and be ready at the places we had to be.

The intersection of Chicago and State was a filthy, human-littered corner. Stairways on all four corners led down into the Chicago subway system. The area was crowded with drunks and beggars. With the weather warmer, the drug addicts were outside in full anticipation of scoring a hit or being able to spot the occasional drunk who had accidentally wandered too far from the Rush Street bar scene and thus could be easily mugged.

And there I was. I wore no make-up and dressed like my pale face — very plain. The quality of my clothes matched that of my vehicle — the beat-up surveillance van. I wore a pair of oversized blue jeans, a sweatshirt with the sleeves cut off, and ratty running shoes. The outfit made me look 20 pounds heavier. I was made up for my role as a poor housewife with multiple children who was inexplicably out late at night, driving a disgusting looking but affordable van.

The van had a stick shift on the floor with a big rust hole directly to the right of it. Luckily, I knew how to drive a manual shift car. However, I had to force myself not to look down as I shifted gears as the image of the street blurring by below was disorienting. Another rust hole behind the passenger side seat poured exhaust in the cab. When I hit a pothole, the sound was explosive and the van bounced erratically. It had no air conditioning or radio, but unlike the other windows, the driver's side window actually operated — thank God for that.

My nerves were frayed from driving that death trap of a vehicle to the drop location that night. I saw the other team members gathered in a parking lot a few blocks away. They leaned on their cars, shot the shit and looked casual. Me...I was nervous. I positioned the van discreetly nearby, but not too close to, the intersection of the two streets, Chicago and State. My weapon was hidden in its holster under my sweatshirt. Next to me on the passenger seat lay a legal pad and pen for surveillance notes, a pillow, my camera bag with the camera fully loaded, and a can of Coke. After I parked, I walked over to the group. They looked up, looked away, and then looked harder at me.

"Elaine? Is that you?" Gene asked, bent over in laughter. Everyone else started snickering after taking after long, hard stares at me.

"Very funny, guys. You didn't know that I'm from true hillbilly stock, did you? All of this blue blood, educated shit is just an act," I replied, playing along with them, trying to brush it off, but actually embarrassed because I must have been shockingly ugly. After a few more comments about my looks, they went back to what they were talking about, and I remained on the edge of the conversation, just like I always seemed to be when in a group of agents.

At about 10:15 p.m., I said, "I'm going to set up and, perhaps, Gene, you better get your ass into the Burger King and have a treat."

Everyone agreed on which direction they'd take so we could catch the Hornet no matter which way it went. Gene took the most illogical one — north — since he was going to be inside the Burger King.

Back in the van, the minutes went by like hours. The street scene was busy and scary for a woman sitting in a car by herself — even if she was carrying a gun. If a thug tried to grab me, he wouldn't know I had a gun. He'd find out when I drew down on him. But to draw down on someone, I had to be alert enough to be able to do that before he got the upper hand. These were uneasy thoughts. At this moment, I was earning every penny they were paying me.

Out of the corner of my eye I saw the gray Hornet. It pulled up in front of the Burger King like it was a miniature racecar. Frankie had told me Micus drove like an old lady because he was afraid of getting caught — not tonight. Then lazy-ass Micus didn't even get out of the car and go into the hamburger joint. He sat behind the wheel looking straight ahead. What the hell did Micus expect? Special delivery of the *bolita* records? I got the camera and took a couple of pictures. They could have been of the sky for all I knew.

Ivan came over the radio. *"I've got the subject parked in front of Burger King facing north."*

Bill replied, *"10-4."* I also replied, *"10-4,"* indicating that I too understood Ivan's transmission. Gene gave us two taps on his handheld, which meant he heard the news.

Then, I saw a man crossing the street and walking up to Micus' car window. Only his back was visible to me. I took a photo of his back. They spoke for about 10 seconds and then he was gone.

Bill said, *"Subject number one approached target's car on driver's side, talked for about 15 seconds and then left. He walked west on Chicago Avenue. Do you want me to follow him?"*

"Negative, Bill. We'll stick to our plan," I interjected.

Ivan reported, *"Target's car is pulling away from the curb heading north. I am going to do a U-turn and follow just to make sure they get headed in the right direction."*

"10-4," I replied. I also wanted to say, "Don't be too much of a hot dog about it, Ivan. We know where he's going," but I refrained.

"Elaine to Gene. Elaine to Gene. The drop has been made outside. Proceed to second location."

Just as Micus' car had crossed some railroad tracks in the heart of Hammond, Indiana, the crossing gates started coming down, red lights flashing and all. There we were, five different cars of FBI agents, idling on the opposite side of the tracks from our pigeon, Walter Micus.

We had laid back so well that when the target had go to the exact location, none of us thought hanging back on the other side of the tracks would be a mistake! Then this freight train rumbled in front of us blocking our view to Micus going into Brothers Restaurant and getting the *bolita* cash and numbers.

Each of the agents tried to recoup by making U-turns and driving parallel to the train tracks to see if there was somewhere to cross over, either in front of or behind the train. Shockingly, none of us could find any street not blocked by this incredibly long freight train. There wasn't a way to the other side. The train had now stopped, blocking every street in town.

Micus and Frankie went into to Brother's Restaurant just on the other side of the railroad tracks. Gene and I independently of each other discovered this and pulled our cars into a parking lot next to the train tracks across from the restaurant. We got out and surveyed the scene. Gene said he was going to jump between the boxcars to see the drop.

"Gene, you have got to be shitting me! You want to climb between the boxcars to get to the other side?"

He gave me his goofy little smirk, and even in the dark, I could see his eyes twinkling in amusement. He knew that the thought of jumping up and walking across the coupling linking the two boxcars was not something someone did every day, and he didn't know that I was absolutely, inexplicably, terrified of trains.

Gene calmly said, "If we don't stop yapping about it, we'll miss the pass-off."

"I don't know if I can do this, Gene," I reluctantly replied, gulping as I said the words no female special agent ever wanted to say.

"Okay, Elaine. Wait right here and I'll go over and see if I can catch it." As he spoke, he motioned with his hands as if to say, "Calm down, I'll take care of it."

As soon as Gene turned to pull himself up between the cars to get to the other side of the railroad tracks, I found myself following right behind him in order to mimic his movements. I crossed over the boxcar coupler, but to this day I still don't know how I was able to do it. Finally I had overcome my fear of trains. The Ken Eto case was mine. I'd be damned if someone else was going to get the evidence and make my case.

Jumping down from the coupling, we were no more than 40 feet in front of the Puerto Rican sandwich shop at which Micus had met the Indiana drop-off. We scanned the area for our man. Micus' car was nowhere to be seen. But a few seconds later, we saw his distinctive greasy, pockmarked face and goofy-looking body come out of the restaurant. A Puerto Rican male somewhere between 5 feet 5 inches and 5 feet 9 inches tall, weighing in between 135 and 160 pounds, accompanied him. As they came out of the door, lucky for us, we witnessed the Puerto Rican guy hand Micus a brown paper bag. Micus then slowly strolled over to his car, which was parked about three feet away with Frankie twitching inside. Micus slid in behind the steering wheel. There they just sat because the damn train was still blocking everyone's way out of this town.

Arm in arm, looking like a couple, Gene and I strolled past their car and around the block to get away from the scene. We tried to appear innocuous. I didn't want anything about us to later trigger vague recollection in Micus' dull brain. As we got around the corner and out of Micus' sight, Gene pulled his handheld radio, commonly known as an "HT," out of the pocket of his windbreaker and said, "*All units can pull off tonight. All units can pull off tonight. We saw the drop, and you can all go home and get some sleep.*"

Ivan replied, "*10-4.*" Bill came back, "*10-4. Looks like you might have to stay over there all night.*" He chuckled. "*See you tomorrow.*"

I learned something about the reality of these criminal activities that night. I thought all criminal drops containing thousands of dollars in cash or valuable wagering tickets might be sealed in clean, white envelopes or in some official-looking container. Now I knew that they were in either brown paper bags, shopping bags, or the most ordinary-looking packages. The crooks, now that I was in the know, usually glanced around their crummy little apartments or homes and grabbed the first thing they could put their hands on. It was with this discovery that I got into the habit of wearing white cotton gloves to avoid contact with whatever — of course, I didn't want my fingerprints on any evidence. Later I found that these gloves were also great protectors of my weekly manicure.

By the next week, my informant, the trusting, goofy, and wonderful Frankie, found out that Micus had rented a room at the Holiday Inn, just outside the Chicago city limits, not far from his house. This room was used to tabulate the wagers — the second element of proof of illegal activity that was critical to my case against "Tokyo Joe".

He was going to trust Micus to tabulate all of the bets and how much they were for and determine how many winners were able to select the random 3 number combination. It was just like Lotto now legally run by every state in the U.S.

Ah! Now Mr. Eto would have to come to this location to proof the lists of bettors names, their wagers, how much they bet, count and see if any of them were winners. This was too good to be true. At whatever motel Micus selected, I would be there to see him go in and out of the room that the FBI knew there were gambling records

Surveillances now became Tuesday nights in Chicago at the Burger King, followed by the shuttle to East Chicago, Indiana. On Wednesdays, we watched the motel parking lot, waiting for Joe Eto to show up. When he was spotted, it was as if I had won the Puerto Rican lottery. It meant I had one more piece of evidence against him. I was thrilled.

Eto always eased his Mercedes sedan into the motel parking lot as casually as a grandpa on vacation. He looked no more sinister than the average elderly Asian businessman — no Italian Godfather look for this mobster. Slowly, he got out of his car, patted his shirt pocket to make sure he had his glasses, and then walked into the motel to do his job. He would proof Micus' numbers and then determine the winners of that night's *bolita* game. He was the *bolita* banker. If there were a lot of winners, people who picked the right three-number combination, it was bad for him — he would have to distribute a lot of his money. But, if he had only a few winners, the profits rolled in. Of course, the odds were in favor of the Mob.

Since Eto's assistant, Micus, was for certain a slow learner — he had in fact attended a high school for academically challenged students — the calculating job took him a very long time. Not to miss the arrival of Eto, we started early and suffered long, hot days waiting and watching from our cars parked in the motel lot. But Eto typically did not show until late in the day. He wasn't going to arrive early to painfully watch his assistant slowly tabulate.

One of the reasons Eto employed Micus was because Sam Sarcinelli, Micus' brother-in-law, had made so much money in the cocaine business that he was looking for places to invest it. So Sarcinelli had become partners with Eto in the *bolita* business by backing him with his cocaine profits. This meant that Eto had also become a partner in the cocaine business by using the proceeds of that business to support *bolita*.

Frankie kept talking to me about Sarcinelli and his cocaine enterprise and how he sold stock issues backed with his coke money. But I told him I could concentrate on only one crime at a time. I did realize that if Eto had cocaine money mingled into his gambling money, he was a goner. Drug money could bring enormous prison sentences. Right now I had no proof of the cocaine connection. I thought Eto must have been desperate if it was true.

Micus resisted telling Frankie what room he had rented at the Holiday Inn, but I found out by calling Micus at the motel and being connected to his room. This was what we call a "pretext call." I pretended to speak

Polish, and he hung up on me. Hang up on me all you want, you dumb shit — and keep registering under your real name, too.

The surveillance crew of three other agents from my squad was always in place by 8 a.m., just in case Ken Eto decided to get up early and pop in on Micus. He never did, but one time he surprised us by making the pickup in East Chicago, Indiana. No matter — George, positioned in his trusty van, got great pictures of him meeting with "Flowers," the *bolita* man in East Chicago.

Bolita, along with every other gambling game and vice in northwest Indiana, the home of harsh, foul-smelling steel towns at the southern tip of Lake Michigan, was controlled by the Chicago Outfit. Flowers was the Outfit's Puerto Rican man, and Frank Guzzino was the local controller who paid tribute to the Chicago bosses. Maybe I could take down Guzzino too.

By the end of July, Frankie had convinced Micus that it would be in his best interest to have Frankie rent the motel room as a cover for little ol' Micus. And those bothersome loser *bolita* tickets? He'd just store those for him in a hole in the back of the garage at his workplace. He didn't own the joint, but Micus went along with that idea also. By this time I was severely stressed but holding up. I learned everything I could about gathering evidence; conducting surveillances; debriefing, manipulating, and making payments to informants; and finally, how to work with the god-like personages called federal prosecutors.

Bill Brown, my supervisor, stepped out of his office one day and said, "Hey, Smith, come on in here." Bill was a much different person than Ray, my yellow-toothed, missing-in-action former supervisor. First of all, Bill was black. At this time, there were so few black agents in the FBI that it would have been difficult to say we were even integrated. But Bill felt good in his skin, and as far as I had experienced, everyone liked him, including me. Secondly, he was interested in the work his agents did and wanted to help us. Lastly, he was opinionated and very stubborn.

I sat down in Bill's office and looked around at the clutter of books, papers, newspapers, and half-empty coffee cups littering his desk, window ledge, and bookcases.

"What's up, Bill?" I sat posed to write down his every word of wisdom. Ready as usual to stroke the boss with respect.

"I know you ain't gonna like this, Smith. I want you to take the Eto case down in the next two weeks."

- CHAPTER EIGHT -
A Fly in My Web

"Smith, you can't make this case your Bureau career." Bill saw the dumbfounded look on my face and that my body had collapsed into the chair like a deflated balloon. A deep-throated laugh rolled out of his mouth. Bill seemed to be amused. "I don't mean that, Smith." He leaned forward with his forearms on his messy desk and picked up the butt of an unlit cigar from an ashtray. Inserting the stubby little brown thing in his mouth, he said, "You've got the goods. Take it down before anything happens."

"I know you're right," I said. Then, unable to stop myself, I asked, "Are you sure we have enough?"

"Look, you have a couple more weeks to surveil Eto and get more records. During that time, you write the search warrant and then, bingo, you take him down."

In my head, taking him down was beginning to sound sort of peaceful. I saw a glimmer of light at the end of the tunnel I had been digging with a spoon. "Well, I do have an appointment this afternoon with Marty Powell at the Strike Force to discuss the case."

"See, there you go," Bill said, extra loud, as if to add enthusiasm.

I wanted to say, "Okay, okay, Bill, I'm not in kindergarten. I get the point," but I didn't.

I got up to leave Bill's office. He stood and came around his desk to pat me on the shoulder. "Smith, it's going to be just fine. You'll see."

As we both walked out of his office, he saw a friend of his and yelled, "Hey, joker, did you hear…" His thoughts were off to somewhere else, and I was left there, holding my proverbial dick. Even women can have one of those.

I shuffled back to my desk and flopped into my big brown leather chair, pulled out the bottom drawer of my desk, put my feet on it and swirled around to look out the window.

Dietzie, sitting at the next desk, said in a fake German accent. "Frau Schmidt, you dun't look so gud."

"Well, Bill wants me to bring the Eto case to an end."

Dietzie picked up his pipe, lit it, and blew a puff of smoke out of his mouth. In 1980, everyone smoked something. He leaned back in his chair.

"I'm afraid I don't have enough evidence," I continued.

Dietzie said, "Well, that, Frau Schmidt, you do. Whether it's enough for the prosecutors to indict him is another question. Aren't you meeting with Marty at the Strike Force today?"

"Yes."

Dietzie went on pontificating. "Well, you tell him what you have now and what you plan on getting in the next few weeks. And see what he says. There's no way Bill is going to want you to take this case down if they won't prosecute it based on what you have. That's what we're about. Prosecution."

"Yeah, you're right on that one. Why waste our time if we don't prosecute these people? Seems to me we do a lot of that around here anyway. These federal prosecutors are pretty powerful, aren't they?"

Dietzie blew some more pipe smoke into the air above him and nodded his head like an old wise man. I went back to work.

I'd been studying the legal manual. I thought I had evidence to charge Eto with violating interstate transportation in aid of racketeering enterprises[16], operating an interstate gambling enterprise[17], and conspiracy[18]. I knew I wanted to search the motel room with Eto inside it and grab him in the act of calculating his wins and losses. I knew I had to write an affidavit to support a search warrant. By now my heart should have been wildly pounding, geared up for my meeting that afternoon with the prosecuting attorney, but all I wanted to do was go to sleep. I desperately wanted to go home, take off my pantyhose, put on my nightgown, and crawl into bed. Maybe I could cancel the meeting and reschedule for tomorrow — claim I have cramps.

Deferring such thoughts for the moment, I headed for the washroom. I sat in the stall for a long time, hanging on the toilet, not peeing, just staring at the ugly gray door inches from my face. This is just too much work, I thought. I've got to cut back. Here I was, only 11 months out of new agents' training school, on the cusp of breaking a case against an organized crime figure that no other agent had touched in 30 years, and all I could think of was my nice warm comfortable bed at home.

Relieving myself, I got off the toilet and looked at my watch — lunchtime. No wonder I felt so badly. My biorhythms were down. I needed my usual pick-me-up — a grilled cheese sandwich with a chocolate shake.

I grabbed my purse and saw Dietzie. I got his attention and made the universal sign for eating by pointing my finger at my open mouth. He shook his head no. Recently much of my conversation with him was pantomime. His days were spent wearing black earphones, proofing the transcriptions of hundreds of hours of taped conversations taken on the wiretap of Caesar DiVarco's hangout.

I returned with my lunch and ate it at my desk. While eating, I started putting together all the paperwork I had to prove my case. Dietzie took off his headphones and said, "I'm going to call you 'Agent Amuck.'"

I just looked at him quizzically.

"Why don't you relax and eat your lunch? Why don't you listen to classical music, like me?"

I shot a look at him. "You mean you're not proofing your transcriptions?"

"Well," he said slowly, "not all the time, and not on my lunch hour. You, Frau Schmidt, have to start taking it a little easy." He must have read my exhaustion and overload. Who said men couldn't be sensitive?

The Chicago Organized Crime Strike Force, a group of about 10 attorneys, was independently funded and managed apart from the United States Attorney's Office. Its job was to prosecute mobsters. The Department of Justice wanted these prosecutors to answer only to their supervisors in Washington, D.C., and not in any way to be influenced by the politically appointed United States Attorney in the judicial district in which they were located. There were Strike Forces located in New York, Newark, Miami, Chicago, and Los Angeles. These were the cities that the Department of Justice had determined did not have the prosecutorial resources or balls to hit organized criminals. Most United States Attorney's Offices were offended by the Strike Force's presence and thought of them as interlopers.

As I rode up the elevator to the eighth-floor Strike Force offices located in the same federal building as our FBI office, I was nervous and a little awestruck at the proposition of me presenting my case to the assigned prosecutor. This guy had studied the law, argued federal cases, and put away the bad guys for life. I stepped off the elevator and saw a sign that read *Chicago Strike Force* next to a Department of Justice seal. I entered and approached the receptionist. "Hi, I'm Elaine Smith with the FBI. Here to see Marty Powell." I showed her my credentials.

"Please sign in on the register and I'll buzz you in." I signed. She buzzed. She gave me a sticky white convention badge on which she had written my name with *FBI* underneath it. I took a seat in the tiny waiting room. I noticed her staring at me. She caught my look. "We've never had a female FBI agent up here before," she said.

"Oh," was the only reply that came to my mind at the moment. [19] As I nervously waited, I reviewed the organization of my papers and reread some of my surveillances. I found a few mistakes and made myself a little less than confident in the quality of what I was going to give this prosecutor.

The door that led to the inner hallway opened and a round-faced white guy, around 40, stuck his head out and said with a twang, "Well, you must be Elaine Smith."

I stood. "Yes, I am."

"Well, I'm Marty." I walked over to him and we shook hands. "Come on in." He had a homey accent I couldn't place, but I caustically thought it might be an affectation to try to make me comfortable. He led me to a small office. All surfaces were covered with books, papers, and boxes filled with more paper. His desk offered more of the same. Would I ever see a neat office? An organized office? An office that even had a plant in it?

Marty sat back in his chair, put both of his feet up on his desk, and spread his legs apart. Then, once he was situated in this position, he said, "So tell me, Agent Smith, why are you up here today?"

I was dying to say, "Not to look at your crotch." But I knew that wouldn't win me any points. Why are some men such disgusting slobs when they're in their offices? Do they think they're free to behave in any uncivilized manner they wish? I tried not to take it personally, but at this point, I wanted to go home and go to bed now more than ever. "I have the investigation on Ken Eto."

Mr. Prosecutor interrupted and said, as if he were some sage, "Ah, old Ken Eto, I know him well."

I asked, "How's that?"

"No, no, go on," he said with a wave of his hand.

Forgetting the interruption, I continued, "Well, starting June 17, we surveilled Eto's tabulating man going to Indiana on four occasions to pick up *bolita* wagers. We also watched him pick up from another *bolita* collector here in Chicago. Following three of the four Chicago to Indiana and Chicago pickup combinations, we watched the motel room he is using as his tabulating room. On all three of these occasions, we identified and photographed Ken Eto arriving and departing from that room."

"We have the *bolita* records from the operation since May 5. These records are in Washington, D.C., at the FBI Identification Division, being examined for fingerprints. Next they will be sent to the experts at the Gambling Unit to establish the identities and the number of the various participants, along with the gross proceeds of the operation. From my preliminary examination, I can say with certainty, we do have a minimum of five people involved, over $2,000 a day being wagered, and the operation crosses state lines."

"Well, it sure sounds as if you got yourself a case on Ken Eto," he said.

"Would you prosecute him for what I have?" I asked. I wanted to cross my fingers and toes.

"I'd prosecute Joe the Jap if he spit on the street."

I was elated, but surprised at his forcefulness. "Marty, how do you know about him?"

He came back, "Everyone knows about Ken Eto. The Outfit used him to try to muscle in on the numbers racket. Even had him try to organize the P. Stone Rangers[20] and put them under the control of the syndicate."

I interrupted in a stunned tone, "You mean the Italian mafia tried to muscle the original bad-ass black ghetto gang?"

Marty answered, "You got that right. We think Eto and his buddies even killed one of their biggest policy operators. And then buried him in concrete in the Dan Ryan Expressway construction."

I knew the story of the Dan Ryan Expressway. Chicago's first eight-lane, California-type freeway was built right through the black neighborhoods of Chicago's south side. It displaced close to 100,000 black Chicago residents. The first Mayor Richard Daley "resettled them" into horrific public housing concrete-bunker high rises.

Marty continued. "In the 1960s, two policy operators were convicted of evading $1 million of tax for their operations in Gary and East Chicago, Indiana alone.[21] Then, in 1970, the Strike Force decided to look into policy operators. FBI and IRS agents were estimating Gary and East Chicago were bringing in $6 million to $9 million a year. We also know that Gary and East Chicago are controlled by the Outfit."

"Was Eto involved in this?"

"I don't know," Marty replied. "I do know that in the late 1960s, DiVarco was actually being strong-armed by the Black P. Stone Nation and sent Eto to try to intercede on his behalf. Eventually the black gangs proved too numerous and too crazy even for the Outfit."[22]

"Marty," I said, trying to get him back to the present, "Bill Brown wants me to take the case down in the next couple of weeks. I've never written a search warrant affidavit. Will you help me?"

He nodded. "Sure."

"Excellent. I appreciate that. And with the current evidence and what I'll continue to collect, do I have probable cause to search Eto's motel tabulating location?"

"Yes, of course, of course."

"Fantastic!" I said, a little too loudly. A little embarrassed, I stood up, and then, almost as an afterthought, handed him the typed surveillances of Micus and Eto. I also gave him the debriefings of Frankie, with his name never used. He was only a number on the document. "I will start drafting the affidavit and keep you up to date on my progress. Thanks again. I'll keep you posted." I stood.

"Right, Agent Smith. Here's my card. Do you have one?"

"I do," I replied, as I awkwardly bent over my purse and fumbled to get out a business card. I handed him one. He studied it, nodded, and kicked out a little, "Hmm." I reminded myself to start giving away my card more often. Since the minimum order of cards was 500, it would probably take me a hundred years to pass out that many cards. My card was different.

Elaine Corbitt Smith
Special Agent
Federal Bureau of Investigation
219 South Dearborn
Chicago, Illinois 60604
312-431-1333

No one I knew had a card printed like mine. I chose not to use the FBI seal or any other insignia approved for use, and certainly no one had thought of having their cards printed on ecru paper in script. It always created a reader reaction.

I left the Chicago Strike Force office in a much better mood, even though I was not fully confident that this Marty guy was going to be that much help. He seemed somewhat of a windbag and little too flip about making a commitment to help me. My case would eat into his available time and, by the look of his office, he was already overwhelmed.

I returned to the squad area and walked into Bill's office. He was alone. "Bill, may I talk with you?"

"Sure, darlin'. Sit down," Bill said. When Bill called me "darlin'," it wasn't demeaning or in any way a come-on. From him, it was a southern term he might have used with his daughters, sisters, or friends.

"I just met with Marty at the Strike Force. He said he would prosecute Eto with the evidence we have now. He also approved a search, and he'll help me write the affidavit."

"Just as I thought. Good, good. Now you just have to plan out your schedule for the raid. I'll help you get the people to staff it. I think we should invite along those Vice Control Division detectives you met. It will go a long way for improving our relationship with the Chicago Police Department."

"Bill, that's fine with me, but let's not invite them until the day before. We'll have them come to a meeting at our office and then just happen to go on a raid. I don't trust them. They might mess this thing up. Please?"

"Okay, okay, Smith, you can have it your way," Bill said.

"Also, I rented the adjoining motel rooms for the next two weeks. I planted bugs and cameras in them and want to see what we get from that. So the earliest we can execute the search warrant would be August 19."

Bill thought for a while and said, "That's longer than I had hoped for. A great deal can go wrong in three weeks."

"I know, and we'll just have to make sure it doesn't. In any event, no one can take away the evidence we have so far, right?" Bill just rolled his eyes.

I left Bill's office and walked to my desk. Once again it was late in the day and no one else was around. I thought about the web I was spinning to nab Joe Eto. Bill was right. The longer we delayed, the greater the possibility the web might be broken. Tension was building. It was time to catch the fly.

The night before the raid was scheduled for Eto's motel tabulating room, we did our last Tuesday night surveillance on Micus making his pickups in Chicago and then in East Chicago, Indiana. But, that night, for the first time, we missed the pass-off between Micus and Flowers in East Chicago. I blamed Bill. It was his first time on this surveillance, and he was assigned to sit in the parking lot of Brother's Restaurant. So there he was, a big black guy wearing the grubbiest-looking clothes I had ever seen, sitting in his car, smoking one of his ugly little cigars. According to Frankie, Bill's presence alone apparently scared the shit out of those bad-ass Puerto Rican dudes and Micus. So they made the pass-off on a side street just a few blocks away. Later, I could always get a laugh out of Bill by mentioning this incident. But at the time, I was not amused. I wanted everything to go perfectly.

During those three weeks of intense preparation for the raid, the legal term "absentia" applied perfectly to how I acted as a wife and mother. Sure, I came home each night for dinner, but I came home late. I worked every Saturday afternoon and every Sunday. When I was at home, I made and received calls at all hours, interrupting whatever we were doing. Kim was 9 years old and was an amazingly self-reliant child. Since she was an only child, she had developed that ability to entertain herself. Later she said she was comfortable knowing she could spend time with herself, unlike many of her friends, who had brothers and sisters that they would torment when they became bored. Tom just took it all in and quietly understood my obsession.

My last task that night was to confirm that Micus had gone to the Holiday Inn to begin his routine of tabulating, sleep, and tabulating some more until Eto arrived. Then I went home to try to sleep. It was a stifling August night. The air conditioner rumbled in the background. I tossed and turned, covers on, covers off, and thought of a million things I should have done, or should do the next day. I got little sleep that night.

Tom left for work at his usual time. On his way out, he kissed me tenderly on my lips and, while he held my arms, looked into my eyes. "Good luck today," he whispered. My husband knew how important this was to me. He knew how devastated I would be if anything got screwed up. He also knew how remarkable it was that his wife, the rookie, with less than a year in the field, was about to conduct a raid on an organized crime gambling boss.

"Thanks, honey," was all I could say. I didn't tell him that I really wanted to stay curled up in his arms all day long rather than face what I was about to.

I lingered around the house, had breakfast with Kim, chatted with Grandma, went for a jog, and then showered and dressed. Believe it or not, dressing casually for a raid was a little perk that somewhat compensated for an18-hour workday. Executing search warrants, as I came to find out, always involved very detailed, grueling, grubby work.

I got to the office well before Bill. Everyone else was either keeping an eye on Room 127 at the Holiday Inn or relaxing at home. We were scheduled to hit the room around 4 p.m., the usual time that Eto would appear. Most of our crew was working a 2 p.m. to 10 p.m. shift. Besides being responsible for this whole thing, I had a 12 p.m. appointment with Magistrate Judge Balog and the Assistant United States Attorney. Marty Powell, it turned out, didn't disappoint my expectations. He proved to be a bag of wind.

One of the other attorneys, Marty's boss, Gary, helped me craft almost every word and refine my affidavit, all 34 pages of it. He made me write and rewrite the affidavit until I wanted to scream. At the time, I didn't understand why he was so picky, careful, and insistent that all the details be 100 percent accurate. But, once we got into the prosecution stage of the case against Eto, I understood completely. The very first thing a defense attorney will attempt to do is attack any evidence seized under a search warrant with the goal of suppressing the search warrant to win the case.

I suggested an angle of my own — issue seizure warrants for both Eto's and Micus' cars. Therefore we would expand the search beyond just the motel room to also include and seize Micus' and Eto's cars. Legally, they used their cars to transport illegal goods (gambling wagers) across state lines. We could grab them. This was going to be good. But I was so freaked out about getting everything right and done on time that there was little time to reflect on my "web building" success.

I walked into the magistrate's office in the Dirksen Federal Building nervously anticipating my meeting with the august dignitary. Immediately, the awesome view of the blue waters of Lake Michigan filling the floor-to-ceiling windows captured my attention. Then Marty Powell stepped up. He gestured toward an open door. I followed him into Judge Balog's vast office: dark green carpet, wood paneling, bookcases filled with leather-bound books — an authoritarian design palette intended to humble visitors. Marty greeted the judge with friendly *bonhomie*. I was stiff with fright. Judge Balog directed us to sit. We sat. Seconds passed quietly while he flipped through my affidavit. He stopped on a page and looked up at me. "Agent Smith, do you often knock on the motel door of the target of your surveillance?"

Oh, my God. He really had read this thing. And he found the interesting part of the otherwise boring legal document. "No, your honor, I do not. I went to that door by mistake. When I arrived at the Holiday Inn to relieve the agents already on surveillance, they mistakenly had given me the subject's room number instead of their room number. I knocked on that door. To say the least, I was surprised when Mr. Eto opened it and stood in front of me. But I quickly covered my mistake by appearing confused. I blurted out, 'Oh, you're not my husband.' And at that point, he closed the door in my face."

The judge smiled. "Well, I thought that was a fairly bold move on your part, but now I understand. Good thing you were able to cover it."

I wished I could tell the judge that I wanted to kill those two agents. I still have the vision of them peeking out the door of the room across the hallway and laughing their asses off. But in reality, all it did was make my case stronger. In opening that door, Eto had allowed me to verify he was there, and I was able to get a look inside at an adding machine and loose papers on a table in the motel room.

Judge Balog had no more questions or comments. He signed and stamped the last page of the affidavit, in addition to signing and stamping warrants for the search of the person of Ken Eto, the person of Walter Micus, Room 127 of the Holiday Inn, Eto's Mercedes-Benz, Micus' Oldsmobile (he got this new car from his brother-in-law, Sam Sarcinelli, as partial payment for a cocaine debt), and finally, the ugly green AMC Hornet.

I had 24 hours to execute this warrant, but I sure wasn't going to wait that long. I had only three more hours till showtime, and I was starving. As I left Marty at the magistrate's office, I told him I would give him a call when we entered the premises and provide status update. He shook my hand and said, "Good luck, Agent Smith. Go get 'em."

I muttered in reply, "Thanks, Marty." But I thought, "You are such a goof."

When I got back to the squad area, things were beginning to heat up. Some of my squad mates had arrived and were milling around. The sledgehammer was out on one of the desks, and a big discussion was taking place as to the best technique to use to breech a door. There was laughter and a general air of excitement, which did nothing but make me jumpier and more hyper than usual. I dropped the signed warrants on my desk. I had picked up lunch on the way, and I began eating it at my desk — a nice greasy Popeye's fried chicken breast, coleslaw, and fries, with a real Coke.

Bill came out of his office and saw me. He walked over and asked, "So, Smith, did you have any trouble with the magistrate?"

I swallowed some chicken breast and answered, "None at all, except he did question me about knocking on Eto's door. He thought that was a ballsy move for a woman."

"He didn't say that!" Bill shouted in shock.

"No, he didn't. But he did question me as to why I did it."

Bill threw his head back and laughed long and hard. "That was a good one, Smith."

"Ha, ha, ha," I replied with a fake laugh, making sure my mouth was open and full of half-eaten chicken breast. I swallowed and continued. "We're ready to go. I just have to make copies of these warrants to leave with the subjects and a couple for the file. What time did you schedule the sleaze-ball cops to arrive?"

"Now, behave yourself," Bill shot back as a warning. "They're riding with you. They'll be here at 2 o'clock."

Bill went back into his office and I went back to eating my lunch, but somehow I had lost my appetite. I was way too nervous to do much but worry. I jumped out of my daydreaming to answer the phone, "Hello, this is Elaine Smith."

"Hi, Elaine, this is reception and I have two Chicago detectives here to see you. Should I have them sign in and give them visitor badges?"

"Yes, thanks very much. I'll be down to get them in five minutes. Ask them to have a seat." I thought a five-minute wait was better than an hour wait like they gave me. I really wasn't trying to get back at them. I just needed to copy these warrants, throw out my lunch, and make sure I had everything in my briefcase.

"Welcome, gentlemen," I greeted Garza and Berti as they rose from their chairs in the reception area. Both smiled nervously and fingered the plastic visitor badges hanging limply around their necks. "Come on, I'd like to introduce you to my supervisor, who will explain why he invited you here today."

Berti, who couldn't keep his smart-ass mouth shut, said, "Oh, I think we have an idea."

I offered just a faint smile that neither confirmed nor denied his comment.

The two "*bolita* experts" followed me to my squad area. We walked through the large open-office area, passing numerous other squad sections filled with guys talking on their phones, standing around bullshitting, or dictating memos. Some had just come in from the street — others were on their way out.

I walked them into Bill's office and made the introductions.

"Gentlemen, please sit down," said Bill. "I hope you can spend a couple of hours with us this afternoon?"

Both Berti and Garza nodded their heads in the affirmative.

"Good, good. Because I think we're going to show you a fuckin' good time."

My mind flashed: Whoa, whoa, Bill. You don't have to get down to their level.

Then Bill laughed his usual laugh, lit one of his nasty cigars, and said, "We're going to raid Ken 'the fuckin' Jap' Eto."

My boss was actually taking this thing too far. He was bragging to these two goofballs and we hadn't even banged down the door yet. Oh, shit. "Uh, Bill?" I interrupted him.

"Yeah, Smith?" he said in an irritated tone.

"I need to make just one quick call, and then we should be heading out. Okay?" He waved me off with his cigar hand like I was a fly.

As I left his office, I heard him say, "Oh, the phones, you both know that neither of you can come near a phone until we finish this job, right? Smith there has orders to shoot off your balls if you do." He laughed again. I almost stopped cold in my steps to turn around and straighten out this bit of misinformation, but then I thought — who cares? If they do screw up this raid, I will shoot their balls off.

I got to the phone on my desk and called Frankie at work. "Yo, Frankie. How's it goin'?"

"I'm hangin'," he replied.

"Have you heard anything from the genius?"

"Naw. He don't call me when he thinks Joe the Jap might be comin' soon. He's scared to death of him."

"Well, my eye says he hasn't gotten there yet. Okay, Frankie, just checking in. Keep cool. We are almost there. You're the greatest. Love you."

"Love you, too," Frankie replied.

Over the summer, and with the intensity of me having to rely on this uneducated and so-called "intellectually limited" person, my attitude toward him had radically changed. He and I were now trusting allies. The "love you" phrase was my way of telling him I cared about him more than the case and would do anything I could to make sure he was safe from harm. At one of our planning sessions, Frankie had accused me of not knowing what I was doing and I replied, "Yes, Frank, I am flying by the seat of my pants, but it's the best I can do. I need your help. Not your challenge. We can figure this out so it turns out the way we need it to." He was instantly contrite.

Bill had done his job on Garza and Berti, and driving with them from downtown Chicago to the Holiday Inn in the suburbs was almost pure torture. Along on the ride, they heard the radio chatter of everyone on the squad going into service and heading for the motel. Of course, they didn't know where they were going. There were 14 Bureau units in service, some with two agents in each car because I had to have extra agents to drive the three cars we were seizing back to the FBI garage. I must say I was surprised when Berti piped up and said, "We sure didn't think you were going to be able to do this. We thought this would be an impossible mission for a rookie like you. Eto is a hard nut to crack. You know we pinched him just a few weeks ago?"

My blood began to boil. "You what?"

"Yeah, we pulled him over late on a Tuesday night. He didn't have anything on him."

"I thought you were going to advise me if you got anything on him?" I shot back accusingly.

"Duh, we didn't, Elaine. He was a cool as a cucumber." Nightmares of these idiots screwing up my case ran through my mind. My God! I guess my web has been hanging by a thread. Bill was right when he said it was time to take it down — the sooner the better.

I turned into the driveway of the Holiday Inn and drove past the surveillance van. In this weather, the van was a hot box for the agent sweating inside. And he held the critical responsibility of spotting Eto's car when it pulled in, taking a photograph of the vehicle, and then taking another photo of Eto exiting his car and entering the motel. In order to remain inconspicuous, he had to sit in the back of the van, roasting.

Parked in a treeless area, the dark brown van with no back windows absorbed all the heat of the blazing August sun. None of us could do more than an hour in this torture chamber. We would emerge drained, sweating, and swearing at Eto for the pain. I wished him luck.

I parked my car at the back of the motel parking lot and led Berti and Garza through the back door of the wing containing Room 127. From there we snaked through the hallways to Room 125, the room adjacent to Eto's. I knocked quietly.

The agents in Room 125 would usually listen through the door to overhear any conversations in the other room. But today's agents waited for the heads-up that "the man" was there and the game was about to begin. The four agents in the room were the dudes who would announce, "FBI, open up!" and then, if it didn't happen instantly, breech the door with the battering ram — really, it was just a very large, heavy hammer. These agents were my most trusted squad partners to assure a meticulous job for me. They all knew how to enter a room safely, take control of the situation, and then conduct an evidence search that would withstand the most vigorous attacks from Mob defense attorneys.

I introduced Berti and Garza around the room and they joined everyone else by sitting on the floor or one of the beds. We chatted quietly, ever so infrequently, because we didn't want Micus in the next room to think we were having a kegger next door. Time dragged. I was anxious, tense, and excited. We waited.

Then the radio crackled. "*Eyeball to Elaine. Eyeball to Elaine.*"

I grabbed Dietzie's handheld and said, "*Go ahead.*"

"*The old man has just arrived and is parking.*"

"*10-4. Sweet words, Eyeball.*"

"*10-4.*"

We agreed we would let Eto get into the room, settle down, and get involved with his numbers — maybe give him 20 to 30 minutes. Then we would hit the door. Finally, we heard Eto knock on the door and Micus opening it to let him in. This guy sure did move slowly. Then — more painful waiting. We listened — some scattered discussion next door, the adding machine tape moved forward on its electric roller, a toilet flushed. I was going nuts. I stood up and whispered, "I've had enough. Let's go."

My case. My ass on the line. I get to knock on the door and say, "FBI, open up!" But I'm not a total fool. No one would be frightened by my announcement, even if I said it in my most bitchy voice. I gave the announcement and pounding honors to Jim Q, who had the deepest, most authoritative voice in the universe and was hot shit with the battering ram. When he yelled, "FBI, open up!" at Room 127, I almost peed in my pants.

He gave Micus and Eto 10 seconds, and as he drew back the battering ram, Micus opened the door. Agents flooded the room, guns drawn, barking orders for everyone to "put your hands up and get down on your knees." Eto and Micus immediately complied. But then Micus, on his knees, leaned over and puked.

Oh, my God, what a smell. I was reminded of elementary school — some kid puking in class — the terrible stench until the janitor brought a bucket of sawdust to cover it up. The gagging reflex often makes others respond in kind. Luckily, none of us did.

Well, that was all we needed to have happen in a room we were going to spend the next several hours in, painstakingly cataloging all of the wagering slips, tallying sheets, and other evidence. Someone brought in a towel from the bathroom and covered the puke, turned the air conditioner on high, and opened the window. That odor left, but then we were assaulted by Micus' body odor. This guy needed a shower and a change of clothes. How repulsive can someone get? Ah…my glamorous FBI job.

Meanwhile, Ken Eto was cool as a cucumber, unfazed by anything he saw or smelled — FBI guys busting through the door, being handcuffed and kneeling on the floor, and watching his employee vomit all over himself. Eto was handcuffed from behind and he needed help with his balance to get up. I helped him to his feet by simply holding his right elbow firmly to pull him up from a kneeling to a standing position. Then I took him into the adjoining motel room and had him sit down in the chair next to the desk.

Oh boy, now I was face to face with my target, the big bad murderer, the gambling kingpin, but I felt…nothing. He looked like a little old Asian man with very hooded eyes without emotion on his face or tension in his body.

"Mr. Eto, I am Elaine Smith, a special agent with the FBI. Here is my business card." I slid it over to him.

He said, "May I have my glasses out of my pocket?"

"Oh, certainly. Sorry." I leaned over and took his glasses out of a black plastic case that snapped in front. I then placed his glasses on his face.

He looked at the card and uttered, "Hmm."

I then said, "Are you comfortable, Mr. Eto?"

He said, "Oh, sure." Just as if he was basking in the sun at a Miami Beach retirement village.

"Do you know why we are here, Mr. Eto?"

"I can guess," he said.

"What would your guess be?"

"Well, Agent…" he started and then looked at my business card. "Well, Agent Smith, you know better than I do." He laughed.

I thought, well, we have a joker here — Grandpa Joker — who is not rattled by anything.

While I was figuring out if I could look really mean at Joe the Jap or even call him that, my friend Dietzie came into the room and introduced himself to Ken Eto. Then he said, "I think we are going to try to charge your partner in there, Walter Micus, with assaulting a federal agent's olfactory senses." Both of them laughed again, this time together. I was a little put off by the frivolity of it all and asked Dietzie if he could stay with Eto while I went to check on the progress of the search teams, both inside and out.

As I walked out of the room, I heard Eto ask Dietzie, "Is she in charge?" I heard him say, "Oh, yeah. One hundred percent running this show."

I walked into the dimly lit hallway and from there outside into the bright light of the afternoon. I squinted to adjust my eyes. It wasn't just the sun. Camera lights blasted in my face. Unbelievable — the parking lot was filled with TV station newsmen. How the hell did that happen? Who snitched to the press that there was a raid going down here?

I shielded my eyes and saw Bill giving an interview to a news reporter from one of the local TV channels. Oh, no. What would he say? I walked around him, out of the view of the cameras' eyes. A couple of agents were going through Eto's Mercedes. They had everything out and were painstakingly cataloging it under the blazing sun. Nearby, a couple of other agents began to work on Micus' black Oldsmobile. This activity was the first step of our search process, which begins with very detailed photos of what we search, from every angle, and each photo being matched with a detailed description.

I quickly returned to the cool darkness of the hallway and went up to the front desk. I sought out the manager, who hustled in from a back room. "Sir, I'm Elaine Smith with the FBI. We are conducting a search in Room 127 that should take only about two hours and should cause no disturbance to your business and no damage to your property."

"Oh," he said. "Somebody named Bill has already been up here, and he assured me of that. In fact, I have his card here in my pocket." He pulled out a business card and flashed it quickly, but I did see the gold seal of the FBI on it.

"Good," I replied. "Bill is my boss, and I'm glad he got here right away. If there are any questions, please just come and get us in either Room 125 or Room 127. We'll tell you when we leave, and we thank you for your patience."

His response surprised me. "I think the excitement is fun, and I think the guests do too."

"Oh! Well, thanks!" I then toddled off to the pay phone in the lobby. I called Frankie just to let him know about Micus' puking and that we had pulled it off.

Back in Room 125, Dietzie processed the contents of Eto's wallet. We had a search warrant for Room 127, the vehicle, and the person of Eto. That included his wallet. We would keep the wallet but give Eto an itemized list of its contents. If he wanted something in it, his attorney would have to appeal to the United States Attorney's Office. Eto had $579 in his wallet. I called Assistant United States Attorney Marty to ask what we should do with the money.

"Let him have it back because he'll need that much for the cab fare back to Chicago."

I reassured Mr. Prosecutor that I would be in his office tomorrow to return the executed search warrants to Magistrate Balog around 1 p.m. "Is that okay?" I asked.

"Sounds hunky dory." We hung up. What a hunky dork that one was.

In the end, I had a list of everything we had taken from Room 127 and Mr. Eto's pockets, wallet, and car. Micus and Eto were not arrested but were detained to ensure there was no danger to themselves or the agents. Micus' person and wallet were searched and his cars were seized. A copy of the search warrant was ready to give to the prosecutor. The whole thing had taken about two hours from start to finish. Berti and Garza hitched the first ride out of there with one of the agents driving Eto's car back to the federal garage. Micus was uncuffed and told he was free to go. However, he had been served with a subpoena that demanded he come in to produce his fingerprints and give handwriting exemplars.

Basically, it was just Dietzie, Eto, and I who remained. I said softly to Eto, "You know, most of all, Joe, we want your cooperation about certain people."

He said to me, "I know you have your job to do, and I have mine. That will not happen."

"You have my card, yes?" He did not reply. "You have a subpoena to provide fingerprints and handwriting exemplars in two weeks. We will meet again at that time. Thank you, sir." I stood to shake his hand.

He gathered his papers and feebly shook my hand. It was a weak, dry, just-the-front-of-his-fingers shake. He then ambled out of the room, looked both ways down the dimly lit hall as if he didn't know where to turn, decided to turn left, and headed outside.

- CHAPTER NINE -
Eto Wants Me

I turned to Dietzie and said, "It's just you and me, baby. Let's have a drink."

He looked at me, rolled his eyes, and said, "Frau Schmidt, you sexy thing. I don't think I've had a better proposition all day." He extended his arm to escort me to the bar in the Holiday Inn.

I reminded him that before we lost our heads, we'd better make sure we locked up the rooms and put our briefcases in the car. "That way we can let our hair down."

"Ah, yes, Frau Schmidt, you are always thinking, but you are the only one with much hair." Jim Dietz had a case of thinning hair syndrome.

We made everything secure and then moved to the motel bar. Small, dark, and only for serious drinkers, the décor of the lounge reminded me of the outrageous outfits the "Fat Elvis" wore in Las Vegas — puffy white leather stools decorated with brass studs and chrome trim and backlit bottles of booze on a background of beveled mirrors. Except for Dietzie and me, the place was empty. Micus and Eto didn't stick around, but I bet they knocked down a few stiff drinks when they got home. It was one of those days.

I knew one gin and tonic would make me loopy. I didn't care. How sweet it tasted and how welcome it felt to be buzzed. The gin relaxed me — the good feeling moved quickly from my head to my feet, and I wanted to get up and dance, to shake my thing, to celebrate. A black friend once commented that FBI parties weren't fun because no one danced. That comment struck a chord with me. When I partied, I too wanted to dance. Damn — I wanted to boogie. But tonight I guess I had to settle for mature mellowing instead of raucous romping — just a drink or two with my trusty partner Dietzie. The built-up tension of the day slid out like an ebbing tide, leaving in its place only peace and satisfaction. My raid on Joe Eto was a total success.

After the raid, my world quieted. I resumed a normal life for the time being. I didn't see Joe Eto again until about three weeks after the search when he came in to provide fingerprint samples and handwriting exemplars. This was in compliance with a grand jury subpoena we had given him on the day of the search.

He showed up with his Mob attorney, Mr. Samuel V.P. Banks. Bob Cooley, a Chicago detective who went to law school at night and then moved up the food chain to become a "fixer attorney" [23] for the Outfit, and still later became a government witness, wrote about Samuel V. P. Banks, "… (Banks) was, in my humble opinion, the biggest buffoon practicing criminal law in Chicago. He even dressed the part of your Mob lawyer, with crazy sharkskin suits and loud ties." He also wrote, "…representing Patty DeLeo was a lawyer as far removed from Webb (this was Dan Webb, a nationally regarded defense attorney) as I could imagine — the clown prince of the criminal courts, Sam Banks. He was just an idiot in every way. How stupid can Patty be to use an incompetent like this?"[24]

At this time, though, I knew nothing about Mr. Banks, and surprisingly, when he arrived at the FBI office with Eto, he only cautioned me: "Mr. Eto is represented by counsel." Legally, I did not know how to interpret this advice. With that admonition, he left the office. Eto and I stood alone in the reception area of the FBI office. My thoughts: Well, so much for that legal representation. Eto's thoughts must have been: "How much am I paying him"? In any event, Banks' disappearance made this whole process easier for me. I got a visitor's badge for "Mr. Eto" (which, now that he was in my charge, was how I intended to address him from this point forward). I escorted him back to the tiny fingerprint and mug shot room.

I had to take "major case prints," as they are called. They are the bitch of the century to take. Since Mr. Eto was not under arrest — which continued to piss me off — he was no threat. I wore no gun and I was able to do this job by myself. Every surface on his hand had to be printed. The sides of his fingers and palm had to be rolled to capture every crevice, ridge, and whorl. If you smudged one part, you had to do it over. If someone says they found a fingerprint at a crime scene, it doesn't only mean a fingertip. It could mean a palm, or the side of a palm or a finger. The FBI printing process captured all of these possibilities.

During this time, I figured I could schmooze and develop some rapport with Mr. Eto. He was friendly but reserved. He didn't display any humor, but considering the circumstances, perhaps I too might be a little flat on my funny side while being printed. He was a heavy smoker with a deep and persistent smoker's cough. We even took a break in the process for a cigarette. He appeared to enjoy the break, and it relieved some of the tension inherent in this tedious and precise chore.

I got a good set of major case prints on my subject, and then I pressed a doorbell-like button located on the wall of the room. This "high tech" contraption was connected to the photo lab to notify the photography clerks that we had someone ready for a mug shot. When I rang the bell, George, the photographer, who had been sweating in the van for weeks with me, came galloping in. He knew in advance that "the man" was scheduled to come in today and he was excited. He positioned Eto carefully with the rectangular black placard hanging from Eto's neck that read *Federal Bureau of Investigation – Chicago, September 16, 1980*, and the sequential number of the photo. Now Ken Eto was forever captured in the federal system with these fingerprints and this photo, which I would submit to Washington, D.C., today.

All of this processing was decidedly detailed and boring. It was excruciating for me. I had little patience for slow-paced activity. Eto went into some sort of Asian trance during the process and every once in a while I jolted him out of it. He was an intriguing fellow.

After the fingerprinting and photography process, Eto and I went into a conference room where I had set up the materials needed to follow the procedure proscribed by the Bureau to take handwriting exemplars from a subject. Handwriting exemplars are used in court so that a document examiner from the FBI Laboratory in Washington, D.C., can testify at trial that in his expert opinion, Mr. Eto wrote these numbers and words on those sheets of paper. So now I would be able to link Eto to the gambling records, not only by the fingerprints he left on them, but also by matching his writing.

I believe the sampling process has a psychological component that encourages subjects to crack. They are required to write three pages of their name and ten lines of the number "6." This repetition will eventually catch the writer accidentally using his natural or unique style of handwriting, if in fact he is trying to disguise it. The additional trick played on the subject is that the agent must re-create the writing circumstance as closely as she can to the actual evidence. The type of paper, writing instrument (pen or pencil, roller ball pen or fountain pen), whether the paper was on a pad or hard surface, and so on. The best part is when you dictate something to the subject that he knows he wrote before and you make him write it verbatim, over and over. When Micus did this, he broke down and cried as he wrote and I dictated the words of a note he had written to Eto on one of the tabulating sheets.

Eto, the Zen master, was another story. Although he did get a little sloppy in his numbers and letters after several pages, he never sighed, rubbed his head, closed his eyes, twisted his neck, or complained. We stopped after about an hour for another cigarette break and for my squad mate, Gene, to take him to the restroom. I took a restroom break also. On a whim I also ran down to the government cafeteria on the second floor and got both of us cups of coffee. This act of kindness, a cup of coffee, was the one that seemed to register with him.

After we had finished our excruciating morning together, I stood and shook his very dry hand. All morning I had been anxious about how and when I was going to ask him if he would consider cooperating with the government. It was now or never. I couldn't let the chance go. I couldn't be afraid of being shot down. "You know, Mr. Eto, we would very much like you to cooperate with us. We need the help of people like you to defeat the Outfit."

Surprisingly, Joe took both of my hands in his, looked at me directly through his hooded eyes, and said, "I understand, Agent Smith, that you have a job to do. And trying to convince me to be a snitch is part of it. But that is not who I am. I could never do that. I know I may go to prison for some time. But I can do that standing on my head." He then waved his hand as if to push the hardship away and continued. "I cannot help you, but I respect that you had to ask. I understand what you have to do, but I will never cooperate. This is nothing to me."

Damn — he turned me down. It was like asking your dream date to the prom and being refused. Every time a special agent approaches someone to become an informant, it is as if you are putting a little bit of yourself on the line. My solicitations to others were usually appropriate and not extraordinary, so I was not accustomed to being turned down. I was disappointed, yet not defeated; it seemed as if today's encounter with Mr. Eto was strangely personal.

I escorted him out of the conference room and into the FBI reception area. Smiling, I shook his hand again. Expressionless, he released our handshake, turned, and slowly walked out of my life. I watched him calmly enter the elevator. The doors closed on Joe Eto. Two years would pass before I would see him again.

Family ski vacations for mothers are filled with putting on and taking off layers of children's clothes — each day you bundle them up; find and match boots, poles, and skis; and deliverer them to ski school on time. Always you have to deal with the incessant disputes as to whether they will ski with their parents or stay home and watch TV while their parents ski — lots of complaining, negotiating, commanding. Ah, the joys of motherhood.

In spite of all of these duties, my family and my friend JoAnn's family always managed to have some of the best times of our lives, just trying to live through these moments, enjoying each other's company and the pleasure of being with our children in picturesque mountain villages. JoAnn and I always found time for long talks as we sipped cappuccinos in the sun or while shopping at ski boutiques that carried the finest European ski gear.

Each year, she and I would take private ski lessons. Eventually, we began each lesson by telling the instructor that we just wanted to look good while skiing and we wanted to take frequent rest breaks. While our husbands preferred to ski in a manner they called "balls out," we were more inclined to glide relaxed and graceful down the slopes.

While on one of these vacations on February 10, 1983, I received the early morning call from Bill Brown about the shooting of Ken Eto. I was awakened from the skier's sleep, dead to the world, but I quickly fought to regain my senses. "Ken Eto's been fuckin' shot," I sat upright in bed and shook my head.

Bill went on, excitedly, "He's not dead — the damnedest thing ever, hc was shot three times to the head, and his only problem is that he can't hear all that well now." I could hear the excitement in Bill's voice and was surprised I could understand his words. When Bill got excited or heated up about anything, his speech morphed into slurred Ebonics.

In spite of Bill being easily revved up, I didn't have to imagine much to visualize what a zoo it must be around him. I guessed a lot of agents had been awakened from sleep to hear this news. I knew not many of them would get much sleep tonight either.

"He was shot in the head and he's still alive?" I tried to convince myself that this could be true.

"Listen, Elaine, it's a little crazy here now, but I need to ask you: Who do you think could have done it? He's not telling anyone. Eto got to the hospital, blood pouring out of his head, and told the doctors he had been shot. Then he asked to talk to you. Since then he has refused to let anyone in his room but FBI agents."

Bill said it again. Eto asked for me. My heart jumped a beat as if a lost lover had found me again, if I ever had a lost lover. With that news, my mind jumped on an adrenaline-induced kick. I racked my brain for the names of men who may have tried to kill Eto. "Bill, give me one second." I tried to think of the other guys in the Vince Solano north side crew. Shit! Why would they want to kill Eto? He's nobody. He's never going to cooperate with the FBI.

"Elaine…any idea who did this?"

Thoughts of all kinds blew in and out of my head: If Eto dies, I'll lose my most significant statistic of having convicted an organized crime figure. I've got to sound smart and all knowing. Umm, thinking, thinking… Out of my butt came these names: "Ronnie Ignaffo or Jasper Campise?" I hoped Bill didn't start laughing at my two suggestions right then and there.

Instead, he said, "Anyone else?" He was prodding for more.

I sighed, "I don't know, just give me a moment." I squeezed my eyes shut and rubbed my forehead, thinking: Okay, if made members usually do the hits, who could have been the made members on the north side crew capable of this? Or was it someone trying to make his bones?[25] Finally I gave up. "I just don't know, Bill. Really, it could've been anyone." I opened my eyes and saw a sleepy Tom looking at me, no doubt wondering what the hell was happening.

"Well, call 210 [26] if you come up with any other names," Bill said. "I've got to go."

"Okay, Bill." I laid my head back into the pillow.

"What was that about?" asked Tom.

"Joe the Jap got shot three times in the head and is alive," I answered, now awake and back in business.

Tom rolled over and said, "He won't be for long." Almost immediately he fell back into sleep.

I took this as a sign that the conversation was over and I closed my eyes, but behind the peaceful look that may have been on my face, my mind was working overtime. Eto actually asked for me specifically. Damn. I could have been there for his deathbed tale of who killed him. I saw the headlines: *Mob Hit Solved by Rookie FBI Agent.* What a shit I was, always thinking about myself.

I rolled over in bed again. Now my eyes wouldn't stay shut. What would make the Outfit want to kill Eto? His words came back to me: "I understand what you have to do, but I will never cooperate. This is nothing to me." That statement had even made me want to experiment with a little police brutality, but physical confrontation was not my strong suit.

My gambling case would give Eto maybe 18 months in prison and five years probation — a walk in the park for someone as composed and dedicated as Tokyo Joe. But during the previous two years, I had tracked Sam Sarcinelli and Larry Bradi's[27] cocaine money, which had been financing Eto's *bolita* business. If that case could be made, Joe Eto would receive another 20 years — serious time — enough to make a man think differently about whether to do the time or talk, even the stoic Mr. Eto. Had Vince Solano heard about that?

I stared into the dark and wondered what it was all about until little dots crept into my vision and I finally gave in to my exhaustion. I felt I had been sleeping for a few moments when I was jarred from the comfortable, warm oblivion by the phone ringing again.

This time I sat up in bed. "Hello?" I said, expecting it to be Bill again.

"Elaine?"

I recognized his voice immediately. It was Bob Walsh, my new supervisor. In the FBI we had a saying: No matter how good or how bad your supervisor is, he won't be your supervisor for long. So it goes.

"This is Bob. I'm just letting you know that Eto's cooperating. He's named his shooters."

"He has? Who are they?" I was holding my breath.

"He said it was John Gattuso who shot him, but Jasper Campise was there as the set-up guy."

Wow, I thought. I had named Campise as one of the shooters when Bill called, but I hadn't actually expected to be right.

"Bob, I'm coming back on the first plane I can get on tomorrow morning."

"No, you're not," Walsh shot back.

"What?"

"You're not coming back."

I took a deep breath before I started to swear, but said instead, "Bob, this is a major break in the case. I need to get back to help." I imagined he was trying to subtly take me off the case. This was clearly going to be bigger than anyone had imagined. If Eto survived this shooting and was able to finger the guys who had done it, it would be the first Mob hit ever solved. Of course they would want me off the case. I was just a rookie; three years in the Bureau was nothing to these guys. To top it off, I was a woman. I started preparing myself for an angry argument, defending myself and my ability to stay on the case.

Walsh stood his ground. "Elaine, no. Stay in Vail. Finish your vacation."

I started to protest again. "But…"

He plowed through: "You'll need all the rest you can get. The case is yours when you get back."

As I tried to tell him thanks and how much I appreciated it, he hung up.

The case was still going to be mine when I got back! This was the break of a lifetime. I couldn't wait to see where all of this was going to lead. I decided not to think about it for the rest of the vacation. That is, if I could. Walsh had said I'd need my rest. I was willing, at least, to try.

On the last night of our vacation, the Federal Express truck delivered a package to me at the condo. Inside the document envelope, Walsh had sent me the rough transcript of the recording taken of Ken Eto on the night of February 10, 1983, talking while in his hospital bed at Northwest Hospital in Chicago.

I excused myself, locked the bedroom door to discourage any accidental interruptions, and, with the excitement of someone opening a love letter, I started to read the words of the man I knew would become one of the most important in my life.

Reading the transcript, I could just imagine the scene. I knew exactly where the hospital was and what it looked like from the outside. I guessed the hospital room was small and nondescript, but private. Eto would be propped up in the narrow hospital bed, wearing one of those tie-in-the-back hospital gowns. His head would be completely encased in white gauze bandages. Intravenous tubes would be hanging from a pole, dripping antibiotics and fluids into his arm. A heart monitor would be mounted on the wall next to his bed, graphing, in green lines, the rhythms of his heart.

Next to him would be Supervisory Special Agent William I. Brown, my old supervisor, who justifiably was there. The case had been made under his command and he knew the subject. He would be sitting in an uncomfortable metal chair holding a white notepad and pen. A small handheld tape recorder would be on the table next to Eto's bed. Bill would be nervous as hell because he knew he couldn't mess up one of the biggest breaks the FBI had ever been given in the history of the Chicago office. Carefully, I read each word and thought about the implications.

Eto: *The reason why I say I must have a little time to sort things out in my mind (garbled) this is it.*

SA Brown: *Again, let's, let's, let me ask you one, a couple questions about the shooting, okay? How many people were with you when you were shot?*

Eto: *I don't understand. What did he say?*

SA Brown: *How many people were with you when you were shot? One? Two?*

Eto: *Um, you see, uh, you see, uh, Brown, you know that one question leads to another.*

SA Brown: *No, okay.*

Eto: *Is that what you mean? Is that, is that, the reason why I only gave my name and address was a simple reason, they used to ask, do I have kids, do I have a wife. Eh, eh, I took the Fifth … the simple reason is that it just leads on and on and on and on. You see at this point …*

Nurse: *(Nurse enters.) … Excuse me.*

SA Brown: *Mmm hmm.*

Nurse: *I've got to …*

SA Brown: *Go ahead.*

Eto: *At this time and point …*

SA Brown: *Mmm hmm.*

Eto: *You understand what I mean?*

SA Brown: *Yeah.*

Eto: *Let me think this out.*

SA Brown: *Okay, we are willing to offer you the protection, okay?*

Eto: Yeah, if, if it, if it, if it …

SA Brown: For you and your family.

Eto: If it cost me that.

SA Brown: Mmm hmm.

Eto: But I don't want the protection. If it's gonna cost me, then that.

SA Brown: What do you mean gonna cost you?

Eto: Okay, cost me, by, by, by, by, in other words … trading.

SA Brown: Mmm hmm.

Eto: I won't trade.

SA Brown: Okay.

Eto: I won't trade. I'd rather, I'd rather they come and hit me again. You see, I won't trade. You understand what I mean?

SA Brown: What do you mean "trade"?

Eto: I won't trade with, with, with you …

SA Brown: Okay.

Eto: … or anyone.

SA Brown: Okay.

Eto: I won't do it ….

SA Brown: You'll do it because you want to do it.

Eto: I will do it voluntarily.

SA Brown: Mmm hmm.

Eto: I will do it because I feel comfortable doing it.

SA Brown: But they, you owe those people nothing.

Eto: Huh?

SA Brown: You owe them nothing now!

Eto: I realize that right now! I realize that right now!

SA Brown: *Mmm hmm.*

Eto: *Okay, I realize that, but just because I owe them nothing, it is still against a principle of mine, you understand what I mean (garbled) …*

SA Brown: *Ah, (garbled) we're talking about …*

Eto: *… a long time.*

SA Brown: *Mmm hmm.*

Eto: *To be an informer or to say things with him, but I had to, I had to satisfy myself.*

SA Brown: *But you've a family to look out for.*

Eto: *Huh?*

SA Brown: *You have a family to look out for.*

Eto: *They don't hurt my family.*

I paused for a moment in my reading and thought. These were the first words of any meaning I had heard Ken Eto say, and even after taking three shots to the head, he was still a wily bastard. At least he confirmed the supposition that the Italian Mob had some standards: They wouldn't kill your family — just you. Bill was trying his hardest here — a lot of "mmms" and "hmms" — a very delicate situation for sure. Riveted, I returned to my reading, only vaguely hearing the sounds of everyone coming in from skiing and the children begging to do something.

Eto: *They only want me, for whatever reason. Oh, my God, they're so silly. That, you know, and everything I think of the substantial time that I was going to get on the 20th, 25th, right? [February 25 was the day Eto was to be sentenced in federal court on my gambling case.][28]*

SA Brown: *25th, yeah.*

Eto: *Yeah, they expected me to get substantial time.*

SA Brown: *They did?* [You could hear the shock in Brown's voice just about jump off the page. None of us thought Eto would get anything more than 18 months. Stupid Samuel V.P. Banks must have been telling the Outfit bosses something completely wrong. Just like Bob Cooley had said, "He was a clown for an attorney."][29]

Eto: *Yeah. It's ridiculous. Ridiculous. (garbled)*

SA Brown: *Can you tell us anything more about, or will you tell us anything more about, the guys that shot you? Were they two people?*

Eto: *I am going to let you guys know, but first I gotta put it in my mind and I got to, got to tell the whole world or them people that I am set.* [What does he mean by 'set'?" Guess if I had just been shot I wouldn't make sense all the time.][30] *Somehow that, uh, and this is gotta be put in such words, you know, it's us, you see, when I left home tonight, I knew I was going to get it.*

SA Brown: *What time did you leave home?*

Eto: *Goddamn right, I knew it.*

SA Brown: *You knew it when you left home?*

Eto: *Goddamn right, when I left my home.*

SA Brown: *Why did you know it?*

Eto: *Don't worry, I got insights.*

SA Brown: *Mmm hmm. Mmm hmm. Did you say anything to your wife where you was going? Anything at all?*

Eto: *I give her, eh, my name is to them, now they had their shot. Heh, heh, heh, heh, right?* [Does Eto mean he gave his wife the names of the people he was going to meet? Did he expect her to testify against these mobsters if anyone brought them to trial for the murder of her husband?][31]

SA Brown: *How many people with weapons ...*

Eto: *Huh?*

SA Brown: *... was, was with you tonight when you got shot?*

Eto: *Come on, Brown.*

SA Brown: *Okay, right.*

Eto: *You're just, you're just generalizing the (garbled) ...*

SA Brown: *Okay.*

Eto: *Now how, is he, hmm, how do I play this game and be happy playing it, okay? I've played games and many (garbled). I'm happy. You know, I never was mad, bitter, or anything.* [This is just amazing! Eto is strategizing about cooperating or not. Most people would be screaming the names of the people who just tried to murder them, not looking at all the angles they could play.][32]

SA Brown: *Mmm hmm.*

Eto: *(Garbled) ... my games.*

SA Brown   *Mmm hmm.*

Eto: *This is another game.*

SA Brown: *It's an entirely different ball game.*

Eto: *It's another game, right?*

SA Brown: *It sure is.*

Eto: *Now the way I play this game and be a little happy about it, uh, you know, um, since life is supposed to be fun. (Laughs)*

SA Brown: *What time, what time, did you leave home tonight?*

Eto: Huh?

SA Brown: What time did you leave home tonight?

Eto: I left home about, uh, damn close to 6:30.

SA Brown: You, you still live out in Bolingbrook?

Eto: Huh?

SA Brown: You still out in Bolingbrook?

Eto: Hmm.

SA Brown: Did you leave home alone?

Eto: Yes, mmm hmm.

SA Brown: Did you have a meeting with someone after you left home?

Eto: Brown, you know ... we been going around this for years and years and years and years, me and you. [Bill had been the case agent on a policy/numbers case in which two of Eto's most trusted workers, Challe Oda and Raymond Tom had been given immunity. Then they were found in contempt of the grand jury when they wouldn't testify against Eto's involvement. While they sat in jail for 18 months, Eto supported both of their families.][33]

SA Brown: Yeah.

Eto: Maybe you've learned something from me, I don't know by the way you pound.

SA Brown: Mmm hmm.

Eto: But like I said, Mr. Brown, I have to sort things before I could justify my action.

SA Brown: But you will tell us ...

Eto: Huh? [Is Eto always saying "Huh?" to Bill because he can't hear him or doesn't understand him? I think he is giving himself time to think.][34]

SA Brown: You will tell us who was with you tonight?

Eto: I'm sure.

SA Brown: You will? [I was so happy for Bill. He has worked hard to get this information. He has earned his pay.][35]

Eto: I'm sure. Uh, I have to have some time. I have a good reason, not only because they ...

SA Brown: You gotta reason.

Eto: Huh?

SA Brown: You have a reason. You got shot. What other reason do you have to have?

Eto: Something for my guts, and my heart and my soul! Bodily wound is that? [Oh, my God! This man wasn't thinking of revenge as his main motivation. Would I ever understand him? Or was he playing another game — this time with SA Brown?][36]

SA Brown: Okay. We're gonna let you get some rest.

Eto: Huh? See if I can have a cigarette? If I can't, that's fine.

(Monitoring discontinued.)

[What happened in between Eto asking for a cigarette and the next thing he says, I don't know, but it's amazing to me.][37]

(Monitoring continued.)

Eto: I'm going to have fun just, just spill, spilling guts.

SA Brown: But, just, just give us the ...

Eto: Huh?

SA Brown: ... shooter's name tonight.

Eto: Huh?

SA Brown: Just give us the shooter's name tonight and we'll let you get some rest and we'll, you can think about these other things in your mind.

Eto: *I beg pardon?*

SA Brown: *Just give us the shooter's name tonight. The people you were with when you got shot tonight. And these other things we'll work out later.* [Bill must be getting pressure to get the name of the shooter so an arrest can be made and Eto's "flip" to the other side can be finalized, because once you walk over that line, it is impossible to take it back or go back. Eto, on the other hand, is not to be pressured or rushed.] [38]

Eto: *Let me talk to a lawyer.*

SA Brown: *Your lawyer?*

Eto: *Yeah.*

SA Brown: *Okay ... Jeremy!*

Eto: *Let me talk to him alone.*

SA Brown: *Okay.*

                (Monitoring discontinued.

                  Muffled conversation.

                Monitoring continued.)

Jeremy Margolis: *Phil Cline from Chicago Police.* [During the time that I was waiting for Eto's indictment and arrest, I began working on Sam Sarcinelli et. al. and his drug ring. In doing that, I ran smack into Sergeant Phillip Cline, working on a joint task force with United States Drug Enforcement, who was also targeting Sam Sarcinelli. The FBI, me in particular, had certain talents and skills that his group didn't. Chicago Police and Drug Enforcement had certain talents and skills I certainly didn't have. We joined forces. It wasn't a great marriage, but it was working, and we were beginning to start to put away a lot of people for very long sentences. Sergeant Cline knew about my information that Sarcinelli's cocaine money had backed Eto's gambling enterprise. He must have been on duty that night and raced to the hospital to see if he could get the edge on this break in the case.][39]

Eto: *You are now giving me immunity.*

Margolis: *Ken Eto feels that Thursday, February 10 is the past and Friday, February 11 is the present and the future. It's now a new day. They tried to kill him. All old bets are erased. It's a new ball game and, as I understand it, what he and I are talking about is, he's guaranteed federal protection for him and for the family — depending on however he and his family wish to work that out and his personal things we'll discuss in the future, but whatever they desire, uh, whether it's together or not, that's up, that's up to them. And for what he tells us, the information he provides us, he will have no criminal liability. Is that the FBI's wish?*

SA Brown: *Okay.*

Margolis: *Chicago Police agrees to that?*

Cline: *Yes, yes.*

Margolis: *Okay. I'm now telling you as Jeremy Margolis, Assistant United States Attorney, okay, and here's my badge and here's my commission (he places his badge in his hand and Eto's on top of it), I have the power to tell you and bind the federal government, okay?*

Eto: *With immunity?* [This man is very smart. He was making sure Margolis used the word "immunity" and that it was recorded.][40]

Margolis: *With immunity. I told you there are two things we want from you. You only have two conditions. Ya tell the hundred percent truth and you answer every question fully and completely. In return for your truthful*

answers to all questions — truthful, complete, answers —
you'll be protected; your family will be protected. You will
have no criminal liability. You have immunity for the
information (garbled) ...

Eto: *(Garbled) ... later?*

Margolis: *Pardon me, and I'll give you a paper*
later.[41]

Eto: *You see, there's no way I'm a free man no*
more.

SA Brown: *I agree.*

Eto: *They took my freedom away. I can't walk*
the street. I have to fight them. They had their shot. They
muffed it. I think I would be better off if they didn't muff it.
But as long as they muffed it, maybe I shall go this route.

SA Brown: *Okay.*

Eto: *There is an alternative. This is justified,*
right? I cannot, uh, be very dishonorable or something and,
and did something really against my grain ... oh yeah,
maybe I should shoot myself in the head. But I can't shoot
myself in the head just because somebody else tried it. They
don't leave me no alternative. And if they don't leave me
no alternative, why should I, I can't understand, why
should I feel bad I cooperate in another side now. Well,
however, that's best way to put it. Believe it. This really
isn't in my position, I don't think, when I got hit with three
or four bullets or five bullets that I am an informer. Okay,
then you should get what you asked for tonight for the
simple reason is, we'll see how well you hold your deal.

Margolis: *We will hold our deal.*

Eto: *And I'll give you my deal first.*

Margolis: *I will keep my fucking word to you. That I
promise.*

              (Nurse enters room to examine patient.)
              Monitoring discontinued.

[Could the nurse have entered the room at a worse time
than this? I can't imagine how frayed everyone's nerves
were and how they may have wanted to shoot her.][42]

              Monitoring continued.)

Eto: *Okay. The reason why I expected a lot of
foul play and everything else was because of prior meetings,
what had been said, and it was all phony. You understand
what I mean?*

SA Brown: *Mmm hmm.*

Eto: *It doesn't make sense to me. So I come to
the conclusion I'm going to go. I'm going to get hit. I'm
going to go and get hit tonight anyway.*

SA Brown: *Mmm hmm.*

Eto: *I had a dead bang feeling that was going
to happen, you understand?*

SA Brown: *Okay.*

Eto: *But I went anyway. I went anyway. And
when they told me to get into my car, I thought, this is it.
When they told me where to go and then they told me the
last part of where to go, I said forget it. (Laughs)* [My sense
of survival and understanding that this man has could not
be in more conflict. Why would anyone drive to one's
death? And on top of it all, he laughs about it.][43]

SA Brown: *What did they tell you?*

Eto: *They directed me, right? They directed me
where to drive. Now you know where my car was. Or you
guys should know. You know that's a hell of a spot to go tell*

me to park! After all, with the intuition that I had.
(Laughs) ... So you got what you wanted tonight. [Unless I
was missing pages, I saw nothing in this transcript that
named Jasper Campise or John Gattuso as the killers. Did
Eto tell Brown and Margolis this when the nurse came in?
I was beside myself sitting there on my bed in the condo
in Vail and being so clueless.][44]

Margolis: *Was he, uh, was Jay in the back?*

Eto: *Huh?*[45]

Margolis: *Where was, where was Jay, when he shot*
you?

Eto: *Who? Jay?* [If this all hadn't been so
serious, it would have made a great comedy with Eto's
hearing problem.][46]

Margolis: *Yeah.*

Eto: *Jay was sitting next to me in the front seat.*

Margolis: *Okay.*

Eto: *Johnny was in the back.*

Margolis: *Johnny, okay.*

Eto: *See, he's the one that hit me.*

Margolis: *Did he say anything or did he just ...*

Eto: *Huh?*

Margolis: *Did he say anything to you or did you just*
hear shots?

Eto: *No, not, no word, no. Why should he say*
anything? He's gonna get it done, that's all.

Cline: *They told you to pull back there by the*
railroad tracks and that's when Johnny shot you in the
head.

Eto: *After I parked.*

SA Brown: *What happened after you got shot?*

Eto: Huh?

SA Brown: After you got shot. What did you do?

Eto: I thought I was going to die, but I'm conscious, I shouldn't be conscious, so I start shaking, like make believing that I'm, I'm, I'm finished, you know. And I'm on the, on the seat, but I hear bang, bang, I mean, uh, the doors close, that means they're taking off.

SA Brown: Mmm hmm.

Eto: Well, I give them a little minute to take off and I got my head, uh, my hand on my head like this, holding the, the blood in, so I figured that, uh, they are, uh, gone, I open the side of my car and walk the other way to, uh, Grand Avenue.

SA Brown: You walked down the alley?

Eto: Yeah, wherever that, that empty lot or wherever. There's blood, gotta be blood all the way down. I went on Grand Avenue, turned right and, uh, found me a drugstore and asked them to call, uh, an ambulance.

SA Brown: Did you see another car?

Eto: Huh?

SA Brown: Did you see another car?

Eto: Yeah, but I don't know what it was. I couldn't recognize it or nothing.

SA Brown: Was the car there after you got shot, or did they take it?

Eto: (Laughs)

SA Brown: Did you hear the engine start in the other car?

Eto: No, I heard them, uh, they run out of the car, I hear footsteps.

SA Brown: Mmm hmm.

Eto: Running, okay? I thought they might be running towards the restaurant over there. I didn't even think about the car over there.

SA Brown: Mmm hmm.

Eto: In fact, I was laying down in the front seat. So, so, uh, my thoughts were that they ran, I don't know if this is true or not, it's just in my mind, that they slammed the door, and I heard, uh, foot, you know running steps and, uh, it just, this, I just figured that they were going, uh, on the other side of the street that we came in. I didn't pay no attention to the car when I parked. I noticed there was one car there. After I got shot, I didn't notice if it was there or not, because, what the hell, I'm holding my head and I don't hear no more, uh, running, uh, footsteps and I don't hear nobody in the car.

SA Brown: You want some water or something? Want anything?

Eto: Yeah, coffee. Give me coffee. Black.

(Monitoring discontinued.)

- CHAPTER TEN -
Switching Sides

After reading the transcript of Eto's disclosure regarding the two hit men, I was anxious to get back to claim my former subject, now my witness. He was my catch, and there was going to be a fight if anyone tried to snare him into their net. Other than a straight-up battle with my bosses, I figured Eto was mine. He was sitting in a psychologically vulnerable position. My goal would be to shift his loyalty from the Outfit to me, the smart little rookie that had finally caught him after all these years. I knew the ropes of loyalty creation from collecting and discarding boyfriends as a teenager.

In the office on my first day back from vacation, I prepared both strategically and physically. My first move would be to meet with Bob, my supervisor, to thank him for letting me keep the Eto case and to stoke his ego a bit. I'd drop a few admiring remarks about how he took charge of what must have been a tension-filled, delicate situation.

I had already phoned Marc and Joe, the two agents who had temporarily been assigned to begin the massive debriefing and interview scheduling with Joe Eto. Immediately upon my return, I let them know I was ready to begin my work with Eto. I wasn't worried about Marc challenging my territory. He was a very nice guy, a so-called "administratively pure agent,"[47] who was not devious. The other agent, Joe — a crusty old guy who spoke with an Irish brogue — was an entirely different matter. He was an attorney and had the habit of pontificating all day as if from a pulpit. His encyclopedic knowledge of the Mob provided plenty of material for his daily sermons. He didn't like me, and I believed he would just as soon slap me as look at me. He thought I was "too big for my britches," to use an old Irish saying, which meant he thought I was conceited. In my opinion, he was meant to be avoided and ignored.

I was still shaky and nervous when I arrived at my desk. I looked for Bob, but he wasn't in yet. My thoughts drifted to Joe Eto. I suspected he hadn't seen a woman for weeks, except for the nurses on staff and the occasional female agent who might have been rotated into the guard duty roster. There were seven other female agents. I knew none of them would have talked to him, and they would have only dressed for comfort if they had pulled the 12-hour "guard the witness" duty. In contrast, 10 days in the mountains of Colorado had tanned and shaped my body. I wore a pale blue Donna Karan suit with a skirt short enough to emphasize my legs, but also tailored in a fashion that screamed of a quiet sophistication that only money could buy. I wanted to look good for my friend Mr. Eto.

The squad area appeared as if it had been hit by an atomic bomb. There were no agents at their desks. Slowly, they trickled in. All of them had to give me jabs about how I had destroyed their lives and interrupted their work. The Eto thing had a significant impact on them and their workload while I was gone. But soon they tired of teasing me and were drawn to back to the work they had ignored for more than 10 days.

When the squad secretary, Pat, arrived, she grinned, gave me a big hug, and said, "We've saved all of the newspaper clippings. I have them all in a file for you." Perhaps I had been too paranoid. She handed me a folder that was bursting with mostly front-page newspaper articles. I was in awe. In Vail, Colorado, there had been nothing about the attempted murder of a gambling kingpin in Chicago. I eagerly devoured the news coverage.

*   *   *

Chicago Tribune, February 11, 1983, Front Page
"Mob boss Eto shot three times in head"
By Henry Wood

Ken "Tokyo Joe" Eto, a reputed crime-syndicate gambling boss and longtime mob muscleman, was shot three times through the back of the head Thursday night in a theater parking lot on the Northwest Side, then walked for 1 1/2 blocks to a pharmacy for help.

Earlier Eto had told Lt. Arthur Walsh of the Grand Central District, "I'm not going to die, so I'm not going to cooperate."

High-ranking mob bosses apparently fear that the prospect of a long prison term could motivate Eto to divulge crime-syndicate secrets in return for leniency, sources said. The same fears are believed to be the reason behind the slaying of Allen Dorfman January 20, 1983, following his conviction in federal court.[48]

*   *   *

Chicago Tribune, February 12, 1983, Front Page
"Chicago's troubled crime syndicate"

...The defection of Eto could have long-range effects on mob activity, investigators noted, because of the knowledge he is regarded to have as a gambling kingpin and his association with top mob figures.

*   *   *

Chicago Tribune, February 14, 1983, Page 10
"New bonds are set for 2 accused as hit men in Eto shooting"
By John O'Brien

Two reputed crime-syndicate figures were being held Sunday in lieu of $1 million and $1.5 million cash bonds in the shooting of mob gambling boss Ken "Tokyo Joe" Eto, as authorities moved to capitalize on Eto's defection and willingness to tell all. ...federal authorities secured warrants for their arrests on federal charges after hearing that both Jasper Campise and John Gattuso were released when they each posted $50,000, or 10% of their $500,000 state bonds.

A loud voice interrupted my reading, "So do you think you can sit around here all day and read newspaper articles, Smith?" I looked up to see Bobbie Walsh, my boss, grinning ear to ear at being able to bust my chops. And I think he was happy to have me back on duty.

"Hey, Bobbie, how are you?" I reached out for him and our handshake turned into a bear hug.

"Well, we've just been sittin' around here on our asses. Give me second to hang up my coat and get a cup of coffee and we'll get together."

"Certainly," I replied.

I sat on the visitor's side of Bobbie Walsh's desk, with my pad and pen, waiting for him to return and impart his words of wisdom to me.

"Well, we've got Ziegler and Doyle out at Great Lakes holding down the fort."

"You have them where?" I asked.

"Oh, that's right," he said. "You don't know where we stashed our star. He's at Great Lakes Naval Base Hospital. Has the entire 11th floor to himself. We've staked out one entire ward as a command center for Eto's debriefing."

My mind instantly flashed back to the special meaning that the Great Lakes Naval Hospital had for me. On September 21, 1981, I was awakened from a sound sleep, as I had been working a night shift, the day Tom was shot. Someone came to get me. Half-dressed, I ran to the Bureau car that pulled up in front of our house. As I finished dressing in the front seat, we drove at speeds of 90 to 100 miles an hour toward the hospital. My mind also raced ahead. I thought about my Tommy. I tried not to think of the worst. I hoped and prayed he was hit in the arm or foot — not in the gut. But no prayer could alter the course of the bullet that cut through his midsection that day. I was devastated. Six weeks of surgeries, recovery, and uncertainty followed. Then Tom had his third abdominal surgery. My friend Lynnie and I waited for the seven-hour procedure to end. When completed, the surgeon, Dr. Block, approached me and said, "Your husband has one foot in the grave and is slipping fast."

I felt myself slipping, not into a grave but to the floor. Lynnie caught me. Then I reached out and hung onto the arm of the world-renowned surgeon. I pleaded, "I don't care what you have to do, Dr. Block, but you cannot let this man die. Even if he is a cripple, or whatever hardship we'll have to bear, you just cannot let my husband die." He didn't reply but simply put his head down in what I hoped was determination and left the room. As I watched him leave, Lynnie cradled me in her arms while I sobbed — overwhelmed with thoughts of losing Tommy.

Walsh sat before me waiting for me to respond. He might have wondered about the daze he had induced with his talk of Great Lakes. He knew nothing about Tom's accident.

After being shot, Tom initially was taken to the naval hospital because that was the trauma center closest to the FBI's firearms range. Tom was the head firearms and defensive tactics instructor when he was accidentally shot during a hostage training exercise. It was here he underwent his first abdominal surgery. I blamed the Great Lakes' surgeon's lack of competency as the cause of the life-threatening infection Tom developed there. When I saw him getting sicker rather than better, I, with the pull of some friends, had him transferred to the University of Chicago Hospital, where Dr. George Block, the chief of surgery there,[49] did save his life.

"Elaine…you okay? Don't worry, Eto's safe there."

My mind snapped back. "Right, I've been there."

"It's a perfectly secure location," Walsh went on. "At his fingertips Eto has all the medical care he may need. We have the run of the place — from who gets in the front gate and who guards the hospital door to having the only key to the 11th floor either by elevator or stairway."

I put aside my personal thoughts and said, "It sounds incredible! That was brilliant to put him there." And I really meant it. It was.

Walsh jabbered away, "We've got things organized and scheduled to the minute. Eto seems to be in excellent health and spirits. What I want you to do is take over. You will handle all of Eto's information and scheduling. I have given Marc the assignment to investigate Eto's shooting."

"I truly thank you, Bobbie, for letting me have the responsibility of working with Eto."

"You are a pain in the ass, Smith. You tend to work too independently. But you are great with people and you are one of the hardest-working agents I have ever met. There is no reason why I shouldn't give you this." Walsh never pulled his punches. He was all New York Irish.

"Well, thanks." But I was all Chicago and couldn't just let his statement go. "What do you mean a 'pain in the ass'?"

"See, there you go. You had to ask why you're a pain in the ass. Because you asked, that's what makes you a pain in the ass."

I just smiled. I really wanted to ask why he thought I worked too independently but thought better of it. I knew why I worked independently. Lynne, my first partner, had returned to the FBI, but as the wife of our squad mate, the Arkansas Razorbacks football player — God forbid! — only to transfer to headquarters when he got a promotion. Another partner had turned out to be a drunk. I just gave up after that. There just weren't any agents who had the same drive as I did or the freedom from never-ending family responsibility.

That first morning back from Colorado, I waded through the rest of those amazing newspaper articles and the Bureau correspondence that had piled up in my folder. I was able to review the final results of the FBI Laboratory Document Examination Report on the Eto *bolita* operation. Also, the expert who wrote the report and who might be required to testify in federal court had inquired if a trial date had been set. His report confirmed what we needed against Eto. The expert was willing to say, "The materials from the search were those found in an 'office' or a 'clearinghouse' of a gambling operation accepting wagers on three-digit numbers. The total amount of wagers for the four weeks found in the motel room was $220,376.25." He could further testify to the records previously sent, which corresponded to those seized in the search and indicated a total of more than $3 million in wagers from the beginning of May through August. And that these wagers had been accepted by at least

160 writers and 14 controllers. Well, too bad Mr. Expert was not going to be needed. I would have to call him to let him know the subject had agreed to plea after having survived a Mob hit to assassinate him.

Before I left to drive to Great Lakes Navel Base to meet Eto, I stopped in Bobbie's office and asked if he knew of Eto's sponsoring attorney for the Witness Protection Program.

"That would be none other than Jeremy Margolis. Eto seems to think Margolis is his own private attorney also. The two of them have bonded like nothing I've ever seen before. All I can say is that it was our good luck that Jeremy was out socializing with the terrorist task force when, on his way home, he heard the radio traffic and decided to stop in at the hospital." Jeremy Margolis had been the prosecuting attorney on the case of the Puerto Rican terrorists who were planting bombs all over Chicago and the case of the Tylenol poisonings,[50] which were originally considered domestic terrorism. He was the "supreme commander" of what came to be called "The Wonderful World Police" (WWP). Don't ever think that grown men do not play games or want clubs. The WWP was a club of agents and prosecutors who worked terrorism. It was their way to build camaraderie and strengthen their resolve while working some of the most elusive and complex investigations. My husband was one of them and, in fact, second in charge of the squad. He and Jeremy were great friends. Jeremy spent many nights holding my hand while we tried to help Tom fight for his life. No other sponsoring attorney for Ken Eto would be more hardworking and "in your face" than Jeremy Margolis.

Great Lakes Naval Base is located on Lake Michigan and has been used as a United States Navy training facility since World War II. Driving up the wide drive to its enormous white entrance gate is intimidating. Attached to the gate is a 20-foot-high steel fence, also painted white, which surrounds 10 miles of the land side of the base. Two uniformed and armed guards saluted me. This was the U.S. Navy at its best and proudest. I stopped the car next to them and handed my FBI credentials to one. "Hi, I need to find the hospital and hoped you might direct me."

"One moment, please, ma'am," the guard said, as he turned and went into the guard house to look at a clipboard, using my creds as a comparison of some sort. Well, ain't this some hot shit? They had a list of who could enter the gate that day. The guard returned my credentials and said, "You may proceed down the main road to the hospital. It is directly east of this gate and there are signs along the way that will guide you. Thank you, ma'am." Then he saluted again.

"Thank you," I replied, but I didn't know how to salute, and I knew any attempt would be a mockery. There was another guard at the desk inside the entrance to the hospital. This guard checked my name off a list and saluted me. Then, while calling someone on his phone, he said, "Please wait here and someone will be out to get you."

Obediently, I sat down. After about five minutes, agent Marc Ziegler appeared out of an elevator door at the rear of the hospital's main hallway, about 50 yards away. I watched as he walked quickly toward me.

"Hey, Smitty, good to see you," he said with a welcoming smile and handshake.

"I'm so happy to be back, Marc." The enthusiasm in my voice didn't need to be moderated with Marc. He understood.

"Well, we've been working your boy pretty hard, but he is anxious to meet with you. He's told us some pretty amazing stuff. He and Joe Doyle get along wonderfully. It's like watching two old-timers talk about the good old times."

We walked swiftly to the elevator — there was no other way to walk with Marc who, at 6 foot 4, was an efficient machine of a man. No wasted movements or actions for Marc — he was the ideal German. We rode the elevator to the 11th floor and reached two wide doors leading into the ward. Outside sat an agent that I vaguely knew. I gave him a quick wave and greeting, "How you doing?"

"Oh, I'm fine," he replied.

Sure, I bet. He was on babysitting duty — a hated activity for any agent.

Marc led me in to a hospital ward. About 20 empty beds were positioned perpendicular to the windows, offering a magnificent view of Lake Michigan through the barren trees of February. In the second bed from the door, a man sat reading the newspaper. His head was wrapped in white gauze bandages, and he was wearing dime-store reading glasses.

"Hey, Joe. I've brought your girlfriend here to visit," said Marc enthusiastically.

"What?" Then he put down the paper and looked up at me standing at the foot of his bed. "Well, well, well, you sure have."

"So you remember me, Mr. Eto?" I asked as I walked forward to shake his hand.

"How could I forget? You run the show!" he said, and then he laughed while taking off his glasses to look at me.

"Not exactly," I replied. "How are you feeling? How is your head underneath all of that dressing?"

"Oh, I feel fine. The food stinks and the coffee is terrible, but Joe Boyle[51] and Marc here have taken good care of me."

I turned to Marc and asked, "How often do the doctors examine Mr. Eto and…"

"Call me Joe," he interrupted.

"Uh, what are the doctors saying about Joe's injuries and follow-up care?" I finished.

"Nothing, but some rest is recommended, and sooner or later, the bullet fragments will start to work their way out from underneath the skin covering the back of his head, which will be irritating, but not of any medical consequence. We have the X-rays. I'll get them for you."

Marc ran off and I turned to Joe and asked, "May I sit down next to you, Joe?"

174

Joe replied, "That's what I've been waiting for."

I pulled up a chair close to his bed and put down my briefcase and purse. I tossed my coat on the next bed over. I got comfortable and then raised my head to find him looking at me from under his hooded eyes.

"I guess you got what you wanted, didn't you?" he laughed.

This took me a little by surprise, and I paused in my answer. "My God, Joe. I never would have wanted this to happen to you."

"Ah, they're so dumb. You, more than anyone, knew that I was never going to turn informer. But these people, who I've known for over 30 years, couldn't figure that out."

"I knew you were a hard case and you weren't going to help me. I understood your position. But that didn't mean I didn't want you to. Believe me, each time you'd pat my hand and tell me you understood I had a job to do, but you just couldn't help, I was disappointed.'"

Not realizing Joe and I were reminiscing and in the process of bonding, Marc returned and interrupted our conversation to show us large X-rays of Joe's head. He held these up to the light from the windows and explained how Joe had survived three shots to the back of his head. "As you can see, there are distinct tracings each round took when it entered and then exited, all in the lower posterior portion of Joe's skull. These bullets entered at an angle that directed them just under the skin of Joe's skull and then out again. Here is where Round 1 entered and exited; here is where Round 2 entered and exited; and here is the path that Round 3 took. "If John Gattuso had pointed the gun directly into Joe's skull, all three bullets would have entered Joe's brain, causing his death. Round 1 would have entered his brain stem, which controls your heartbeat and breathing. Round 2 would have exploded into his cerebellum, which controls balance and muscle coordination, and, most likely, either Round 2 or Round 3 would have severed his posterior cerebral artery."

"Very gruesome," I said. I thought this would be a good way to make "attempted murder" sound really bad for a jury. "The bottom line is, the angle of Gattuso's gun was wrong and that was what saved Joe's life."

"And will probably cost Gattuso his," Joe interjected. "They might let Jay ride it out, but Gattuso's in a lot of trouble."

"Why would they let Campise get off for screwing up your hit?" I immediately quizzed him.

"Why?"

"Yes. Why would Campise get off?"

"Campise has been a made member for a long time. He has strong family support out of Kansas City. The Civellas are his family and they are the bosses there. Sure, Kansas City is controlled by Chicago, yes, but his relations are the territory bosses."

"What about Johnny?"

"Ah, I don't know about him. Never seen much of him and thought he was something of a mess-up, ya know." Joe started laughing until his smoker's lungs caught him and he started to cough.

Marc and I chuckled at Joe's comment — gallows humor. Gattuso had screwed up — bad.

After Marc's grisly description of what could have happened if Gattuso had aimed the gun correctly, he went on to elaborate that there was some supposition that the rounds were old and the powder had deteriorated. There was also another unproven theory that if there was a silencer on the .22-caliber weapon, it would have further diminished the striking power of the ammunition. But in the end, it was probably just Joe's good luck that the bullets did not enter his brain.

"I have to go dictate some interviews we did this morning. So if it's okay with you two, I am going to go over to the little desk I have and do that. I'll let you two get reacquainted." Marc gathered up his X-rays and headed off to the far end of the hospital ward.

"Where's Doyle?" I called after Marc.

"He had to go to the dentist, and since you were now going to be up here, he decided to go." I looked back at Mr. Eto. He was getting out of bed.

"Why don't we go sit over where they have some chairs and tables?" he suggested.

No time to protest because he had already climbed out of bed and was putting on a bathrobe and slippers. He led the way.

We moved to a setting of government-issued, imitation leather chairs that overlooked the hospital parking lot and sat down.

"Joe, why did they hit you over a gambling case?" It was still incredulous to me that he would be killed for a little gambling case.

"Oh, it's ridiculous. Just ridiculous. But I knew it was coming because of the way Vince was acting. He is a paranoid little man."

"I have a copy of the transcript from the night they attempted to murder you. May I read just a portion of that to you? What you said?"

"Oh, sure." He then relaxed back into his chair, crossed his hands across his chest, and closed his eyes. Great, I thought, I'm going to put him to sleep.

Transcript – Northwest Hospital
February 10, 1983

SA Brown: *When he told you that you were going to have dinner with the old man, who was he talking about? The old man.*

Eto: *Uh, talk about, about Vince Solano.*

SA Brown: *Vincent Solano.*

Eto: *Yeah. Mmm hmm.*

SA Brown: *Okay, did you see Vincent today?*

Eto: *No, I seen him about, about, uh, a week, 10 days ago.*

SA Brown: *Did you talk to him? What did you talk to him about?*

Eto: *Again, I was called, that he wants to, uh, uh, meet me.*

SA Brown: *Mmm hmm. Who called to tell you that?*

Eto: *At that time he wanted to meet me.*

SA Brown: *Who called to tell you that?*

Eto: *Joe Arnold does most of the calling, okay?*

SA Brown: *Where did you meet Vince at that time?*

Eto: *I met him on Belmont. There's, uh, west of Harlem, west of Central. There is, uh, there is a pancake house. An International Pancake House.*

SA Brown: *Okay.*

Eto: *Do you know where that is?*

SA Brown: *Yeah, I know where it is. Who else was there with you?*

Eto: *Just him, just him. That we did not go inside. I parked and he said, and, uh, we took a walk down the street.*[52] *He asked me about this and about that. It was specifically he asked me about, uh, uh, the case.*

SA Brown: *That's the gambling case, right?*

Eto: *Yes, and whether we pleaded the stipulated bench.*

SA Brown: *Okay, mmm hmm.*

Eto: *I said that we pleaded the stipulated bench and then he asked what that was. I explained it to him. That we have the right to appeals and of the, the motions that we put in, that we have the right to appeal. I already had told him this before and that there was no possible way we could beat this case, you know.*[53]

Eto: So I would like to, um, to, um, plea bargain. When I told him before, he didn't object to it.

SA Brown: He didn't object before to this plan?

Eto: No. But this time when I says that we, uh, took the stipulated bench, what, the same thing as plea-bargaining, you know what I mean?

SA Brown: Mmm hmm.

Eto: But not quite the same. He got mad, said, 'What the hell you want to do that? Why didn't you, uh, go to trial?' What the hell, I already told you that I'm going, I'm going to, uh, make the, I can't possibly beat the thing, so I'm going to make a deal, if I possibly can, you know.

SA Brown: Mmm hmm.

Eto: Then he commenced to tell me, uh, you have three choices.

SA Brown: What did he say they were?

Eto: Okay, one, to, um, you got a choice of doing time, you got a choice of appealing the case, you got a choice of taking off. I says, 'Why should I take off?'

SA Brown: Mmm hmm.

Eto: Why should I take off? Sentence won't call for that much. Five years at the maximum. Kind of sounds funny to me, you know. Always they're making out of gambling thing, this guy. We're walking down the street and when he gets through asking me these things, I figured we're through and we're going to go back, and I make a little turn. Then he got really jumpy. He says, 'What are you looking over your shoulder for?' Like, uh, I'm expecting somebody to come up behind me or there's somebody tailing us or whatever.

SA Brown: Yeah.

Eto: *No, that's good for nothing. I thought we were through and we were gonna go on back. Acted very, very jumpy. Okay. And then, uh, finally when we did get finished with our conversation, we turned around and went back, and my car, it was cold, I had my hands in my coat pocket. He said, 'What have you got in your pocket?' Like I've got a gun. Which I never have a gun. I only got a pack of cigarettes. Cigarette. He said, 'Oh, I thought I seen something.' He already planned it that time. (Garbled.) ... Do things that, uh, that, uh, that made me suspicious of what was happening, okay? As all of those idiosyncrasies that he never done before. Edge, what the goddamn hell, for what?*

SA Brown: *How long have you known Vincent Solano?*

Eto: *Jesus Christ, I must know him for 25, 28, 30 years.*

SA Brown: *How long has he been your old man?*

Eto: *Since Dominick Dobell died.*

SA Brown: *Who was your boss before then?*

I stopped reading the transcript, and as soon as I did, Eto opened his eyes and said, "That was some stupid stuff he did. Goddamn, they should have done a good job."

"I could have told Solano you were a hard case,"

Joe laughed. "That would have been a good one."

"So, in terms of your gambling case, Joe. If Vincent Solano is your boss, then he too is involved in the conspiracy to commit the same crimes to which you were going to plead guilty," I interjected.

Eto knew exactly where I was going and said, "Damn right. And so are Rocky Infelise and Louis Marino."

The mention of those two names was startling. Rocky Infelise was the boss of the west side of Chicago and was regarded as the strongest, biggest moneymaker and the most influential of street bosses. He was an organized crime heavy. Louis Marino was his front man, or the "Joe Arnold" for Infelise.

Bob Cooley, the crooked cop and Mob fixer attorney, in his book, described Rocky Infelise as, "…not a guy with a sense of humor. I never tried to pal around with him. I knew the mob bosses reserved him for their most vicious and important hits."[54]

"So, Joe, how does Rocky Infelise become involved in your *bolita* operation?" I was completely puzzled about how the crossover of territorial bosses was taking place here.

"When I first started the *bolita* business I was under Turk Torello. When Turk died, Joe Negal took over. It meant that all of the business, no matter who was my present boss, went to him. Before I started operating again in the late 1970s, I met with Ferriola and Solano at the Diplomat."

I interjected, "Who is Joe Negal?"

"That's Joe Ferriola," he replied in a tone indicating I should have known that. This was the first of many explanations Joe had to give us on understanding the convoluted business ownership and street tax philosophy of the mob.

"How do I prove Rocky Infelise is involved in the *bolita* business?" I asked.

"I met him and Marino every month to pay them the $5,000 street tax. Maybe you saw me meet them once?"

"Fat chance, Joe. If I had, it would have been a day I wouldn't forget. I guess it will be my job to try to prove that part. Joe, you've just expanded my gambling case to include one heavy dude, Rocky Infelise. Thanks. How about a coffee break?" I asked.

"I think that sounds wonderful." He lit another cigarette and leaned back to enjoy the smoke.

"Marc, yo!" I called with exuberance knowing I was getting great information spending the afternoon with my Mr. Eto, the man United States Attorney Dan Webb[55] had called, "…the best break the U.S. government has had since Joe Valachi."[56] "Where do I get coffee?"

"Coffee?" Marc asked with a grin on his face. "Around here we make our own. Come with me and you shall see." He walked me to a makeshift kitchen in which an old, crusty coffee maker was sitting. There was a column of Styrofoam cups, fake powdered milk, and sugar. Yuck. "We made this pot this morning, so maybe you'll want to make another one. Joe lives on coffee and cigarettes."

"Mmm, sounds like my diet." I made a fresh pot of coffee and brought a cup to Joe and a cup for myself. I could barely drink the poison and vowed this had to change.

I figured I had talked enough about business and said, "Joe, why don't I get the newspaper you were reading, and I'll start reading these reports over here. And we'll just sit in the sun together reading. Is that okay with you?"

"Oh, that sounds fine to me, Elaine. You know I am yours now. You know that, don't you?"

"Well, now that you say so…I do, Joe."

He had called me by my first name, and he had told me he was mine. I would clarify exactly what that meant in the weeks and months to come, but it was as if we were getting married. Only this time, I was sure our marriage would last a lot longer than the previous four or five others he had had. As we both sat and read, I felt an easy comfort level being established between us. There was no need for idle chatter. There was no need for me to "wow" him. I guess I had already done that months ago. Someday I would have to ask him about that.

Reviewing the reports, I came to the photos of Eto's car parked where he had left it the night of the shooting. One photo showed the trail of blood on the snow-covered alley from the open car door and along the sidewalk leading to the Terminal Pharmacy. I flashed back to the alley photos of the vacant lot covered in snow which was the murder scene of Santiago Gonzalez in 1956 — Mob hit symmetry.

Other photos included those of his clothing — inexpensive polyester pieces totally inappropriate for the freezing temperatures that night. Dried, brown-looking blood covered his white shirt, plaid sports coat, tan sansa-belt pants, and belted trench coat.

"Joe?" I asked, interrupting his newspaper reading. "Why did you go to that meeting if you knew it was going to be a hit?"

Joe cleared his throat. "I almost didn't. I told Mary Lou where my life insurance papers were located, I took a bath, I put on my nice clothes, and then I went out and sat in the car. I sat for about half an hour before I backed it down the driveway. And it was damn cold sitting in that car because the heater no longer worked."

"You didn't think to call me? To call the FBI? To run away?" Incredulously, I instantly shot back those questions at him.

"No, never those things," he said calmly, as if speaking to an excited child.

"You just drove to your death?"

"Well, I thought maybe there was a small percentage of an edge, but very small, and I had to take it. For me, I had no other choice. But once Jasper directed me to the alley, I knew it was all over." He lowered his head and stared blankly at the floor.

I looked at the little old man who had faced death so bravely. I felt sorry for Joe, but I knew he wasn't the sort of man who would let me hug him while I told him that I felt his pain. But, strangely, I did feel his pain. It bothered me that he underdressed for the cold weather that night, that the heater didn't work in his car, that he had to listen to the lame conversation and laughter of his executioners as he silently drove to his death, that he was shot three times, and that no one was there to help him as he stumbled down that dark, snow-crusted alley, blood gushing from his head.

I returned to reading the shooting reports. It surprised me that Joe stated he was afraid that a Chicago policeman would come and finish him. On the way to the hospital he asked a rookie cop to sit next to him. For comfort? For protection?

"I'm sorry, Joe."

"Don't be silly. This is my job. What do you need?" Joe asked.

"Why were you afraid a Chicago policeman was going to finish you off?"

He laughed. "You know how corrupt they are. You know there are coppers who do exactly what the Outfit wants them to do. Finishing me off would not be a big deal." He smiled.

"You think they would get away with that?" I once again asked in disbelief.

"I don't mean to make light of it, Elaine. It's just a fact. Outfit murders have been committed for years and years. Who has gone to jail? What Mob hit has ever been solved? And you know who knew about the failed hit on me, even before you?"

"No, who?"

"Hanhardt, that's who," Joe said.

"I'm sorry, who is Hanhardt?" I asked.

"Hanhardt is the chief of detectives for the Chicago Police Department. I even paid him off to make sure the police didn't dig too deeply into a murder.[57] On another occasion I gave a gold Rolex watch to a lieutenant in charge of homicide investigations to cover up a murder."

"Whose murder was that, Joe?"

"Uh, he was a troublemaker. Puerto Rican who wouldn't leave our operation alone. We were all just young punks then, but this guy threw a piece of pipe at Angelo LaPietra, who was guarding my game. When Angelo drew his gun from his waist, the carload of them took off. But

Angelo didn't forget it. Let me think. Ah — they made a terrible mess of him, actually disemboweled him. Angelo is like that. He is, what you call it? Sadistic personality."

"Was his name Santiago Gonzalez?" I asked.

"Yeah, that was it. His street name was Chavo. But how did you know that?"

"Joe, I can't tell you all my secrets on our first date, can I?" I laughed.

I was relieved that I wasn't sitting here with someone who could disembowel another human being. I did feel much better about this guy Joe — a lot better.

Later I found a taped conversation Joe had with FBI agents. It gave me greater insight into the man and his business.

> SA Doyle: *What is more important to the Outfit, Joe? Being a tough guy or a moneymaker?*
>
> Eto: *Is their ability to, um, to kill. The ability to enforce. To find people to make money, they find me, they find others, you know. But, uh, unless, uh, we're enforceable, we're not going to do them any good.*

I spent a few hours with Joe that afternoon, and they had been productive. Joe fingered a high-ranking police executive as a puppet of the Mob, to include the covering up of murders. He solved the 26-year-old murder case of Santiago Gonzalez, also known as Chavo, by identifying the four made members who had done it, Joseph Ferriola, Turk Torello, James LaPietra, and Angelo LaPietra. He provided information that included four made members in the management and conspiracy of Eto's *bolita* gambling operation, Joe Ferriola, Rocky Infelise, Vincent Solano, and Louis Marino. Three of these men were territorial bosses: Joe Ferriola, Rocky Infelise, and, the stupidest of all, Vince Solano. As the sun had already set on that February afternoon, I realized I wanted to go home. I was suffering from information overload.

"I think I'm going to pack up my things and go home for dinner soon, Joe."

"Oh, is it getting to be that time already?" he said with surprise when he looked up from the newspaper he had been reading all afternoon. He sure studied things.

"Yes, it is. Your palace guard should have changed at 4 p.m. and it's now 5:30 p.m. I'll go find out who is going to be sitting outside. Or he can come inside and watch television with you, if you wish."

"Yeah. It's good company. Each one of these guys has such a different story. I just don't want the one I had last night."

I was sort of bewildered. "Joe, why not?"

"He ate with his fingers; he ate his potatoes, meat, everything with his fingers. I asked him if he wanted to use his silverware, but he said he liked eating like that better."

"You have got to be kidding me!" I said.

"No, he really did."

Inside I was writhing with anger. Who was this animal? This man represented the whole FBI, and he had left a lasting impression on our star witness, who I imagined had seen everything, but had not expected to see an FBI agent eat like an animal.

I looked at the clipboard that held the names of the agents scheduled for duty and saw who was on duty last night. It was a sloppy, dirty little guy on our squad who had six kids. He brought black bananas to eat and used the same lunch bag day in and day out. His shirts were frayed and grayed, and he had but one or two suits. I guessed money was tight trying to raise six children, but certainly he had to use utensils while on Bureau time. I'd have to talk to Bobbie about this. I didn't need to be known as Emily Post — people thought of me as a snob already — but really.

"Joe, it's not the same guy tonight, and I'll make sure he doesn't rotate back in for guard duty during meal time. I'm sorry that he did that. Let me go out and get our man for tonight and introduce you to him."

After I finished that formality, I said, "Joe, as an FBI agent, I think you have given me the most rewarding day I have ever had. Thank you so much." I held out my hand to shake his. I then added, "Today even beats making Walter Micus puke after we came bursting through the door at the Holiday Inn."

He laughed. "I see you have a mean streak. That's good."

"I wouldn't think that would be a good characteristic. Anyway, sleep well, Joe. Tomorrow we'll sit together in the sun and you can tell me more stories."

We both laughed again and I walked away from the only patient in the otherwise empty hospital ward, Ken "Tokyo Joe" Eto. Above all, this unique man was a survivor.

Of all the Mob hits that were ever done in Chicago, how did I happen to be the case agent on the one close-in, set-up, "take him for a ride and shoot him in the head three times" survivor? Besides all of that luck, the hit seemed to have enormous historical and working knowledge of the Chicago Mob. This was going to be really amazing.

- CHAPTER ELEVEN -
Failure is Forever

A procession and progression of the highest-ranking to the lowest-ranking law enforcement officials were allowed to interview Mr. Eto, as long as they could explain their reason for doing so. We had to allow numerous Chicago Police officials to question and re-question him about the night of the shooting. Attempted murder is a state crime, not a federal one. The state's attorneys, who would prosecute Mr. Gattuso and Mr. Campise, needed to interview their victim and witness. The only way I could tolerate many of them was to know there were good policemen and local prosecutors.

But it was the FBI that would actually break the case open for them and guarantee that when Gattuso and Campise walked in to court, no judge would be bribed nor jury fixed to let either of them off. If any such thing happened, it would create a massive stink and everyone from Chicago and Washington, D.C., would smell it.

Our days were spent being schooled by Joe. Working closely with him, we went from kindergarten to graduate school. Ultimately, I could authoritatively challenge any Mafia bullshit anyone tried to put down for the rest of my Bureau career.

In those first months, he told us that power and rank in the Mob were not achieved by the amount of money brought into the enterprise. It was easy to find people who could do that. Status was earned by displaying the ability to kill another human being. If Joe's theory was correct, then the executives of the Mafia were its most psychopathic members — it would be like an insane asylum run by its sickest residents. How could such an organization succeed?

As February slipped into March, my daily lesson about the Chicago Mob led me to understand what kept the loony bin functioning. The

Mob's perpetual presence was generated by man's desire to gamble, to get something for nothing, and to be sexually promiscuous. It guaranteed its legacy as long as politicians, police officials, judges, and lawyers were willing to accept the syndicate's money and help them. Marc and I learned that vice and bribery always coexisted. And the psychopathic killer bosses made sure no one became too moralistic or humanistic. That could not be tolerated as it would diminish the Mob's strength.

Even before I returned from my ski vacation, Joe had identified more than 100 "made" members or associates of the Mob. He had provided the names of a minimum of 30 businesses that were Mob fronts. He had provided detailed information about the enterprise of the syndicate and how it operated in Chicago, with only small variations in other cities, such as New Orleans, Detroit, Cleveland, New York, and Newark. He definitively stated that Chicago had representatives in, or controlled, Springfield, East St. Louis, and Peoria, Illinois; Hammond and Gary, Indiana; Denver; Milwaukee; Las Vegas; San Francisco; Los Angeles; and Seattle. This was critical to prosecuting Outfit bosses under the Racketeering Influenced and Corrupt Organizations (RICO).[58]

Much of Chicago's control over other cities came from its stranglehold on the unions. The Chicago Mafia had early on infiltrated and taken over the finances and the bargaining power of the unions. When an industry is threatened with a shutdown because its workers are going to go on strike, there is no more powerful tool. Unfortunately, the unions soon became only puppets of the Mob and no longer represented the workers.

I had always been pro-union because my father was a union electrician. His union wages gave me the financial ability to go to college — not to a community college, but a well-respected university, living the life of a sorority girl. Most likely in the early 1960s there were not a lot of daughters of electricians enjoying the same experience. Yet the opportunity existed; if a skilled union worker wanted to sacrifice to send his child away to college, it could be done.

The father of one of my college sorority sisters, JoAnn, had been a union tool and die maker. As adults, JoAnn and I were able to spend our vacations together skiing in Vail, Colorado. With our education and the opportunities it provided us, we were the products of the American dream. Somewhere along the way, the union organizations relinquished control to the corrupt Chicago syndicate, and this may have stolen the dreams of subsequent generations. As Joe spoke of his bosses, you could tell which ones he admired and which ones he didn't. It was clear James "Turk" Torello was his favorite. He used to say that Turk was smart, and every time he said Turk's wife's name, Doodles, it made me want to giggle.

I don't recall talking with Joe about the viciousness of Turk Torello. Perhaps Joe liked him because he was always good to him, but one of the Mob murders attributed to Turk Torello was the brutal three-day torture death of William Jackson. "Action Jackson," as he was called, was a loan shark who apparently stiffed Turk on his cut of the profits. He was also wrongly suspected of being an FBI informer. Squad photos showed the 350-pound mutilated body of Action Jackson after Torello had hung him on a meat hook and poked him with an electric prod. "He was on that thing three days before he croaked," Torello said excitedly on the illegal FBI wiretap. "He was floppin' around on that hook. We tossed water on him to give the prod a better charge, and he's screamin'..."[59]

The detail of the information Joe was giving us was beginning to pile up, and I was becoming frustrated in the role of a listener, not an actor. Joe knew I was anxious to begin gathering the evidence to include Vincent Solano, Rocky Infelice, and Louis Marino in his gambling enterprise. We would brainstorm about how I could do that, trying to tie each of the characters to him through telephone records, surveillances, anything we could think of.

190

My husband Tom also had useful suggestions on how to proceed with the investigation of the attempted murder of Joe Eto. Since the crime was a state charge, Eto's car was towed by the Chicago Police. It had been sitting in an impound lot with dozens of other towed cars. Tom insisted I secure the car for an FBI search for physical evidence that might incriminate Campise and Gattuso.

I called the homicide "dicks" assigned to the case and asked if they would mind if I took the car for that purpose. The detectives didn't seem at all concerned about me taking it, but they had to get the okay from the commander.

To make sure I wouldn't be trumped on this one, I told Bobbie, "I think it's important we get Eto's car back from the Chicago Police pound and do our own forensic search of it. Who knows what we may find — a fingerprint, some hairs, or some fibers? Right now the Chicago detectives don't have a problem with that idea, but they're waiting for their commander's approval. Could you help pull a little rank and call the commander for me?"

"Sure, but Smith, you aren't thinking of shipping that entire car back to the FBI Laboratory, are you?"

"No, Bob. Just the interior."

"You going to do that?"

"No. I already have two guys who want to do advanced crime scene work at Quantico. They think it would look good on their applications. But, Bobbie, when you call the commander — don't make it sound like we are dying to get that car. Otherwise those coppers might think they have something big on their hands, and they won't want to give it up."

"See, there you go again. You have a great idea all worked out, and then you have to go and try and tell me how to do my job."

"Okay, okay," I responded. "Sorry about that," I said without much conviction. But I left his office pleased with the results of my meeting.

In two days, Joe's car was in the basement of the Federal Building. Under the 30-story high-rise federal office building that housed the FBI offices, the United States prosecutors, and the United States District Courts, there were several levels of underground parking. On the first level, the FBI had a small area devoted to executive parking and to what was known as the "radio shop." This was where our technicians installed and repaired our car radios. It was also where we temporarily parked our Bureau cars whenever we brought a prisoner in, because the prisoner elevator was a few steps away.

The area was dimly lit and filthy from cars pulling in and out all day long no matter the weather. It was here that the Chicago Police towed Eto's car, with all the grime and slop of the last month of Chicago's winter weather still on it. It sat melting and dripping filth of its own onto the floor around it.

The two agents, Don and Bruce, who had volunteered to do the painstaking, neck-breaking forensic and evidence recovery, were waiting with me when the forlorn black 1976 Ford Torino was dragged in and dropped. The Chicago Police tow guy unceremoniously unhooked the car from the tow bar and let it bang to the floor. He then pulled himself out of the truck, waddled his 300 pounds over to Bruce, and said, "You gotta sign this release."

Bruce said, "Oh, no. Not me. Her," and pointed to me.

I stepped over and signed the form, took the copy that was mine, and took custody of the car. I breathed a sigh of relief. The baby was finally in our hands.

The agents donned new protective paper clothing that covered them, to include their feet, hands, and head, and got to work. They then spread yards of light brown butcher paper in several layers all around the vehicle. Don turned to me and said, "You can stand here and watch, but what we are going to do is dismantle the entire interior of this car, seal each piece in butcher paper and tape each package as tightly as possible, label it with a distinct numbering system, place these pieces into several large container boxes, and ship them back to the FBI headquarters lab. I figure it may only take us 10 to 12 hours because nothing can drop from this car unless it drops onto that brown paper."

Immediately, I replied, "Oh, well you just go right ahead, because I have enough to do without standing around watching. But then what happens when it gets to the lab?"

Bruce said, "Once everything is unwrapped in the Hairs and Fibers Unit, each part is brushed and all the hairs and fibers collected are categorized by where they came from. If any hairs or fibers are found in our pieces of butcher paper, they are put into the same grouping. Then the hairs and fibers will be examined under a microscope and matched to the known samples or categorized as unknown specimens. After the paper and all the other surfaces have been swept for hairs and fibers, all the parts will be sent over to the Fingerprint Section. Then every surface will be examined for fingerprints with a special light. If a print or partial print is found, it will be lifted and they will try to match it to the known and unknown prints of the case. Known prints will be Eto's, Don's, and mine. And they have the known prints of the two subjects. Of course they will be looking for those. And they may find other prints."

Over my shoulder I heard a new voice, "And, Smith, that is why it is so important that we get those subpoenas served for fingerprints and hair samples as soon as possible." Jeremy Margolis had snuck up behind me.

"Well, how did you get into Bureau space, Margolis?"

"Oh, don't you know the Supreme Commander can go anywhere? Hey, I didn't know you were going to do this, but brilliant idea. Too bad you're married to such an idiot. I feel sorry for you."

"Actually, this was Tom's idea, Jeremy."

"Noooo?" he replied, making fun of me.

"Well, how did I know he would be talking about my case to everyone?" I replied in a disgusted tone.

"I gotta run. Do a good job, guys. We are depending on you," Jeremy called as he scurried off.

"Yeah, yeah," was all that was heard from inside the car as Bruce and Don were already hard at work and didn't have time to be screwing around.

"If you need anything, give me a call, and thanks so much," I said to my two evidence "experts," who were already lifting the front seat out of Eto's car, blood stains and his black leather gloves still in the same place as they were on the night of February 10. The Chicago Police hadn't done a single crime scene examination to that car. Thank God. But damn them for all the murders they could have solved over the years if they had known how to do their jobs.

I left the Federal Building and drove to the hospital to talk again to Joe and to tell Marc about the car. When I got there, Joe was walking around the ward on one of his little strolls, trying not to go stir-crazy. Seeing him, I thought that the sooner we could send Joe out into the real world, the better. This was a restrictive, unnatural way to live. He was fully recovered except for the bullet fragments that would work through his skin. Marc pulled those out with tweezers and then cleaned the area with an antiseptic. Joe needed to go to restaurants, see other people, walk the streets, see movies — be normal.

As I entered the ward and took off my coat, I announced, "We got the car, boys."

"Oh, good," Marc said.

"Yeah, and it was in pristine condition. The coppers hadn't done a thing to it," I added sarcastically.

"Ah, those two were in that car no more than 10 minutes and they had gloves on. I don't know what you think you'll find, Elaine," Joe interjected.

"I don't know, Joe. But that doesn't mean we eliminate taking the step," I replied. Deep down in my heart, I didn't think we'd get anything, but in something this important, we had to try. "Anyway, we get to have a little fun with our two murderers, Johnny and Jasper."

I turned to Marc. "Jeremy met me in the basement and said he'd get a subpoena ready to serve on them for hair samples."

"Okay, I'll check in with Jeremy and then give them to Joe Doyle to serve." Marc walked away like a tall, lanky bird. At his makeshift desk, he wrote a reminder to himself. He was so compulsive; I just loved working with him. I tended to be high energy, all over the place, trying to do a million things at once. Marc was high energy, but he approached everything in a routine, organized manner.

Joe, who loved to watch and listen, must have thought we were a great pair to study. Sure, he liked to talk, but Joe was also content observing. What he did with those observations, I can only imagine, because I never asked. After a while, I surmised that he utilized everything he learned from watching to give himself an edge up on the next guy. Considering he was out on his own at the age of 14 and he belonged to a race that was discriminated against, it was no doubt a useful habit.

"Hey Joe," I said, "Back to the fun part of this search of your car. It gives us the opportunity to flip[60] Johnny and Jasper two more times. Once when we serve the subpoenas and then when they come in to the FBI office."

"Don't I know that?" Joe laughed.

Bob Walsh had put Agent Joe Doyle in charge of trying to convince Johnny and Jasper that their days were numbered and that they should cooperate with us. But so far, Doyle had only been cursed out by John Gattuso's wife, Carmella, the daughter of some mobster. She also tried to push him down a flight of stairs. Doyle had not even been able to gain entry to the front door of the condo building in which Jasper Campise lived. Now we would send Doyle out with some backup help to stake out their houses and discover the best opportunity to serve the subpoenas. Bob Walsh may have been thinking of putting the surveillance squad on the pair, just to see if we could catch the Outfit trying to hit them. Or maybe we could catch them meeting with the bosses. Such a meeting could signal their impending deaths.

Finally, if the two hit men "victims" came in without their attorneys to provide hair-plucking evidence, Marc and I could try to work them over with our charm and convince them to see the light. Every time we had an excuse to flip someone, we didn't waste the opportunity. Mobsters generally didn't stand on street corners waiting to bump into an FBI agent.

"Only when we take the hair samples, I am *not* taking their pubic hairs. Marc will have that honor all to himself," I said loudly.

"Did I hear you mention my name, Elaine?" Marc called out.

"Oh, yes, my dear," I replied. "It was in conjunction with *you* being the one to tweak several pubic hairs from both Johnny and Jasper. You know you have to obtain hairs that are derived from a natural 'combing' and hairs derived from plucking. Ouch!"

I imagined Marc following procedure, combing the pubic hairs of Johnny and Jasper, and then, one by one, pulling the prescribed three hairs from three distinct regions of their pubic areas. Joe and I looked at each other and laughed. Then we retreated to sit together by the window.

"So...can I get my Mercedes back now (Joe had two cars, and the Mercedes was seized at the search)?" he asked.

"What, Joe? I was surprised by his aggressive question. "No, you can't. That car was seized because it was used in the commission of an interstate crime. It has been seized and now formally forfeited over to the United States government."

"Ah, I've never heard that law before," he grumbled.

"Perhaps because the state can't do it and the feds never did it until I decided, why not? Crime is all about profitability, and if having a nice car is one of the perks, then I'm going to try to take that perk."

"I sure liked that big car. You felt safe in it and it rode like you were driving on a cloud." Joe's eyes drifted upward.

In my evil mind I told myself: Remember always to take their cars. It really hurts them.

We dropped the topic. As I checked my notes to see where we had stopped our interview yesterday, Joe picked up a crossword puzzle he was working on. One of the agents started him working them, and now he divided his time between the newspaper, crossword puzzles, walking circles around the ward, and talking to all of his "interrogators."

At our last meeting, we had been talking about Larry Bradi and Sam Sarcinelli's drug business. Joe had received financing from both of them. On the occasions he had visited Sam or Larry, he met a number of their associates and had even witnessed bags of white powder and suitcases filled with U. S. currency.

"So, Joe," I said, grabbing his attention.

"Yeah." He put down his puzzle and pencil.

"Did you ever see Sam's Learjet?"

"Oh, I went to New York and back with him on it."

"You did? When was that?"

"Well, we went to pick up $50,000 in New York right before I hired Walter Micus, his brother-in-law, to help me tabulate. About, uh, April or May of 1980. That trip to New York on Sam's private jet was something else. He smoked cocaine through a water pipe all the way to New York. Even smoked it while riding in the limo through the streets of New York to the Doral Hotel. At the hotel, Sam held a lot of business meetings about his stock manipulation schemes and continued to smoke through all of these meetings. When I asked him about it, he told me it kept him sharp."

"About that same time, Larry Bradi decided he no longer wanted to be a partner of mine in the *bolita* business. He needed to make more money, and he could do that selling coke on Rush Street. Sam told me he was going back into the coke business to raise more funds for his stock schemes. I then introduced Sam to Larry and told Sam that he could trust Larry with $50,000 worth of cocaine. As a result, the two started a business relationship. I kept out of it because I didn't want anything to do with drug dealing."

I didn't mention to Joe that he was already up to his eyeballs in drug dealing. His *bolita* operation was being financed by not one, but two drug dealers. And he had introduced the two to each other — God! Mr. Networker! I'll cover my ears when you talk about drugs.

I then turned to the subject of the Witness Protection Program and how the man in charge of that program was due to show up anytime to interview Joe and set the final details for Joe's return to the real, but exceedingly different, world.

Jerry, the United States Marshal coming today, was a no-nonsense dude whom I trusted. I think he felt the same about me. He had interviewed my informant Frankie, and together we had decided that Frankie could be his own protection program. Frankie had changed his name and moved to Arizona. Joe Eto couldn't do just that. The government had very big plans for him, and his neck was now going to be transferred over to Jerry's crew. They had their hands full. It was said that there was a $100,000 contract on Jimmy Fratianno's head. Imagine the price for Ken "Tokyo Joe" Eto's head.

I knew the Witness Protection Program was the pits. It was the bargain basement of government programs. They didn't provide the witnesses with cosmetic surgery or a total makeover. A new name and valid social security number would be provided, along with educational credentials that tied to previous school and work experience. A living stipend, slightly higher than the national average, would be provided. But this continued only until you found a job, and you better not take too long doing that. They would help you find an apartment, but it would be one you could afford, and it wouldn't be too nice.

Before U.S. Marshal Jerry had even arrived that day, Joe had decided not to take his present wife, Mary Lou, and her three children with him. The marriage had not been so great before the shooting, and the added burden of being in the Witness Protection Program would make it a nightmare.

From my way of thinking, the only thing Joe had left was his life. At this crossroads, how precious was this to him? Wherever he was going, he would have no way of making a living. He could no longer participate in illegal gambling. He had other children but spoke of them rarely. He would have no friends. Strangely, I wasn't afraid or nervous for him. Once again, all I saw was this unemotional, ever-observant human being who quietly and without fanfare portrayed the strength of steel. He'd do okay.

From Jerry's way of thinking, this was "one hot potato" witness, and they couldn't screw up on anything. The credibility of his program rested on keeping Eto alive so he could continue to walk in and out of court as many times as federal prosecutors wanted him there.

When Jeremy Margolis recommended Ken Eto to Gerald Shur, Assistant Director, Office of Enforcement Operations, Criminal Division, Department of Justice, Washington, D.C., for inclusion in the United States Witness Protection Program, he wrote dramatically, "I was summoned to Eto's hospital bed by Chicago FBI Special Agent in Charge Edward D. Hegarty, where I reached an accommodation with Eto, who promised to cooperate and testify. The FBI regards this as the single most significant breakthrough in Chicago organized crime history. Eto has been debriefed at length and has provided a wealth of information regarding organized crime murders, gambling, money laundering, narcotics, and rampant police corruption. At the very least, even without the cooperation of any defendants, identified by Eto, literally dozens of prosecutions are expected, including murder cases against three of Chicago's five street bosses. …(S)ince Eto has already miraculously survived an assassination attempt, the threat level could hardly be higher."[61]

"Hey, good lookin'," Jerry called as he walked up to my chair. I stood and gave him a hug. I then reintroduced him to Joe.

"Don't let me interrupt you," Jerry said graciously.

I knew he always had about 10 balls in the air at any one time and never had enough time to sit around waiting. "Jerry, we were just going over something. But we can get back to it when you are done."

"Well, this might take a while. I have to give Joe a psychological test and then review his entire life. Usually takes me about three hours."

Marc and I looked at each other and shrugged our shoulders. What's three hours to us? We'll barely get started on what we should have done three weeks ago.

Marc said, "Mr. Joe is all yours. Coffee is over there with cookies, compliments of Mrs. Smith, and lunch is brought up around 1:00 p.m. We ordered an extra for you."

Marc and I moved to the far side of the ward to dictate, read and write reports, and make phone calls. Actually, we were anxiously waiting for Joe to go. We had drained his brain of so much information, and it was doing no one any good to have him just sitting with us. It was essential that this information predicate new cases on specific mobsters or supplement old cases that had been sitting, just waiting for a break. It was as if we were the "forward observers" who had gathered the intelligence. Now we had to get back to the troops so an all-out strategic warfare against the Mob could begin.

Little did Marc and I know that it was going to happen so quickly and so sensationally, but on the following Saturday, the United States Marshals flew a helicopter onto Great Lakes Naval Base Hospital's helipad and took our Joe away. Even though this move was our desire, back at work we were both reeling with the emptiness and immediate change of purpose. The fact that we had not been able to say "Goodbye" or "We'll see you in a month, Joe" left us emotionally dangling. I wondered if that would have been good for him or not.

With the immense burden of the issues we needed to address, we found ourselves tabling certain matters for the next time we would see Joe.

Back on the squad, day in and day out, our lives became fairly normal, and my old buddy Dietzie commented, "Frau Schmidt, you don't seem so 'amuck' lately. I've even seen you go out to lunch."

"Ah, my dear," I replied in a manner so laid-back I could barely recognize my own voice, "It's getting to be summer, and I think I want to take life at a little slower pace."

"One has to stay balanced, you know," I lectured in a mocking tone.

I leaned back in my chair and thought about the last four years. They had been the most challenging of my life: Entering the FBI Academy in June 1979; making the case against Eto in August 1980; wiretapping one of the largest cocaine distributors in the United States, Sam Sarcinelli, et. al. in 1981; almost losing my husband to a gunshot wound in September 1982; and five months later, responsible for the handling of a witness that gave the Chicago FBI's organized crime program its best chance to hurt the Mob. I thought I should probably slow myself down and then maybe everything else around me might do the same.

"Hey, Smitty," Marc called as he came lopping over to my desk. "Nick DeJohn just called and he wants to bring Jasper in for hair samples tomorrow at 9:00 a.m. Are you available?"

"Marc, are you kidding? Would I ever miss the chance to torture a man? No way," I eagerly replied.

"Oh, good, we're on then," he said. "I'm going to get the tweezers, instructions, and evidence tissue paper now. See you in the morning."

There was no doubt in my mind that Marc would be prepared like a neurosurgeon going in for this hair plucking. Sometimes this job could be so much fun.

Jasper Campise[62] arrived the next morning with his attorney, Nick DeJohn,[63] who had to be one of the biggest goofballs I had met in a long time. He was the typical Italian stallion, with black slicked-back hair, wearing the light gray shiny suit, but he was mortified to be out in public because the night before one of his front teeth had fallen out. He didn't want to shake my hand because he had to keep it over his mouth so I wouldn't see how funny he looked without his front tooth. Did he really think I cared how he looked?

Jasper was an old sad sack of a man. He was short and stocky, with gray hair and the biggest bags under his eyes I had ever seen. Boy, this man needed either a long vacation at a spa or drastic plastic surgery.

DeJohn explained that he had to rush off to his dentist and hoped we would follow the laws regulating communicating with his client. Mr. Campise was represented and that meant he had selected to invoke his right to remain silent. During all this, Jasper stood silently.

What DeJohn didn't understand was that we understood that law better than he did. Jasper could invoke his right to remain silent only if he was in an arrest situation. Jasper was not. In any event, it was meaningless chatter by DeJohn to make his client think he was doing such a good job.

"Ya! And he told them fuckin' agents that they couldn't talk to me," I could almost hear Jasper bragging to Vince Solano.

I am sure he wouldn't tell Vince how we were going to make him laugh and show him we were respectful, intelligent, and honorable people — all the qualities missing from the people with whom he hung around.

The hair pulling wasn't as dramatic as I hoped it would be. Jasper didn't scream out in pain when Marc plucked three hairs from three different regions on his head, plucked hairs from his arms and legs, and then took him to the men's room to do the genital hair plucking and combing.

And I must say, all of our talk and pleasantries went right over Jasper's head. He was catatonic. He had no personality or, as a psychologist would say, "no affect." God, this guy was in bad shape.

Later Marc told me about John Gattuso's hair pulling because I was not able to witness that. But Joe Doyle was there. And as luck would have it, Mrs. Gattuso, along with her husband's attorney, Joe Carbonara, was also there. Marc and Joe Doyle would not allow Mrs. Gattuso to accompany her husband into the conference room, and she apparently verbally lit into Doyle with, "Fuck you for harassing my husband, you mother-fucking bastard," again. It might have been fun to see, but I think it would have made me angry to witness someone treat an agent with such disrespect. I might have been tempted to "bitch slap" her, but that would have been very bad for our side.

The hair samples were sent to the FBI Laboratory, and Marc and I went back to work. We were attempting to corroborate every word of Joe Eto's information and develop the predication for new cases. It was a task I enjoyed doing because somehow I knew I'd eventually get the evidence we needed to put away a lot of bad people. Anyway, it was summer and life was grand, and that night was bridge night.

Held every other Thursday night, bridge night was one of my favorite social evenings. After work that July 14, I drove to Annie's house. I wheeled through the streets of the north side of Chicago to her Lincoln Park townhouse. Finding a parking spot in Lincoln Park, Chicago's hippest neighborhood, was close to impossible, but when I drove a Bureau car in those days, I never let that bother me. I just parked illegally.

The members of the bridge club were sorority sisters, except for one, so there were years of shit between us. Most of it was good, and that bound us together tighter than anything. We had all chosen Alpha Chi Omega as our sorority at our *alma mater* — the University of Illinois. Alpha Chis were high status. We loved it. We all came to expect that same standard in everything in life.

Annie, the homecoming queen, had a big job at a top advertising agency in Chicago and had remarkably remained unmarried. JoAnn had gone on to marry her college boyfriend, supported him through law school, and was now the epitome of Lincoln Park high status. She had a personal shopper, a maid, a huge diamond ring, and a multimillion-dollar house just off the Chicago lakefront.

Marvin was the only male member of the group. Obviously he was not a sorority sister, but he was tough enough to hang out with the likes of us. He was hysterically funny, witty, and a consummate pessimist. He was the perfect downer to the snobby group of one-up women the rest of us were. An accomplished architect, very artsy, he was cutting edge in everything he did or liked.

And then there was me. Notably, I was the least intellectually gifted of the bridge players, but I was just as happy and, most might say, more successful than all of them. I had entered a career unknown to women and was making a name for myself. I married my high-school sweetheart — a letterman in football at the University of Illinois. Tommy was my hero. I had always been in love with him. I even idolized him a bit — a strong, capable man who could sweep me up in his arms and take away all the bad in the world.

There we were, four old friends. No matter what we accomplished, we were still the silly girls who would steal food from the sorority house fridge and have late-night bridge sessions over cigarettes. Yet, in addition, we had not added another woman to the group, but this single guy, who fit in perfectly and with whom we all felt at ease.

The hostess of bridge night would always serve great food, dessert, wine, cigarettes, and laughs. No one could make you laugh harder than an old friend. We all knew each other's business and that made for uproarious evenings. I had just arrived at Annie's house, the site of that night's bridge club. It was one of those unbelievably hot and humid July evenings that Chicago is famous for. I quickly changed out of my work clothes into some short shorts, a T-shirt, and flip-flops. I got a Coke from the fridge and grabbed a handful of baby carrots off the table that had been set out for snacks.

We had dinner first, and then coffee was made, desserts passed out, and cards dealt. It was somewhere in this process that my beeper went off. I excused myself and went to use Annie's phone in the kitchen. I dialed the call-back number, realizing it was located somewhere in the western suburbs of Chicago.

It was Walsh. "Hey, 'angel of death,' seems like you did it again. We think we've got Gattuso's and Campise's bodies in the trunk of a car out here."

Walsh used a nickname I had recently acquired, "the angel of death." First, one of my informants had been shot, rolled in a rug, and set on fire. Later, an Eto associate, Anthony Crissie, whom I had approached to cooperate, had been gunned down as he got out of his car. After that, everyone started calling me "the angel of death." The boys had even made a sign and put it over my name placard on my desk.

Walsh continued, "There was a car found in Naperville. It's been sitting in some apartment building's parking lot for God knows how long, and the residents have been complaining about the smell. The police ran the plates and say it's registered to Campise. Ziegler and I are heading up there now. You should probably be there."

"I'm leaving right now!"

Walsh gave me directions and hung up.

"Holy shit!" I said as I ran into the dining room to grab my clothes, purse, briefcase, and keys. "I have to go. I think the two guys who tried to kill Eto are dead in the trunk of some car up in Naperville."

My bridge buddies were well filled in on the details of the case. In fact, we had been skiing in Vail with JoAnn and her family when I got the call about Eto being shot and surviving. I had definitely ruined bridge night, but I could not have cared less.

My Bureau car was a beige box — actually a Plymouth Volare, one of the ugliest vehicles on the street — complete with plaid plastic seats, beige plastic flooring covering, and a "call number" of Chicago 69. The fact that I was given this car may have been a subtle sexual jab.

I awkwardly ran down the block with my briefcase and purse banging against my legs. My work clothes were thrown over my arm and flew in the breeze. I fumbled with all my junk, trying to open the door. When I finally was able to juggle that open, I threw all my stuff in and then jumped in. I jammed the key into the ignition and turned it. Nothing.

"The god damn kill-switch!"

At the time, the Bureau was fond of putting kill-switches into their cars. They were well-hidden switches that would not let someone hot-wire and steal FBI cars. If an agent's keys were stolen or lost, no one could start the car, even with the keys, until they found and turned the kill-switch off. I fumbled underneath the ashtray and found it, flipped it, and jammed the ignition on.

Before pulling out of my spot, I groped around on the back floor, found the red light, plugged it into the cigarette lighter, opened the window, and stuck it to the top of the roof. I then turned on the siren, the one that sounds like the ones the French police use (high-low pitch); I just love France. I sped to the nearest expressway entrance that would take me to the suburb of Naperville.

Driving this piece of shit car was really a treat — especially at speeds greater than 60 miles per hour when it developed a disturbing front-end tremor. No matter, the car and I were impressive that night — red light flashing, siren blaring, traveling at more than 80 miles per hour on a Chicago expressway — it was both exhilarating and terrifying at the same time. Terrifying because so many cars outright ignored my approach. It was as if they were deaf, dumb, and blind. Some ass always gets in the way. It seems ridiculous but it happens. Even though I was almost temporarily deaf from the siren, some nincompoops in front apparently couldn't hear a thing. Nevertheless, as I drove with red lights and a siren, I was filled with a surge of adrenaline, sweaty palms, and the loss of any concept other than the space and time inside that car.

Hell, it was even fun on the Fourth of July when Tommy or I would drive some of the neighborhood kids around in the car with the cherry on top and the siren blaring. The feeling of being above the law and the respect it garnered was a big buzz to me, but when I was in a legitimate law enforcement rush and the public ignored me, it made me almost homicidal.

I wanted to call Tommy to tell him about the killers, but this was before the era when everyone and their 3-year-old had a cell phone. We had beepers, but it wasn't the same. Tommy was my touchstone. I needed his calm reserve and advice. I had a tendency to react before thinking, and this was one time I sure as hell didn't want to do that.

Then I saw it, on the left corner of my horizon — lights, commotion, people, and news camera trucks. I had been able to follow Walsh's directions perfectly, and the disturbance to this peaceful apartment complex was clear from blocks away.

"Oh, my God!" Marc was the first to speak after we opened the trunk.

I tried to say something along the lines of "Oh God," but the gag reflex in me made it sound more like a grunt. I knew Marc had to be holding his lunch back, but we both knew better than to let anybody see us wretch. Our faces instinctively turned away from the scene in the back of that car, making it even easier to disguise the feeling. My thoughts turned to the ridiculous — what were these two guys doing in a Volvo — a pretty "old school money" class of vehicle?

"Hey, there are two of them in there." It was Marc again. He grabbed me back from ruminations about the incongruity of a Volvo and Campise into the nasty reality of looking at two dead bodies. I looked again. There were two guys crammed into the trunk — the spare tire was even still in there. I could feel the heat coming off the bodies. They seemed uncomfortably hot, even though I knew they were dead and not really feeling much of anything. Blood was streaked and spattered all over their bodies, their clothing, and the car. It was brown, dried, and peeling off like a really bad sunburn.

After sitting in the trunk of the car for a couple of those 90-degree Chicago summer heat wave days, they had bloated up, expanding their midsections to more than twice normal size. It's like they were fish and had grown to neatly fit the space that was provided; skin and bloat filled every spare inch of the trunk. And the smell... I tried to only breathe through my mouth, but I found myself having a rather sick inclination to smell it again, just to check that it really was that bad. It was indescribable but at the same time carnally familiar. The smell of human life expired and rotted. The dead had a distinctive smell. And once experienced, it is never forgotten. It was a smell impossible to endure for a long period of time and utterly unforgettable — the smell of evil, malice, and hate.

I didn't see such horrors that often, but when I did, I'd go home and thank God that I had a separate existence from all of it — if only to cover it up for a while. It was ironic to witness one of these nasty situations and then return home to my other life — my blonde-haired, blue-eyed little daughter waiting to eat spaghetti for dinner and to tell me about sixth grade and all the innocence it entails. Very strange.

Getting the bodies into to the trunk was an easier job that the disgustingly physical job of removal that faced the crime scene technicians who were being flown in from D.C. We stood there, looking down at the bodies. Jasper Campise's shirt looked like he was trying to relive his more youthful days and try on some of his "thin" clothing. He was bursting out of his shirt from the stomach. But it was the position of his pants that told of the shame of his death.

His gray work pants, belt and all, were pulled down around his knees. The ridiculous pair of blue bikini underpants he had been wearing still covered his private parts. Had Mrs. Campise found these bikini shorts sexy? Did Jasper think that as a 65-year-old man, grossly overweight, it made him sexually attractive? It was pitiful beyond my comprehension.

Marc, ever playing the scientist, explained to me, "His face is distortedly large and black, Elaine, because the blood pooled there after he was garroted. They twisted a thin piece of wire around this guy's neck, suffocating him, but also breaking the neck with the force of the twist."

There were also various puncture wounds on Campise's torso, one with a portion of his bowel protruding, making me think it looked like his penis had popped out of his pants. But Marc explained it as being the bowel, much to my relief.

John Gattuso, or the hideous distortion both Marc and I had identified as him, looked as if he were bursting out of his clothes too. Poor doe-eyed Gattuso, husband of Carmella, the bitch, had been the proverbial screw-up, the constant loser in life. One of his relatives had told us he was always thinking up new schemes and they always went bust — except for John's Popcorn, a small shop that sold popcorn in downtown Chicago. You had to sell a great deal of popcorn to live well.

Now Johnny was stuffed into the trunk of a Volvo, his skin blackened in the process of baking in temperatures that rose to well above 170 degrees.[64] His cheap working man's clothing also had pulled away from his bloated body. There were various puncture wounds visible up and down Gattuso's torso and his neck also had a very tight thin wire around it.

It had been a mortifying experience when I arrived at the apartment building parking lot and was eyed by every Naperville copper because I had foolishly not changed back into my work clothes. I had a difficult time convincing them of who I was, and I was so self-conscious in my short shorts and T-shirt that it inhibited my ability to do my job. Besides that, the mosquitoes were having a field day with my bare legs.

The Naperville Police Department had graciously offered the use of a large repair garage to the FBI, to which they towed Campise's Volvo. Jasper and Johnny would wait patiently for the examiners to arrive. We were ready to leave. Marc walked me to my car. It was almost midnight and I was feeling like shit — hungry, sleepy, and itchy. But at least I was with a friend and could talk business and not be looked at as if I didn't belong there. Marc and I went over the facts of the past week.

"It must have been the lab report I sent over on Tuesday of last week to Paul Nealis, you know, the Assistant State's Attorney prosecuting Gattuso and Campise for attempted murder," said Marc.

"Oh, yes, I know him," I replied sort of impatiently. The report had revealed the entire miraculous discovery of both Gattuso's and Campise's hairs being found in Eto's car. It couldn't be mentioned casually to me. It also had to have expressions of gratitude and credit given to Tom and those great evidence agents who undertook another one of the unglamorous FBI jobs that often bring headline-smashing results.

"Well," Marc continued in his careful, always so meticulous manner, "that report did say the FBI lab had found Jasper Campise's hair in the front seat of Joe's car."

"But how did the Outfit find out about that evidence so quickly?" I asked.

"You're asking me?" Marc replied a little testily.

"I'm sorry, Marc. It's been a long night." We could only guess how the word got out about the lab findings. "(An) evidence hearing in criminal court and the records disclosed that FBI forensic experts had found hair of the same type as Gattuso's in the backseat and on the back of the front seat of Eto's car. The FBI said the hair strands from the car matched those removed from Gattuso's scalp."[65] That evidence must have been the reason the big boys decided they had to say bye-bye to our guys in the trunk there.

We later learned that Carmella had said Johnny left their apartment on Tuesday, July 12 around 9 a.m. to get some construction materials he needed for the remodeling he was doing to their apartment in the Little Italy neighborhood of Chicago. And Josephine Campise, wife of Jasper Campise, said he had left their condo between 9 a.m. and 9:30 a.m. on Tuesday, July 12 to meet his brother at a funeral chapel to make final arrangements for the wake of a friend. When Jasper failed to appear at the chapel to meet his brother, or at his "antiques store," his family became worried.[66]

Until we got the maggot report, [67] we were figuring Jasper and Johnny had been killed on Tuesday, July 12. One of the neighbors had reported not seeing or smelling the car until that day, Thursday, July 14. This guy always parked in the same spot, which would have been next to the Volvo, and he said he would have noted the car's presence.

It was really late now, and I was miles and miles away from home. There was nothing else I was going to be able to do here. The bodies were going to stay where they were until 6:30 a.m., when Walsh had volunteered to pick up the examiners from the airport.

I decided to take my inappropriately dressed self home, slather some lotion on my legs to stop the itching from the mosquito bites, and go to bed. My first call in the morning would be to Jerry, the U.S. Marshal, to ask him to have Joe call me. I hoped Joe would feel some sort of revenge, but there was a nagging thought in my mind that retribution was not part of his life strategy. His philosophy was all about honor and not bringing shame to oneself. But, me, I was someone different, and I still couldn't wait to tell him.

- CHAPTER TWELVE -
Who Killed the Killers?

After I slipped into my nightgown and eased my drained, insect-stung body into bed that night, my mind screamed with painful, violent thoughts. Was I a victim of my own success? Violence now followed me as part of my life and my career. Joe Eto had been shot three times in the head and left to die on a freezing winter night. The two men who had botched Eto's execution had been strangled with wire, then stabbed, and finally stuffed and obscenely baked in the trunk of their car. Other people who crossed my FBI path were quickly rubbed out because of my association with them. The perpetrators and the victims of these crimes had all known each other for many years. They had been associates in a very violent and disgusting business, and I bore witness and was a party to their carnage.

Random thoughts penetrated and pulsed into my brain. I remembered the day when I unexpectedly found the bloody shirt that Tommy had been wearing when he had been shot. Staring at the relic, I pushed my little finger into the bullet entry hole and then on through the exit hole — Tommy and death had battled each other in the small front-to-back space between these tiny apertures. My beloved husband somehow won his battle. Joe Eto had also grappled with the deadly bees and survived — the recognition of this strange, intimate, and violent symmetry in my life caused me to shiver. It had been a long, stressful evening — there was little left of me. I was exhausted. Dark thoughts were my pillow that hot July 15 night as I tossed about in my bed on an ocean of nasty dreams.

When I awoke, I realized I had slept in late, but I didn't care. Lying on my side, I looked out my bedroom window. The sun shone on the leaves of the tree that grew between our house and our neighbor's. I was cozy.

The dreams and painful thoughts no longer concerned me. The only thing bothering me now was my itchy legs. Damn those mosquitoes, and damn me for wearing shorts last night.

I wanted to relieve my irritation. A shower was my first priority. Afterward, I applied soothing anti-itch gel to my legs. Something I would bring to work today for sure. Getting dressed was sort of a no-brainer for me after being an agent for four years. I had a delightful wardrobe in which just about everything was new, stylish, and fit me well. I was blessed to fit into a size four or six of Max Mara or Armani.

Tom hated it when salespeople from Saks called me. "How much do you spend to make them personally call you?" he asked once after taking a message from a sales clerk.

"They are just calling to tell me about a sale. That should be good news for you," I replied, brushing him off. I was never going to admit how much I spent on clothing. First of all, he'd die, and secondly, I didn't really want to add it up myself. It was better not to know and keep enjoying life.

When I got downstairs, the house was empty. Where were Kimmy and Grandma? I looked outside and realized Grandma's car was not there. Kim was now 12 and had taken a part-time job with one of her friends as an assistant camp counselor at a nearby park. Grams must have driven her over there. The camp counselor thing had surprised me. Kim had hated babysitting, and I never thought being a camp counselor to a bunch of 7- and 8-year-olds would be fun for her. In fact, she had never played with dolls and had never shown any interest in child care.

Kids are always amazing. I know I continued to dumbfound my mother by not quitting work when Kim was born, by going to night school to get my graduate degree, by leaving home for four months to train to be an FBI agent, and by working 12-hour days — all things she thought took me away from being in the home and being a full-time mother and wife.

I often wondered what my dad would have thought. He had been vastly more impressed with my degree than my mother, so proud I had even been a school teacher. Once, as a beginning teacher, I mentioned I needed a wristwatch because I had to time the breaks in my lesson plans. My dad went out that day and bought me a Timex watch. I wore it every day and planned the cadence of my constantly changing "teaching show" to keep my students' attention. I wore it in honor of how thoughtful he had been.

Since no one was home to "kibitz"[68] with, and I knew Marc and Bobbie would be on the lookout for me, I jumped into my car, old number 69, and headed down to work. It was after rush hour and traffic was light. Once in the office, I stopped at Tommy's squad to sip my coffee and tell him about last night.

"The worst of it was the mosquitoes, although the smell was something I didn't need to experience," I said.

"You should have smoked a cigar. That's what all the homicide dicks do," he advised me.

"Right. That would have made me sicker. So I think I'm going to tell everyone that these two murders are your fault because you were the one who insisted we get that car and have it gone over for evidence. Finding their hairs is all your doing. What can I say? Those two murders are on your hands." And with that quick jab, I got up and walked away, waving and saying, "See you tonight."

Once I got to my squad area, our secretary, Pat, told me that Bobbie and Marc were out in Naperville with the examiners and probably wouldn't be in all day. Good. That meant they would leave me alone. I picked up the phone and called Jerry.

"U.S. Marshals," Jerry answered the phone.

"FBI," I replied.

"Hey. How ya doing, beautiful?" Jerry asked.

"You know how to get on a girl's good side, don't you?"

"Never been there. I must not be doing the right thing."

"Fat chance, Jerry."

"I think I know why you are calling."

"I think you probably do, and if I could talk to him, I would greatly appreciate it," I replied.

"Well, we're not as dumb as you might think.[69] I've contacted Eto's handler and he called me. I told him about the murders. But I'll call him again and he can call you, okay?"

"That would make my day. Thanks so much, Jerry."

"Okay, will do. Take care. Bye."

Well, that son of a bitch just went and took all the pleasure I was going to have in telling Joe about Gattuso's and Campise's murders. He just had to tell him. Shit!

In about an hour, Joe called, and I heard his raspy, low, familiar voice on the phone.

"Yeah, I kinda thought it might happen to Johnny, but Jay, um, um, Vince musta been awful mad."

"Joe, I don't think we have talked to you since we got the lab results back from your car. Inside your car, they found hairs from both Gattuso and Campise. Marc sent the FBI's laboratory results to the Assistant State's Attorney on Tuesday, July 6. The State's Attorney had a hearing on Thursday, July 8 at which they told Nick DeJohn and Louie Carbonara of the evidence found in your car."

"Oh, that did it. That did it. No ifs, ands, or buts. That did it," he said. He chuckled. "So you found their hairs in that car?" he asked incredulously.

"Yeah, Joe. Isn't that amazing?" I said. "So, now we flew in some people from D.C. to go through Campise's car and go over the bodies to see if they can find any trace evidence to lead us to someone. But, let's try to think about who could have done it."

"Two at once," he said. "You have to have several people to make sure you get them."

"Joe…they were not shot. They were garroted and then knifed — like deeply jabbed several times," I interjected.

"Well, Vince would want to make sure it was done right this time," he said.

"So you think he would have been there?" I asked.

"Oh, I would imagine so."

"The car was found in Naperville."

"That's close to where Vince lives," Joe said.

"It is? I didn't know that," I replied.

"Well, you have to look at the crew, and they would be the ones to do it. Getting anyone else would be a sign of Vince's weakness, and he's already in a vulnerable position," He paused for a moment. "So you got hairs in that car? Any fingerprints?"

"No fingerprints, Joe. Just hairs." I replied. "Hey, Joe?"

"Yeah."

"Will you call me back next Tuesday when Marc is here?" I asked.

"Sure, I don't think they'll mind. Next Tuesday about this time?"

"Perfect. About this time," I answered. "Joe, take care now."

"Oh, yeah. I'll do that." He said it as if it were a silly thing for me to say. He had been taking care of himself for 49 years and now wasn't the time to get a mother. "Bye."

The line was dead. "Look for the murderers in the north side crew," he had said. What a joke. They were the oldest group around. I didn't think Gattuso or Campise would just sit down and say, "Oh, okay, I know I fucked up Eto's hit. You go ahead and strangle me with that wire. I won't mind the deep, organ-destroying stab wounds you're going to give me up and down my torso. Ah, and don't forget to pull down my pants. That will be a nice humiliating touch."

No, someone had to do these hits fast. And they had to be done by someone strong. Instantly the name Ronnie Ignoffo came to my mind. Yeah. He was young, strong, and an up-and-comer. He had been at a

Christmas party in 1979 and Joe had to ask Tony Juliano who he was. Juliano had told him, "He's one of the guys who work for Caesar in his bookie operation. He's a black belt in karate."

Eto told me Ronnie looked like a weight lifter. He remembered he had been a bouncer at a nightclub, FACES, on Rush Street — the spot for the cocaine-using hippest crowd in Chicago and for mobsters trying to show off their tough-guy personas.[70] Other than that, we knew nothing about this north side crew member. In my way of thinking, he had to be a good candidate for the murder squad.

Eto, as an older man, had always done what he had been told. Vince hadn't realized how keen Joe's intuition was or that Joe had understood Vince's paranoia. He didn't think Eto saw the hit coming. Jasper and Johnny had been okay to do the job on Joe. Eto would have been alone and compliant. If Vince had really thought out the success of this Eto hit, he might not have chosen Jasper. He could have recalled that Jasper had been arrested for a previous killing when the coppers caught him running away from the scene. If Campise hadn't been able to get the case fixed, he might have been convicted.

The Gattuso and Campise hits had to go perfectly. Joe said Vince Solano was a hothead. Vince may have been one of those bullies who make you think they are going to punish you, but then have to recruit some of their buddies to do the job because they aren't brave enough to do it themselves. Maybe he was afraid that if he got in there to mix it up, he might lose or get hurt. This was how Joe taught me to think about the character of Vince Solano. According to Joe, he had been there. He would have had to make sure the job was carried out and the two fuck-ups were dead. Vince could take no more chances. His life depended on it. In my mind, the killing party consisted of Vince Solano, Ronnie Ignoffo, John Mattassa, and Babe DeMonte.

By the time Marc and Bobbie got into the office the next day, both of them were grim-faced and had little to say about what it was like to watch the forensic examiners do their thing with the bloated, rotting bodies of the two hoodlums. Bobbie did say he smoked a cigar, but Marc said he'd rather tolerate the smell than have the taste of a cigar in his mouth.

Marc could be a little prissy about things. In fact, he said he had never even tasted a beer. That, to me, was implausible. I couldn't wait to taste beer, wine, a martini, or any forbidden alcoholic drink. I had hated the taste of them all, but that hadn't stopped me from swilling my share of beer in college. I had never developed a taste for a martini. I first ordered one at a pretend grown-up lunch with a girlfriend while shopping. Result: the urge of wanting to projectile vomit onto the table . Not cool.

I got Marc's attention as soon as he had settled down, and I was able to talk to him about my conversation with Joe and my thoughts of likely suspects.

"Round up the usual suspects, Smitty," he playfully replied to my carefully reasoned killing squad.

"Very funny, Ziegler. Who do you think did it?" I asked.

"Oh, crap," he swore.[71] "I haven't any ideas. I think I'm so exhausted and shell-shocked from all of this that I need some time to recharge my batteries."

"I understand, Marc," I said as I rose from the visitor's chair next to his desk, "but the first thing you should do is order the phone records for the two corpses to see if we can figure out who set up this meeting."

There was an inertia that settled over us for the next couple of weeks. Marc had been given the case to try to solve the murders of Gattuso and Campise, but it seemed as if we were all waiting for the evidentiary miracle to happen again. Those experts would surely find something in the trunk of that car or on those bodies that would point us in the right direction, wouldn't they? I would have rousted every last one of the north side crew down to the FBI office for fingerprints and hair samples just to screw with them, because logic and Joe told us that it had to be them. Who knows which one was the weak link and would break under whatever pressure we could put on them? But I wasn't the case agent, so I didn't push the matter.

Then, on August 8, the Chicago Police found John Gattuso's "black Chevrolet Silverado parked near a construction company where Gattuso last was seen alive on July 12, the day he disappeared ...." [72] I never knew there was a construction company he had gone to in that neighborhood, but I did know that Frank Orlando's porno shop was no more than 20 feet from the corner at which Johnny parked.

"Marc, we have got to go rattle Frank Orlando's chain. This is where they lured Gattuso and Campise to kill them. I've driven by there a million times. It's a dump and it looks as if the porno shop is the only occupant in the whole building. What a perfect place!" I was off and running with my imagination.

"Maybe you've got something there, Smitty," Marc said. "I'll call Jeremy and get a subpoena we can lay on him when we interview him."

Good, good, I was thinking. "While you're at it, get a subpoena for Ronnie Ignoffo. You know he is one of the strong-arm guys, and Vince and Caesar would rely on him to subdue Gattuso once he realized it was time to get tortured to death."

"I'll ask. It can't hurt," Marc said.

"Okay, let me know when you get the paper. I can't wait."

Marc got the subpoenas in just a couple of days, and we planned our calendars to interview both Frank Orlando and Ronnie Ignoffo on the same day. We'd make an afternoon of it. Marc wanted to start out at this Italian bakery he had found just west of the downtown area. They served pizza bread that he loved — enormous hunks of bread with miniscule bits of tomato on top. He would eat two large pieces and be full for days. No wonder. I nibbled on it but found the hunk of bread less than satisfying. Nevertheless, I enjoyed hanging out and watching Marc savor every bite of his total carbohydrate lunch. I was into carbohydrates too, although I enjoyed a little fat with mine. Finishing the pizza bread, we moved on to porno.

In the late 1970s, the FBI had conducted a lot of raids on the publishing house of a porno king. Once they got their hands on the stuff, the government decided to back down on prosecuting him. That decision left the Bureau with a case that was not going to get prosecuted and virtually tons of pornographic magazines, sex toys, and videos stowed in its evidence files. Some clever and horny agent had discovered this stash, and whenever there was a Title III wiretap[73], the wire room[74] was always well stocked with porno to help agents pass the time. Today that wouldn't happen, but when I sat on wires, I learned all about the kinkiest, sickest sexual behaviors from those magazines.

We cruised over to Frank Orlando's dumpy porno shop, located in a cruddy neighborhood. The storefront façade had been "rehabbed" in 1960s Aspen wood siding. It was a dirty piss pot building at the end of a wet dream rainbow. I had never been in a porno shop, so I was a bit apprehensive about entering.

We opened the door and entered a room filled with glass display cases like those found in an old candy store. Little peep show booths lined one wall, running the full depth of the building. Just inside the entryway behind the cash counter, a very dark-skinned, black-haired, little old wizened guy sat reading a magazine.

"Sir, is Frank Orlando here?" Marc asked.

"Who wants to know?" he replied.

Marc whipped out his credentials and said, "I'm Marc Ziegler with the FBI and this is Agent Smith, also with the FBI." I dug out my ID from my purse and waved it at him.

"Well, I'm Frank Orlando. What can I do for you?"

"This is an interesting establishment you have. Could you explain the layout to us?" Marc bullshitted.

Mr. Orlando, who apparently took great pride in his operation, got off his stool and told us about the live peep shows that were ongoing 24 hours a day in the 12 booths. He had copies of almost every sexual periodical published in English and now many in Spanish and Polish. He laughed when he told us about the change in his clientele. Orlando was just warming up. "Over here in these glass cases, I have a nice selection of sexual toys. I have vibrators, dildos, whips, chains, lubricators. You name it, it's here." He laughed. Then he looked at me and said, "Come over here and I'll give you a preview of a peep show."

I always wanted to see what one was like, so I said, "Okay," and walked over to where he stood. Marc was close behind. Poor guy, maybe he thought Frankie was going to kidnap me into sexual servitude. The three of us entered a small booth made of painted green plywood. A lone folding chair was located in the middle of the tiny booth, and a mechanical coin collector was positioned just below a picture window at the back. When Orlando put a quarter into this slot, the curtains covering the window drew back, and lo and behold, not 10 feet away was a young Filipino woman dressed in a G-string and pasties. Immediately she began a suggestive dance. It lasted about 10 seconds and the curtains closed.

"Want to see some more?" Orlando asked.

"Yeah, one more time," I said.

Orlando dropped in another quarter and the curtains whipped back. The woman resumed her dance — another few seconds of titillation — then the curtains slashed closed.

I commented to Frank, "I can see how a guy could drop a lot of quarters in the slot before seeing what approximates a partial dance."

His reply was simply a grunt. Guess he had used up all his charm. The peep show was over. We filed out of the little viewing room. Marc and I spent some time pretending to be looking at the bins of porno magazines, just killing time while we checked out the place. Orlando went back to his stool in front of the window.

Marc finally had enough and wandered to the counter to talk to our suspected murderer. Well, I'll say "suspected accomplice to murder" because this little old man weighed no more than 120 pounds, and fighting him would have been like fighting me, only maybe easier.

Marc leaned on the counter, looked at Orlando and began a long series of questions. "When was the last time you saw Jasper Campise?"

Orlando responded and Marc continued his questioning. Orlando ducked and dodged every question. Surrounded by dildos and sex toys I grew hot — but only under the collar. Listening to Orlando's bullshit, disrespectful answers to Marc's questions made my skin crawl. Finally, when the porno master answered, "I've met a great number of people in my day," like he was some kind of late-night talk show host, I could no longer control myself and jumped into the interview.

"We have cause to believe you were involved in the murders of John Gattuso and Jasper Campise. If you think we are going to stand here and let you think we don't know you are one big fucking liar, you are fucking mistaken. You know each and every person my partner asked you about, including Ken fucking Eto, who told us all about you. If you ever need your skinny ass saved, you have our cards." Frankie Orlando appeared stunned. I walked out and Marc followed me.

We walked down the street. "Well, I guess you told him," Marc said. He looked at me and together we started laughing.

"Oh, shit, Marc. I couldn't take it anymore. I wanted to slap him. I was just enraged that he treated your questions with such disregard."

"Do you think his 'skinny ass' will call us if he ever decides to flip?"

We both started laughing until I had to stop walking and cross my legs so I wouldn't pee in my pants. These Mob old-timers were hardcore assholes. I'd swear they killed Johnny Gattuso and Jasper Campise in the basement of that porn shop, but Joe Eto thought it could have been in Vince Solano's house. I doubted that.

Next we headed for Ronnie Ignoffo's house. It was a two-flat brick apartment building in a lower-middle-class neighborhood. The neighborhood gangs had sprayed graffiti on fences and garage doors. Ronnie's world was definitely not participating in the re-gentrification taking place in much of Chicago. This was a kick-ass, "send your kid to Catholic school" neighborhood. Marc and I went up to the front door and saw "Ignoffo" written in pencil on a label under one of the three doorbells. We rang the bell, not knowing if Ignoffo was at work. It didn't matter, if we didn't get an answer we would wait in the car. We rang it again. We could hear the bell inside the apartment on the first floor. At least we knew it worked so we didn't need to pound on the door. Door pounding with my fists didn't come easy to me so instead I usually kicked at the door. That was always effective. Maybe this technique was a bit brat-like and disrespectful, but a girl has to get attention somehow. This time I pushed the bell with no result.

There was no one home at Mr. Murder Incorporated Ignoffo's house, so Marc and I returned to his Bureau car. Since Marc was our supervisor's pet, he had the nicest car on the squad. We settled in for a quiet wait. This was something you learned to do in the FBI. Wait. And wait. And wait. That is why so many of us work crossword puzzles. I always have something in my purse to read. "We can sit for an hour and barely get settled in," is what I told Kimmy's flute teacher when I would wait outside her house each Saturday morning while Kim took her flute lesson.

We didn't have to wait long, because a vehicle pulled into a nearby parking space and out stepped Ronnie Ignoffo. He walked toward his door. Marc and I exited our car, which was parked right in front of his house.

"Excuse me, sir," Marc said.

Ronnie turned around as both Marc and I approached him. We made certain he had nothing in his hands. I noted he was wearing no jacket. Both Marc and I knew exactly how we were going to get our guns out quickly. None of these tactics had been discussed, but we both knew that this was going to be a confrontational interview with a very strong man. Not to put Marc's strength in question, but I was shooting first and asking questions later if Ignoffo came after me.

"Excuse me, sir. Are you Ronald Ignoffo?"

"Yeah," Ronnie replied.

"I am Marc Ziegler with the FBI, and this is my partner, Elaine Smith, also a special agent with the FBI. We have a few questions we would like to ask you."

Ignoffo nodded his head.

I could see he was not going to be a man of many words. I noted he was trembling ever so slightly, and he had instantly begun to sweat.

Marc used the warm-up question of, "Where is it that you work, Mr. Ignoffo?"

"I work for the Chicago Department of Streets and Sanitation and have worked there, uh, uh, maybe 16 months." Then he gave the name and number of his boss.

I thought, well, aren't you a wealth of information, and isn't it convenient that you have a city job, particularly in a department known for its corruption and close ties to organized crime.

"Well, Mr. Ignoffo, we are here to talk to you about the deaths of Jasper Campise and John Gattuso on either July 12 or 13 of this year."

"I was at work," he immediately replied.

Marc retorted, "You weren't at work 24 hours a day for both July 12 and July 13, were you?"

"You can call my supervisor at Streets and San and he'll tell you," Ronnie said.

"He'll tell us what, Ron?" I interjected.

Now Ron switched to looking at me.

"What?" he asked.

"What will your supervisor tell us?" I repeated.

"I was at work on those days," he said.

"Will he tell me you worked all day on July 12 and all through the next day on July 13? Was there an emergency at Streets and San?" I asked, but not in a snotty way because I didn't really want to piss off this guy. He looked scared.

"He'll tell you I came to work on whatever days he said." He pointed to Marc.

Marc must have decided I was a loose cannon due to my "fuck your skinny ass" routine with Frankie Orlando, so he took the interview back into his own hands.

"Where did you work before you got your job at Streets and Sanitation?"

"I was a bouncer at Blondie's and I worked for Ken Dino and Billy Smith." Ignoffo felt compelled to tell us who his bosses were so we could go check with them. Maybe he thought that we would believe everything he said if they verified he had worked for them. What a joke. We knew Billy Smith was a front for Vincent Solano, Jr. and that Vincent Solano, Jr. was a front for his old man.

"Did you know John Gattuso very well?" was Marc's next question.

"I don't know John Gattuso," Ronnie said. "My father was a good friend of Jasper Campise's and he was a friend of my family's for a long time. I never talked to him about his business and he seemed very private about his doings."

Well, this boy was a regular magpie. He was telling us stuff, all bullshit, but information that we weren't even asking for. Then it dawned on me where we were. We were just blocks away from Jasper Campise's "antique store" and the neighborhood hangout next door, the "American Legion Hall."[75] Perhaps old man Ignoffo went in there to play cards and hang around.

"Do you have any idea why Jasper Campise was murdered?" Marc asked boldly.

"I only know what I read in the papers. I think there was fear that organized crime might think he would turn informant."

Marc continued on asking Ronnie if he knew Vic Arrigo, and the answer was yes since Vic's car lot was just a few blocks from his house.

Did he know Joseph DiVarco?

"Yes — family friend for years."

Had he ever met Ken Eto?

"Um, on one occasion," he said, but he couldn't remember what, or where, that occasion was.

Finally, even I was getting bored, so Marc finished the line of questioning that was getting us nowhere. But Ignoffo was now sweating like a pig and had big circles of sweat under his arms.

"Do you know the martial arts?"

"Uh, I know about the martial arts. I work out every night at the Irving Park YMCA and really don't spend much time getting to know, you know, the people of the street."

I perked up and found this answer very tantalizing. My husband had been a devoted member of the Irving Park YMCA since he was 15 years old. There would be very few regulars who were weight lifters who he would not know. Maybe Tom knew Ignoffo and could give us more of Ignoffo's weight-lifting partners to talk to.

Marc was at the end of his rope, so as a courtesy to me, and being very daring because he never knew what would come out of my mouth, he turned to me and formally said, "Agent Smith, do you have anything to ask Mr. Ignoffo?"

"Yes, I do, Agent Ziegler," I shot back.

I turned directly to Ronnie Ignoffo and looked at him until our eyes met. As I was staring at him, I said. "You killed Jasper Campise and Johnny Gattuso, didn't you?"

The hair on Ignoffo's arms stood straight up and goose bumps appeared all over his arms. He abruptly stopped looking at me, turned, and walked up the stairs into his house.

"Well, Marc, he didn't deny it."

"Geez, Smitty, sometimes you scare me."

We walked to the car and silently drove away, both of us contemplating our afternoon and Ignoffo's reaction to our interview. If only we could begin to squeeze him somehow. Ignoffo was our weak link.

When we got back to the office, we told Bobbie about our experiences with Frank Orlando and Ronnie Ignoffo and then went back to our desks. Marc would dictate the interviews while they were fresh in his mind. The FBI had a saying: "If it wasn't on paper, it didn't happen." That was actually the truth. Every step you took and every interview you conducted had to be documented. The trail of the investigation could be proven and laid out before the prosecutor and hopefully the jury one day. It was a discipline that did make us the best law enforcement agency in the world. J. Edgar Hoover did not mess around. You followed procedure or your ass was out. You followed procedure and your cases were tight and ready for prosecution. Hoover had his personal issues, but on this topic he was dead on.

By September, Marc and I had already visited with Joe Eto in Oklahoma City, Dallas, Houston, and Little Rock. These were "neutral cities" — cities in which Joe had never lived. On our trip to Oklahoma City, we were accompanied by Dan, the attorney who prosecuted Eto on the gambling case. He was a very busy man and could stay only an hour or two. In that short time, he warned Joe about his immunity and that he could never lie. He also warned Joe about never going back to Chicago — generally he acted like an arrogant ass. However, he did say the government was going to try to work out a plea agreement to six months suspended probation to satisfy Joe's gambling conviction. That sounded good to Joe and us.

We planned on staying for three days in Oklahoma City, and we did, but it was the first and last time I allowed the U.S. Marshals make any hotel arrangements for us. The Marshal in Oklahoma thought staying at a Holidome would be a thrill beyond words for both Marc and I. Marc had no children and didn't particularly like to swim. I was a snob and was horrified to be staying at a Holiday Inn — breathing the chlorine fumes that seeped into the room all night from the pool just outside my door, listening to the little children screaming and running around and in the pool, and seeing their obese parents wallowing in the hot tubs every time we went to and from our rooms.

The Marshals explained that due to "security reasons" they had to provide another motel room to be our "debriefing room" and it had to be at a third hotel. That hotel turned out to be a Motel 6 on the major interstate that ran through Oklahoma City. If you opened the door of the room, you heard the noise of hundreds of trucks traveling across the U.S.A.

After Dan, the prosecuting attorney, left the room, I turned to Joe and Marc and said, "I can't stand sitting in this room, in this dump of a motel on an interstate. Let's go find out where the rich people live in Oklahoma City and scope out where we are going to make reservations for dinner tonight." We had been bright enough to tell the Marshal that he shouldn't come and pick up Joe until 10 p.m. because we had a great deal of work to do with him.

So off the three of us went in the Lincoln Continental I had rented. I had found out that Budget Rental Cars would give the government rate of only $5 more a day for a luxury car. So each and every time we met Joe, we rode in style, usually Marc and I up front and Mr. Eto, smoking his brains out, in the back.

This was our game in every town we went to. We would find the fanciest neighborhoods, the best hotels, and the finest restaurants. I would always drive a luxury vehicle, and after a while the Marshals allowed Joe to stay at the hotels with us. They would drop him off on Monday morning and pick him up on Friday afternoon.

Every day we'd meet for breakfast at 8:30 or 9 a.m. because Marc and I liked to run first. Joe would have coffee, black, and a toasted English muffin or bagel. Marc and I would have whatever struck our fancy. Then we'd return to either Marc's room or mine for the entire day. Joe would be interrogated by the prosecutor about his knowledge of people, places, or events in preparation for the government's cases against the mobsters. We would break for a light lunch, go for a short walk, and then go back to work.

Dinner was at 6:30 p.m., and it wasn't until Joe had his first martini, "dry, dry, dry, with a twist of lemon," that he relaxed. I know he was the most relaxed and comfortable with me because he always sat next to me and deferred to my wishes at all times. We were easy with each other and could sit without talking for long periods of time, or talk about all sorts of things having nothing to do with the Mob or the cases. When I would get particularly snobby or outrageous, he'd laugh at me and say, "Elaine, you are somethin' else."

One hot, humid Houston evening federal prosecutor Jeremy Margolis joined our trio for dinner. As we sipped drinks at a table near the hotel pool, Jeremy pulled a trick on us. Earlier, unknown to Joe, Marc or me, he asked the beautiful daughter of the hotel manager to approach Joe. Out of nowhere, in the middle of our conversation, she walked over to our table and stood next to Joe. Marc stiffened and placed his hand on his gun hidden in his gym bag. But her approach was friendly, and her movements were hot and sultry. She leaned over and sensuously pressed herself up against Joe's body. Then slowly she licked his ear before whispering into it.

"Hi Joe. I hear they call you Donkey Cock, and I'd love to find out why." Her husky voice was loud enough for all to hear.

Startled, Joe took a moment to gather his thoughts, then he smiled and looked up at Jeremy who obviously was doing his best to restrain a reaction. Almost immediately, Joe caught on to the set-up. He laughed hard and said to Jeremy, "If you could get her to do that, I'd follow you anywhere!"

They thought it was the funniest thing in the world. I, on the other hand, thought it was disgusting, and I was embarrassed to be at the same table with them. I said so, then got up and left.

Joe came after me and said, "Yes, Jeremy was being childish, but the woman apparently wasn't offended, and I should just ignore his actions because they weren't directed at me."

I didn't want to be the goofy bitch who storms off in a huff, so I came back to the table with Joe and told Margolis, "You are so disgusting, Jeremy. Don't do that again when you're with me, okay?"

He replied with something like, "Yeah, yeah, yeah, and you know what…," and continued on with the story he was telling Marc. Sometimes he acted like a child with Attention Deficit Disorder who had just committed some socially inappropriate act. However, I also needed to understand the world of male bonding. I realized it had nothing to do with disrespect for me, and in his mind his actions were not offensive to the young woman — I guess. I just hoped no man ever had a little fun with Jeremy's daughter that same way.

Our week long trips to meet Joe were tightly planned and took place almost every month for the first 18 months Joe was in the Witness Security Program (WSP). It was a relaxed, unstressed schedule.

When it came time for Joe to testify for the first time, both Marc and I were as nervous as parents at the recital of their only child. The prosecutor walked Joe through the types of questions he would ask him on the stand.

I offered my advice to help him become a credible witness, suggesting he open his eyes wider. He would try and then laugh at me, saying, "They are open as wide as I can get them." I would coach him to make sure he remembered to look at the jury. They were the people he had to convince and who had to believe him.

When Joe appeared for testimony, his transportation and safety were in the hands of the U.S. Marshals. I thanked God I didn't have to plan the security for getting him into Chicago and to the courthouse. The time Joe walked onto the stand to testify was always prearranged with the judge so that he was whisked into the courtroom and then removed immediately after his testimony.

Marc and I would always see Joe the night before he testified, usually with the prosecutor, who would review the types of questions he was going to be asking him once again. Joe never wavered. Over a 17-year period, he never changed an answer in response to any of the questions he had previously been given by us, or any of the prosecutors. This was the most stunning capability he possessed.

When Marc and I had talked about it, we came to the conclusion that Joe was an expert gambler because he could count cards. He had a remarkable if not almost photographic memory.

Watching Joe testify was anticlimactic for me. He did it with ease and aplomb. "Oh, sure," he would say, or "Certainly, it would be that way," or "Hi, Louie," greeting the defense attorney approaching the witness chair for cross-examination. From the witness chair, when he was asked to point out Louis Marino and Rocky Infelice, two murdering sons of bitches, he waved at them and then told the prosecutor they had been his friends.

This was not some crazy man up on the witness stand. It wasn't a man trying to prove something to himself or to the world. It was simply a man telling the world the truth because, as he said: "They took my freedom away. I can't walk the street. I have to fight them. They muffed it. ... There

is no alternative. This is justified, right? I cannot be very dishonorable. …
If they leave me no alternative, why should I … feel bad?"[76]

- CHAPTER THIRTEEN -
The Last Supper

"Are you ready, honey?" I asked Tom.

"Yeah, just let me get my creds and gun." Tommy always carried his gun, a Sig Sauer .45 semiautomatic. It was a Bureau rule, and we were meeting Joe, who still probably had a contract on his life.

But that evening I would not be carrying my gun, a 9-mm semiautomatic Glock. The color of the weapon matched my dress, but there was no way to conceal it. Tonight I wanted people to look at me, not my gun. I wore a short black silk sheath, hand-painted with a few subtle colored flowers. Hand-painted — that's why I bought it. It was like wearing a piece of expensive art. I did a final check in the full-length mirror. I fit the mood of the evening perfectly — outside a band playing Hawaiian music gently filled the night air, and ocean sounds drifted into our Mauna Lani Bay hotel room on soft, warm, salty breezes — the dress I wore was short and accentuated my best attribute, my long, shapely legs. I slipped my tanned feet into a pair of black silk open-toed heels. It was one of those moments when I felt almost too cool for any man to handle.

"Did you let Kimmy know anything about tonight?" Tom asked me as we walked out of our hotel room.

"I just told her we had a dinner to attend and we'd see her tomorrow," I replied. Kimmy, our 28-year-old daughter and only child, was on the Big Island of Hawaii with us, along with her husband Greg. What did she care? She was also vacationing in paradise and didn't need her parents to show her a good time.

The Canoe House restaurant was located on the beach. Tom and I, holding hands as we often did, enjoyed the short walk, listening to the waves, smelling the faint fragrance of saltwater and the lush, moist vegetation just inches from our noses. The ebony sky was filled with stars, and the slight breeze cooled our skin just enough to make it pleasant, but not so much as to give you goose bumps. This was good.

Entering the restaurant, we crossed a small wooden bridge. I looked over the rail. The pond below was filled with koi fish that darted about playfully and shimmered in the underwater lights. Beyond the bridge, the pavilion-like restaurant was aglow with candles and torches. And then, as we neared the entrance, I saw Joe Eto sitting sideways on a barstool, obviously situated so he could watch those entering the restaurant. Next to him sat his daughter, Linda. When Joe caught a glimpse of us, he immediately got up and walked toward me. Years had passed since I last saw him. We hugged lightly and a little awkwardly. This small gesture signified the end of our "official" relationship and the beginning of our personal one. It was now a private friendship, and I no longer had to greet him with a handshake. As we hugged, I felt the soft cashmere of his sports jacket, his one luxurious piece of clothing. A white polyester shirt, cheap tie, and sans-a-belt slacks completed his outfit. These years had not been prosperous for my reformed Mob friend. In fact, they had been downright poverty-stricken. Yet, when Joe found out Tom and I were coming to Hawaii for a vacation, he insisted on treating us to dinner. I had told him that it was too extravagant, but he was insistent. He had to do it. He had to take me out for dinner for the first time in 15 years. I relented. And with that, I allowed myself to step into a private bond between the two of us.

In all our meetings over the years while he taught me about the inner workings of the Chicago Mob, I used government funds to pay for every breakfast, lunch, and dinner we had. I had taken him to the best restaurants. It was no easy task to find a decent place to eat in some of those towns. But I did it purposely, and this act was something that he appreciated.

I had always treated Joe as if he was an important business associate who held my future in his hands. That was simply the truth. Joe was the most important business associate I had or ever would have. His business was running organized gambling. Mine was stopping his business, putting him in jail, and finding and seizing whatever money he had made — a strange association. But neither Joe nor I took our adversarial roles personally. It was just the way business was conducted. He understood it, as did I. There was no personal vendetta. No competition.

People have asked me if I was afraid. I was, but not for my life. The Mob wouldn't kill an FBI agent. That would bring the entire United States Department of Justice down upon them. They knew that would be disastrous for business. The Outfit was all about money, money, and more money. If anyone thinks there is an honor code or trust among comrades, they just haven't listened to hundreds of hours of wiretaps. During my long boring hours of monitoring Outfit phones, hangouts, restaurants, and offices, I can't remember one discussion I heard that had to do with being generous or showing someone an act of kindness. The Chicago Mob, Joe's corporation, specialized in prostitution, pornography, gambling, loan sharking, theft, and scams of every sort. The bribery and corruption of the Chicago Police Department, the Cook County judicial officials, and the Chicago politicians was, de facto, the legal department of the corporation. This department was necessary to ensure that the whole money-making machine kept going without interruption. Murder was also part of the business. If you screwed with the Mob, or you were a threat to the continued success of their business, they would kill you. My fears were always for Joe. Every time he testified in court, he was a target.

The Outfit has a planned procedure, an oral history, so to speak: "How to Commit a Mob Hit." Since 1919, when the Chicago Crime Commission started keeping records, there had been 1,111 gangland slayings, but only 11 had ended with convictions for the killers. Three more cases were "cleared" before the suspects could be arrested because they too became victims of gangland slayings.[77] I wondered which law enforcement agent or judicial official had leaked information to the "boys" that these three were going to be arrested, thereby guaranteeing their deaths. Such information was always appreciated by the Outfit and could earn the source thousands of dollars.

But here was Joe. He had made it. He had been living in Hawaii outside the Witness Protection for the past few years. Linda and I smiled at each other. "Hello, Linda. It's great to see you again." I stepped aside to bring Tommy forward to meet her. "This is my husband, Tom. I think your father has told you about him and our daughter Kimmy." Joe had always referred to our daughter as Kimmy because she was only 12 years old when we'd first met.

Linda replied with a slow, chopped Hawaiian accent, "Oh, yeah, I know all about them and how much my father admires you and your family."

I thought to myself, well, that felt good, but I was saddened that Linda could not have enjoyed a youth as untroubled as the one we had hopefully created for Kimmy. In 1989, in Hawaii on a previous vacation, Joe had insisted I meet his daughter Linda, of whom he was very proud. During that short barhopping evening with her, she had confided to me that it was "a bitch" growing up and attending Catholic schools in Chicago where the nuns and her classmates looked down on her because she was the daughter of a reputed mobster. I guess there wasn't any glamorous fascination surrounding her life, as there was for the New York gangster John Gotti's brats or the fictional children of the HBO superstar Tony Soprano. I felt that Joe would do the honorable thing and take care of his children, but I also knew that Linda's mother had been a gambler and heavy drinker. A mobster father and a gambling, drinking mother sure didn't sound like the ingredients of a blissful childhood.

Joe stepped over to the maitre d' and asked for the table he had reserved under his witness protection name. I had asked him never to tell me his name, or where he lived, while he was in the Witness Protection Program. I had teased him, saying, "All they need to do is threaten to ruin my manicure and I'll give you up." With that silly warning, he had never told me. That night, I learned for the first time that his "chosen" name was Joe Tanaka. It sounded so easy, so common, and so Japanese. I guess those reasons made it a good selection.

Joe lived in four different cities before he moved to Hawaii. Several times the United States Marshals Service made some mistake that caused them to move him on a moment's notice. Norfolk, Virginia, had been the second of his four different "home cities." One time they hadn't screwed up, but Joe, on a chance encounter, had walked past a Chicago Outfit guy in a shopping mall in Norfolk. Their eyes met for just a blink and Joe saw a look of recognition.

After finding out about this, I said, "Oh, shit, Joe. Why did you have to tell him?" By him, I meant Joe's witness security marshal in Norfolk. Joe quietly and patiently explained to me, as a teacher would to a slow student, that he knew the Outfit guy had recognized him, and he knew he would go back to Chicago, or even pick up the phone within minutes, and snitch him out. Joe further justified his actions to me by saying, "I liked my marshal and didn't want him to get hurt or lose his job." When in our next meeting Joe told me what he had given up by leaving Norfolk, I realized he was a very honorable man. Joe proved to me over and over — especially on the night of his attempted assassination, February 10, 1983 — that he was a very brave man.

The waiter took our drink orders and, as usual, Joe ordered a martini, straight up, with just a dash of vermouth and a twist of lemon. Linda ordered a whiskey on the rocks. Damn, these two were grown-up drinkers.

Tom had a beer and I had a glass of white wine. A few sips of the drinks and Joe and I tried to pick up where we had left off years ago. We always had a lot to talk about. We had talked together for thousands of hours. We had eaten breakfast, lunch, and dinner with each other for weeks at a time. We had stayed locked up in hotel rooms all around the United States for 10 to 12 hours a day together, day after day. We smoked our brains out while Joe would teach and tell, and I would ask questions and write down his answers. Now we were here at this fancy restaurant, with the whole evening ahead of us, and the conversation started slowly and awkwardly. I knew it was the inclusion of Tom and Linda. Each individual in this quartet was different from the others.

Linda was a successful businesswoman in Hawaii. Joe was a retired gambler and mobster and Linda's father. Tom and I were FBI special agents, husband and wife. Tom was on the Terrorism Task Force, and I was now a mid-level manager of investigations concerning bank fraud and money laundering. In time, these differences melted away as we ate, drank, and soaked up the setting. Joe and Linda got a little tipsy. Tom and I were sociable. We celebrated my long, strange, and successful relationship with Mr. Eto.

There was another reason for Joe's magnanimous mood and this dinner in Hawaii. He had just received a lump sum payment from the United States of America. With this payment, he told his "handler," the Witness Protection Program Marshal to whom he was assigned, that he was leaving the program. He now had the money to travel and live the life he wanted. He foresaw a life of fishing, relaxing, getting to know some of his children and grandchildren, and, finally, a degree of financial security.

Financial security is an unknown state for a mobster. The earnings from an illegal business or the proceeds from stealing from someone else were constantly threatened by the possibility that some "rogue" law enforcement officer might shut it down. Fixing this could cost a fortune in either legal fees or bribes to avoid jail time. Afterward, the mobster would have to start over, scrapping again in the very competitive gambling or prostitution businesses — somehow surviving by scamming and stealing. Then there were always the bosses who eyed a bigger cut of the profits. At a moment's notice, the boss might want a little more to cover whatever financial hardship he might be experiencing. These upper management mobsters had a way of demanding: "Whatever is yours is mine."

The sum I was able to justify as Joe's lump sum payment was six figures. It had taken him a decade and a half to earn it and it had never been guaranteed or promised. I had told Joe that I would do my best to get him payment but that I could not guarantee anything. Joe took that as the word of a woman whom he began to like and trust even from the first day of our relationship.

We reminisced. Joe was obviously enjoying the evening. He remembered our first meeting had been while I and other FBI agents searched the hotel room that was his gambling "back office." Joe recalled that I had called him "Mr. Eto" and had treated him with respect. "Funny thing," he said, "whenever the Chicago police arrested me, they had been rough and crude, and one even had said, 'Well, I got you now.' You, Elaine, were never arrogant, and I could see you were running the show and that impressed me."

Life is funny sometimes. There are people who think I am one arrogant piece of work. Apparently Joe did not. He had endured 16 years of the United States Witness Protection Program. I was told by one of the national directors of this program that Joe had been the longest participant in the history of Witness Security Program. When he signed on, he understood his job was to work "…until the FBI doesn't need me anymore. I am the property of the FBI. My previous bosses gave me no choice. I now work for you."

The average time anyone is in the WSP is less than three years. Joe's tour of duty was amazing. The inner discipline and personal fortitude to stay in a program that gives a person virtually no direction on how to live his life, other than to not contact previous acquaintances, is unique to Joe. His ability to shift his focus from the action-filled life of a Mob associate and gambler to that of a restaurant owner and a used car entrepreneur enabled him to continue on with his promise to be a witness as long as he was needed. Joe moved on more than one occasion and had to endure leaving behind everything in his newly developed life. This is the reason that most people in the WSP fail; they can't do this once, let alone a few times. The usual cause of failure is contacting an old friend or crony and then being exposed. The other reason for failure is returning to one's old ways, becoming a criminal again.

Joe always had the culture of his Japanese heritage. The inner strength that helped him endure the years as a hobo and migrant worker, and the internment during World War II, prepared him well for this, his greatest challenge. In the end, the strength of his Japanese upbringing and culture, coupled with the ability to accept any circumstance, was his key to survival. Joe's background of independence, ingenuity, and complete mental and emotional control made him the best witness and longest member of the WSP. Joe was the star, and I rode on his coat tails.

This dinner in Hawaii was like Joe's retirement party from the Witness Security Program. He went out with a big bonus. He reconnected with a part of his family and was living in paradise. The "golden years" had come to my friend Joe. He and I knew those "golden years" had turned to shit for his former Outfit bosses — they were either spending them in jail or they were buried six feet under.

Dinner had been magnificent. The four of us relaxed in the glow of the candles and the warm feelings we had for one another. I still felt uncomfortable letting Joe pay for what had to be a very large dinner tab, but after glancing at the bill ever so quickly, he peeled off hundred dollar bills and placed them discreetly in the leather bill holder. Old guys never change. I remembered that he had paid his street tax with hundred dollar bills, slipped under the table at various restaurant meeting places — not that Sammy's Pancake House or Aunt Sarah's Kitchen had much in common with The Canoe.

Both Tom and I thanked Joe and Linda for the great meal and for extending themselves to travel from Oahu to the Big Island just to see us. Joe then said, "I will forever be grateful to you, Elaine, for all you have done for me. For all these years, you have been my friend and one of the few people I have ever trusted." It was a speech of only two sentences, but it was given with such warmth and love that to have made it longer or more eloquent would have not made a difference.

Joe was a man of few words and a man who relied on no one else to make his decisions. I had studied him, watching him interact for 15 years with numerous federal prosecutors, at least 50 FBI agents, 20 police detectives, and countless U.S. Marshals. I had written down and then dictated each word he had spoken. His manner was always the same. He listened to what they said in a concentrated, focused way. When he was debriefed or prepped for trial, he noticed and sensed things about the men and the lone other woman (a federal prosecutor). He exercised all the skills he had developed as a runaway son at the age of 14, a migrant farm worker, a worker on Cannery Row, a bum riding the rails of western America, and a Japanese American who had been interned in Idaho during World War II. He was wary of everyone. He was a man of the streets who was very, very street smart. Joe Eto was not only street smart but also gifted. He once explained the logarithm he had devised to code telephone numbers and it left my mind numb and puzzled.

"You had to decode each phone number every time you wanted to call someone?" I had asked him.

"Yeah, sure," he replied.

To me that would have been like trying to solve an algebraic problem each time I made a phone call. For a moment, I thought that I must have been twice as smart as him since I had caught him at his game. Then I checked my thoughts: it wasn't my street smarts that made the federal case against Joe Eto. It all started with my premier informant, Frankie — the first crack in the wall of the fortress of the Chicago Mob.

Linda brought me back to the present. "My father thinks of you as a daughter."

I tried to be as gracious as possible and not start crying, as I mumbled, "Oh, Joe, thank you so much for what you have done for me and how you have always shown me concern and esteem."

We had reached the end. We got up to leave. On the bridge over the koi pond, I hugged Joe again, this time a little more comfortably, and then I hugged Linda. We had allowed ourselves to celebrate for one evening. We had been victorious against all the odds. Joe had made sacrifices unlike anyone I knew. My daughter and husband had given me the freedom to pursue my need to prove I was good enough to be a special agent of the FBI. Both Joe and I were pleased with ourselves and each other. We parted company knowing this might be the last time we would see each other.

Tom and I walked on the beach, heading back to our hotel room. Once again we held hands. We said nothing for a time — just absorbing the night, the ocean, and thoughts of our dinner with Joe. Then Tom broke our silence and said, "Joe is really grateful to you. It was a wonderful thing that you kept your word, tried your best, and were able to get the money for him."

"Yeah, I guess he is. He deserved a lot more. How much can you pay a person for giving up his life?" I whispered.

"Well, honey, you didn't force him to do that," Tom corrected.

"I know, I know," I replied very softly. I snuggled against his arm and smiled. I knew I just wanted to be quiet and return to being a wife, a mother, and of course, a fashionista. Damn. Joe hadn't even noticed how exceptionally cool I had dressed for that night, but neither had my husband.

- EPILOGUE -

"Hey, what the heck," was a cliché Joe used, either as an introduction or as a conclusion to a topic. He'd say, "Hey, what the heck," and he would flip his hand in a dismissive fashion; usually this hand held a cigarette between his first and second fingers. What Joe meant when he said, "Hey, what the heck," was "I had no other choice." "It was the best option." "Those were the best odds available." "It's no use crying over spilled milk." "I couldn't stop myself." Or, "It's just who I am, take it or leave it."

During my 17-year relationship with Ken Eto, I often said, "Hey, what the heck, I had to do it!" By that, I mean the countless personal matters I tackled for him in order to ease his transition into his new life. Two legal arrangements I took care of for him were selling his nightclub and distributing the funds to pay his mortgage and debts and arranging a quiet divorce from his wife Mary Lou. These tasks went well beyond the usual things an FBI agent do for a witness.

I could have passed Joe off to another agent when I was promoted to supervisor in 1986. By then I would have felt as if I was giving up my child up for adoption. No one would have known him the way I did or have been able to care for him the way I could.

In 1998, Joe traveled with the U.S. Marshals to Hammond, Indiana, to testify against Nick Guzzino, northwest Indiana's Outfit boss. I met Joe at the courthouse there. One of the marshals took me aside and told me that when they went to pick him up, they saw he was living a very impoverished life.

It broke my heart. I immediately went back to the office and did the paperwork to begin subsistence payments for Joe. As long as the FBI needs a witness, they will make sure that person can stay positive and healthy. The U.S. Marshals were to provide the situation in which they could stay alive. The FBI could not turn its back on this loyal witness of 15 years.

I then went to Mitchell Mars, Chief of the Organized Crime Section in Chicago's United States Attorney's Office, and begged him to let me state that the government did not foresee any future testimony for Ken Eto. That statement would allow me to write Joe up for a lump-sum payment from the Department of Justice. Mitch agreed that Joe had paid his dues, and if needed, the prosecutors would have to eat that[78] when they put him on the stand.

My write-up justifying this payment took me a Sunday evening, sitting at my dining room table. The words, sentences, and paragraphs that told about the extraordinary information and testimony Ken Eto had divulged just flowed through my fingertips and onto the page with an ease that nothing else I have written before or since has.

The justification for the lump-sum payment went up through the chain of command in Chicago and only one boss commented, "Isn't he kind of old to be getting this much money?" The response I gave him was, "Isn't that known as age discrimination?"

Apparently, FBI headquarters thought they were getting off cheap, [79] because within two weeks the funds were in Joe's hands, and he called to tell me, "All of my worries are over. I can live the life I want." And with that, and without my knowledge, he left the witness protection program and moved to Hawaii to live with his daughters, two of which I never knew he had. Hey, what the heck, Joe?

As a youngster I had been a potential abduction victim. This chilling experience caused me to be alert to car makes, models, and license plates. I was also intrigued by the aura of the glamour of the Outfit. As a teenager I had been fascinated with organized crime news, and for fun my friends and I would sneak into a deserted mansion on the shores of Lake Michigan. The house, which was surrounded by a thick tangled and overgrown wooded area, was rumored to be Al Capone's hideout.

As a FBI agent I had been fortunate to investigate organized crime cases, and then with amazing luck, have "one-on-one tutoring" from Joe about the Chicago Outfit. With the information he imparted, I was able to pass along these meticulously recalled facts and intelligence to other agents. They then, with numerous other informants and witnesses, along with countless bright and driven prosecutors, have since 1983 devastated the Chicago syndicate; Chicago's evil judicial system; Chicago's corrupt politicians; and Chicago's degenerate police department.

Today, if Joe were still alive, I am sure he and I could stand on top of the Willis Tower and scream at the top of our lungs, "Hey, what the heck, you gave us no choice!"

- In Memoriam -

Upon his death in 2004, Joe's family held a memorial service for him as they scattered his ashes over the windy Pacific shore of California. They asked that I say a few words. I will never forget what I said because it was something from my heart that I wanted everyone to know.

"Few people realize or recognize the determination and bravery it takes for a man to turn his back on his wife, home, friends, way of life, and the city in which he lived and worked for 40 years. It is a rare person who can sustain the pledge he made; that he would testify against his former friends and associates, each and every time he was asked — whether it was one year or 17 years later. This is what Ken "Joe" Eto did.

There is no medal the Department of Justice awards to men such as he, because there have been none as loyal and truthful as he was. For you, the sons and daughters, aunts and uncles, nieces and nephews, brothers and sisters, Ken Eto has brought honor to you.

Please delight with me in all he accomplished. Please be thankful to him for the fortitude and perseverance he showed through the hardships of loneliness and poverty. Because of Ken Eto, life in Chicago can be lived more freely, more safely, and with the justice America promises each one of us."

- JOE'S ACCOMPLISHMENTS -
IMPACT ON THE CHICAGO MOB

I.   Within a day of being shot, Eto was presented photographs and names of individuals known to the Chicago FBI as possibly being involved with organized crime. It was explained to Eto that if he knew or had met any of these individuals, he should indicate such to the interviewing agents. These individuals would be recorded in the FBI files as people known by Eto to be organized crime members or associates in Chicago. Eto agreed to this procedure and stated as follows:

Name	Remarks
Tony Accardo	Boss of bosses (deceased).[80]
Joseph Aiuppa	Boss of bosses.
Harry Aleman	Street boss and a notorious killer.
Joe Amato	Known to Eto as "Black Joe."
Don Angelini	Introduced Eto to attorney Sam Banks.
Joe Arnold	Made member and right-hand man to Joseph DiVarco.
Dominic Blasi	
Herbert Blitzstein	
Louis Briatta	Known by Eto as a Rush Street liquor store owner.
Frank Buccieri	
Marshall Caifano	Made member and money man for Las Vegas.
Frank Calabrese	Made member and boss of near South Side of Chicago.
Phil Caliendo	

Tom Campione	
Jasper Campise	Made member.
Jackie Cerone	Made member and underboss to Tony Accardo, et al.
Anthony Cirignani	Known to Eto as "Tony Juliano." Made member.
George Colucci	
Dominic Cortina	Known to Eto through Angelo LaPietra. Made member.
Tony Crissie	Juice loan operator and president of a bank that the Outfit controlled.
Willie Daddano	Known to Eto as Willie "Potatoes."
Tony D'Antonio	Known by Eto as an individual who had been killed.
Jimmy D'Antonio	Known by Eto as a possible driver for Joe Accardo, and described as a tall man.
John D'Arco	Known by Eto as constantly being at racetracks in the Chicago area. City official.
Louis DeRiggi	Known by Eto as someone who had possibly been shot in the head.
George Dicks	
Joe DiVarco	Street boss of Chicago's north side (Rush Street).
Allen Dorfman	Explained by Eto as having met only once. Union contact and money man behind Las Vegas.
Tony Eldorado	Known to Eto as "Tony Pine."

Chuckie English	Made member of the Mob's western suburban area.
George Erckman	Known to Eto as "the jeweler."
John Fecarotta	Known to Eto as "Big John," who had a justifiable homicide rap through a shooting at one of Eto's games years ago.
Joe Ferriola	Underboss.
Sidney Finzelbar	Degenerate gambler.
Albert Frabotta	Known to Eto as "Obbie."
Nicholas Garambone	Known to Eto as "Mousie."
John Gattuso	
August Giovenco	Known to Eto as "Gus." Made member.
Joel Glickman	Known to Eto by reputation only.
Joe Glimco	Described by Eto as a taxicab union man.
Joe Grieco	Made member.
Angelo Imparata	Described by Eto as skinny and small.
Rocky Infelice	Made member and powerful underboss.
Ronald Jarrett	
William Joyce	Described by Eto as only a possible acquaintance.
Irv Kahn	
Joe Barbara	Described by Eto as having returned to Buffalo, New York.
Angelo LaPietra	Made member and boss of Chicago's South Side.

Jimmy LaPietra	Made member and right-hand man of his brother.
Robert Lewis	Known by Eto by reputation only as having a reputable loan service.
Sam Lisciandrello	
Frank Loverde	
Leo Manfredi	Known to Eto as "Big Leo."
Pat Marcy	Described by Eto as "connected" with John D'Arco.
Jimmy Martin	
Willie Messino	Made member.
Nick Nitti	Described by Eto as the "old man" at the Nitti Travel Agency.
Dominic Nuccio	Known to Eto as "Libbie."
Ron O'Hara	Known by Eto as a policeman and a "money man."
Sam Pesoli	Known by Eto as a policeman and as "Blackie."
Don Peters	Known by Eto as a "union guy."
Leonard Gianola	Known to Eto as "Needles."
Butch Petrocelli	Made member and street boss of the west side (deceased).
Al Pilotta	Known by Eto by reputation only as a one-time South Side boss.
Ben Policheri	
Bernard Posner	Known to Eto as "P.P. Posner." Gambling operator.
Mike Posner	

Rocky Pranno	Described by Eto as a "Stone Park guy."
Sam Rosa	Known to Eto as "Slicker Sam."
Frank Schweihs	Known to Eto as "Frankie."
Chris Serritella	Described by Eto as a gambler who is always on the "short end" in his gambling.
Moe Shapiro	
Vince Solano	North side boss and president of a local chapter of the AFL-CIO.
Joe Spadavecchio	Known to Eto as Joe "Spa."
Tony Spilotro	Made member and in charge of Las Vegas.
Mike Spilotro	Known by Eto to be the brother of Tony Spilotro.
Joe Testa	Described as having been introduced to Eto through Joe Stein.
Albert Tocco	Known by Eto by reputation only.
Frank Tornabene	Known to Eto as "Frankie T."
Joe Varelli	Known to Eto as Johnny "Bug."
Nick Visco	
Angelo Volpe	
Irv Weiner	
Frank Zizzo	Known to Eto as "Cease."

II. Eto then provided a detailed description of the role and status in the Mob hierarchy of each of the above 85 individuals and how they brought money into the coffers of the Mob.

252

III. He gave the United States Justice Department the "Rosetta Stone" of how the syndicate worked in Chicago, such as who the overall bosses of the city were, along with the boss and underbosses of each geographical territory or crew.

Information from Eto's personal observations and experiences over more than 38 years was able to establish that the Chicago syndicate was in fact "an enterprise" and was justifiably prosecutable under the most powerful statute in United States law, the Racketeering Influenced and Corrupt Organizations Act (RICO) (U.S. Code Title 18, Section 1961).

IV. On April 22, 1985, while wearing a hood so that he could not be identified by his neighbors in the new town where he had been relocated, Eto testified before the President's Commission on Organized Crime. During this testimony, Joe explained how the City of Chicago was divided into geographical areas under designated bosses.

He then testified that north side crew boss Vince Solano's position as president of the Local Laborer's Union was nothing but a front for his Mob activities. He further stated that Babe DeMonte, another north side crew made member, who was a business agent for the same union, had laughed and said "no" when Eto asked if he ever went to the job sites. His testimony went on to confirm the sham positions that Salvatore Gruttadauro and John Fecarotta held in Chicago unions as well.

This testimony began the civil proceedings that resulted in the Teamsters Union (AFL-CIO), the strongest and largest union in the United States, being taken over by government-appointed trustees and the firing of all Mob officials.

V. On December 17 and 18, 1985, Eto testified in the case of United States v. Carl Angelo DeLuna, Joseph John Aiuppa, John Phillip Cerone, Joseph Lombardo, Anthony John Spilotro, Angelo LaPietra, Milton John

Rockman, John Joseph Balistrieri, Joseph Phillip Balistrieri, and Frank Peter Balistrieri.

This case charged DeLuna, the boss of Kansas City; Aiuppa, the boss of Chicago; Cerone, the citywide underboss of Chicago; Lombardo, a territorial boss of Chicago; LaPietra, a territorial boss of Chicago; Rockman, boss of Cleveland; and Frank Balistrieri, boss of Milwaukee, and his two sons, with skimming money from the profits of the Mob-controlled casinos in Las Vegas.

Eto was able to personally identify and articulate particular business dealings he had conducted in furtherance of the Mob's success with Aiuppa, Cerone, Lombardo, LaPietra, and Balistrieri. He cited them as all being part of the same organization and all co-conspirators in this enterprise called the Mob.

In his testimony, Eto stated that he purchased Lefty Rosenthal's[81] apartment overlooking Lake Michigan, with all its furnishings, when Lefty moved to Las Vegas to watch the Mob's skimming interests there. In fact, he gave the money he owed Lefty for the apartment and furnishings to Michael Spilotro to give to Tony Spilotro, already in Vegas with the purpose to develop and control the Mob's interests.

At the end of the government's questioning, for the first time since the trial began 52 days before, all defense attorneys agreed to forgo cross-examining this devastating government witness. To that date, 71 witnesses had been called by the prosecutors and Eto was the first one to be let off the hook and allowed to avoid the vicious cross-examination.

On January 21, 1986, Aiuppa, Cerone, and LaPietra all gave up the fight and pled guilty to concealment of ownership of the casinos. On March 27, 1986, Aiuppa and Cerone were sentenced to 28 1/2 years' incarceration. LaPietra was sentenced to 16 years' incarceration. He died shortly after his release in 1999.

VI. The wiretap of the phones of Rocco Infelice, Louis Marino, Salvatore DeLaurentis, Dominic Cortina, and Donald Angelini by a brilliant young agent is the next most significant accomplishment of Joe's cooperation. This young agent took Joe's new insight into the Ferriola group and, together with day and night surveillances and the use of every other witness and informant he could find in the FBI, wrote an affidavit that in 119 pages convinced the Chief Judge of the Northern District of Illinois that the Ferriola crew was using preindentified telephone numbers to conduct the illegal business of the enterprise called the Outfit.

Joe's information gave the agent the names of the members, the chain of command, the various means of support (illegal activities), and the knowledge that gambling was the Outfit's largest source of income for this crew. Furthermore, it included Eto's statement that the Chicago Outfit controls all illegal gambling in the Chicago area through "street tax." If you do not pay street tax to the Mob, you have two choices. Give your business to the Mob or be killed. There is no gambling operation in Chicago that does not pay "tax" to the Outfit. They have a monopoly on vice.

This wiretap led to the eventual indictment of: Rocco Infelice, Edward Stevenson, Louis Marino, Robert Covone, Salvatore DeLaurentis, Michael Sarno, Robert Bellavia, Michael Zitello, Robert Salerno, Harry Aleman, William Jahoda, William DiDomenico, Robert Garrison, James Coniglio, Thomas McCandless, Paul Spano, James S. Nicholas, Ronald DeRosa, Frank Maltese, and James Damopoulos.

They charged the group with extortion and the murder of Anthony Reitinger, who had come to Eto for protection but had not listened to his advice. The bosses had asked Eto to tell Reitinger to comply with their requests, and he communicated to Reitinger that "his non-compliance would cause him physical harm." This same crew had extorted and murdered Robert Plummer and Hal Smith, both gambling operators who owed street taxes to the organization.

What really had pissed off Infelice, et al, was that in a search warrant executed by local law enforcement, $600,000 was seized from Hal Smith's house. This meant Smith's sports booking business was enormous and he was cheating them out of their 50 percent.

During the trial, the government went on to cite more than 25 different extortion victims. The subjects were also charged with bribery and income tax evasion. To make the indictment sting even more, the government added the seizure of Infelice's and DeLaurentis' homes in addition to any and all bank accounts.

Joe called Rocky Infelice and Louis Marino "old friends." When Joe was escorted into the Chicago federal courtroom, all three parties exchanged waves as Joe walked up to the witness stand. After the friendly wave, he then got down to business and clearly stated that he understood that he had to pay $5,000 a month to Joe Ferriola through Infelice in order to operate his gambling business. He fully realized that if he didn't obey, it would mean his death. He elaborated on the more than 30 years he had worked for the syndicate with Ferriola and alongside Infelice and Marino, both of whom he knew to be murderers.

The jury found the 20 defendants guilty. On August 19, 1993, Judge Ann Williams sentenced Infelice to 63 years in prison (release date 2056) and the forfeiture of various assets that were worth $1.58 million, along with $3 million in cash found in bank accounts or his house.

On subsequent dates the judge sentenced Marino to 28 1/2 years in prison (release date 2021) and DeLaurentis to 18 1/2 years in jail.

All the other defendants were found guilty by the jury or pled and testified against their bosses and fellow Mob associates. They have each served a variety of sentences of incarceration.

VII.   The indictment was returned on April 25, 2005, a year after Ken Eto's death, and 22 years after he became the FBI's top witness. But this indictment charged Chicago mobsters as never any federal indictment had before. The 14 defendants were accused of committing 18 murders and one attempted murder from 1970 to 1986 to further the organization's business. Tom Bourgeois, a now retired FBI case agent for the above indictment, code named "Family Secrets," was quoted as saying, "…Eto gave the FBI its first real insight into the importance of Calabrese, and we then targeted him."[82]

This case indicted the criminal enterprise called the Chicago Outfit, also known as the Chicago Syndicate or the Chicago Mob, with conspiracy, including committing murder and attempted murder to further the Outfit's illegal activities, such as sports bookmaking, illegal gambling businesses, and loan sharking, and using extortion, threats, violence, and intimidation to protect the enterprise from law enforcement.[83]

In this groundbreaking indictment, the Mob members charged were:

1. Joseph Lombardo, made member, murderer, and territorial boss, 75 years old when indicted.
2. James Marcello, made member and murderer.
3. Michael Marcello, made member and murderer.
4. Nicholas Ferriola, son of Joe Eto's boss, Joe Ferriola, who had passed on his legacy to his son. He was accused of furthering the enterprise by meeting Frank Calabrese while he was in prison and then relaying the boss' instructions to other members. These actions helped further the Outfit's murders and its illegal businesses.
5. Joseph Venezia, committed crimes on behalf of the Outfit. (Detailed activities disclosed during the trial.)
6. Thomas Johnson, committed crimes on behalf of the Outfit. (Detailed acts not disclosed until the trial.)
7. Dennis Johnson, committed crimes on behalf of the Outfit. (Details not provided in the indictment.)

8. Frank Saladino, made member and murderer, who was found dead the day the agents arrived at his "rent by the week" motel to arrest him.

9. Frank Schweihs, made member and murderer, who committed crimes on behalf of the Outfit. (Activities not detailed until the trial.)

10. Nicholas Calabrese, made member, murderer, and brother of Frank Calabrese, who became the government's star witness.

11. Anthony Doyle, retired Chicago Police officer, who assisted Frank Calabrese by passing on information regarding the murder investigation of John Fecarotta, which was committed by Frank Calabrese and Nicholas Calabrese, along with other illegal acts detailed in the indictment.

12. Michael Ricci, retired Chicago Police officer, who also assisted Frank Calabrese while he was incarcerated by passing messages from him to other Outfit members, along with collecting extortion money and providing false information to the FBI.

13. Frank Calabrese Sr., made member, murderer, and even though incarcerated, through Ferriola, Doyle, Ricci, and others, continued to rule the criminal activities of the Outfit. Frank died in federal custody in December 2012.

14. Paul Schiro, made member and murderer, who also committed other crimes on behalf of the Outfit. (Detailed acts revealed during the trial.)

Murder Victims In Family Secrets Case

The men and one woman executed by the Chicago Outfit were killed in a variety of violent, cruel, and degrading ways. The reason for their murders was usually to protect the criminal enterprise's actions but most of all because of greed. There is nothing honorable about anything the Outfit does. If the bosses think you are a snitch and that will threaten their bottom line — you are dead. If they think you are not giving them their cut — you are dead.

The 18 murder victims were: Michael Albergo, Daniel Seifert, Paul Haggerty, Henry Cosentino, John Mendell, Donald Renno, Vincent Moretti, William Dauber, Charlotte Dauber, William Petrocelli, Michael Cagnoni, Nicholas D'Andrea, Richard Ortiz, Arthur Morawski, Emil Vaci, Anthony Spilotro, Michael Spilotro, and John Fecarotta.[84]

VIII.   In May 2002, William Hanhardt pled guilty to racketeering, actually running a sophisticated jewelry theft ring, for the benefit of the Chicago syndicate. At the age of 72, he was sentenced to serve 16 years in federal prison, had his police pension revoked, and was forced to forfeit $4.8 million to the government (release date 2018).

From 1953 to 1986, Hanhardt was a Chicago Police officer. When Ken Eto was shot on February 10, 1983, Hanhardt was the Chief of Detectives; as protocol, he was immediately notified of the spectacular bungled shooting. If Eto had not demanded the presence of the FBI, Hanhardt may have found a way to complete the job.

With the first confirmed information of someone (Eto) who had actually paid Hanhardt for a "fixed" murder case, the FBI began its long investigation into the highest-ranking Chicago Police officer ever convicted of a federal crime.

Co-defendants of Hanhardt were three "made" guys, Paul Schiro, again indicted in the "Family Secrets" case; Sam DeStefano, a brutal torturer and murderer for the Outfit; and Guy Altobello, a member of Rocco Infelice's crew. Hanhardt had a working relationship with Tony Spilotro that dated back to the 1960s. According to Frank Cullotta, another Mob witness, "he figured out the Spilotro-Hanhardt relationship after he pulled a spectacular robbery in the Mallers Building. It was an inside job, a $500,000 score."[85] While writing this book, due to sitting on a wiretap for two months and hearing George Erkman and his cronies bullshit and knowing his contacts on the phone or in his office, I figured out that the inside man was Erkman, a jeweler who had his office at 5 South Wabash, Chicago, Illinois.

IX. Eto's testimony on November 16, 1989, was short and simple. It pertained to how he got rid of his parking tickets (each time he'd hand over approximately 20 to 30) without having to pay for them and without any penalties for not handling them within the time given by the city.

His testimony was given in the trial against James DeLeo, the secretary of the Chief Judge of Traffic Court for the City of Chicago, James LeFevour. DeLeo had been charged with being the "bagman" for Judge LeFevour. LeFevour had already been disgraced by being found guilty in the first of the string of prosecutions that had rumbled through the federal courthouse in Chicago. This news was heard around the United States as evidence of how shockingly corrupt the judicial systems of Cook County and Chicago were. This testimony demonstrated the Outfit's close link to the judges in Cook County.

Eto testified that his Mob attorney, Samuel V.P. Banks, had years before advised him on how to "dispose" of his pesky parking violations. Banks also had Judge LeFevour's son, Terrence, as his law partner. Finally, Banks represented Judge LeFevour in federal court and, knowing already Banks was a doofuss of an attorney, it was no surprise when LeFevour was found guilty of violating the racketeering statute and filing false income tax returns. Former Judge LeFevour was sentenced to 12 years in prison.

Surprisingly, LeFevour's secretary DeLeo was found not guilty in federal court, but he later pleaded guilty to misdemeanor income tax evasion. This is the only federal case against the Mob in which the defendant won.

X. On March 18, 1985, Joe extracted a small amount of revenge against Joseph "Caesar" DiVarco, the Mob underboss who had set him up to be murdered. After more than 40 years of paying DiVarco between 30 to 60 percent of every penny Eto earned, DiVarco had agreed with Vince Solano's paranoia and assisted him in Eto's attempted assassination. To extract his revenge, all Eto had to do was describe his relationship with DiVarco, the set-up for attempted murder, and DiVarco's status in the Chicago syndicate. DiVarco had already been charged and tried in federal court and at the age of 73 was sentenced to 10 years in prison and fined $60,000 in court costs. Along with him that day, Ronnie Ignoffo also was sentenced as being a participant in the illegal gambling and extortionate enterprise.

So while DiVarco was ensconced in his prison cell, I was the one who decided to mess with him, and I requested the President's Commission on Organized Crime to order DiVarco to appear before them. I told Joe that being transferred from one federal prison to another, across the United States to Washington, D.C., was a nightmare of an experience for a prisoner. In this case, it was a death sentence. Joseph "Caesar" DiVarco died in transit.

XI. On July 4, 1985, Joe once again earned some sense of retribution when he testified in federal court during the sentencing phase of a case the government brought against Joe Arnold and Joe Grieco. Both were accused of attempting to bribe a federal grand juror. Joe's testimony reiterated how Arnold had called him on numerous occasions when either Vince Solano or Joseph DiVarco, the bosses, wanted to meet him. Arnold's last call to Eto was to set up the time and place he was to pick up his two designated killers, Gattuso and Campise. Essentially, although not charged, both DiVarco and Arnold were guilty of conspiracy to commit murder. Sadly, the government had not tried them for that, so the judge sentenced each Outfit "worker" to five years of incarceration.

XII. You don't get any higher than "The Commission" of La Cosa Nostra. Don't get me wrong, the New York mobsters did not kill, torture, or have better control of their politicians than the Chicago Outfit — their playground was just a little larger.

On December 21, 1988, Joe testified in the government's case United States v. International Brotherhood of Teamsters, Chauffeurs, Warehousemen and Helpers of America, AFL-CIO. The government was out to take over the AFL-CIO, and Joe testified about the Chicago Mob's involvement in the unions and the pervasive use of these positions to further their own illegal activities. As part of that testimony, he read a list of every high-ranking mobster in the United States. He went on to name the top mobster boys from New York City.

XIII. From the beginning of our relationship with Joe, he told us that George Ryan was a crook. There was nothing in 1983 that we could pin on the political nobody. But that small seed of suspicion stayed with Ray, a squad mate of mine. Over the years, and many cases later, Ray started hearing more and more about Ryan being a crook and a buddy of organized crime.

He started investigating and began uncovering some amazing things, particularly after a truck dropped a brake pad that ripped into the gas tank of a van carrying a family of five children. The van caught on fire and before the father driving could pull over, the van became engulfed in flames. All five of the parents children were killed. The public outcry over this tragic accident focused on Ryan, who was then Secretary of State. When it was found that the truck driver who caused the accident had purchased his commercial driver's license and had not attended truck-driving school, the proverbial "shit hit the fan" for Ryan, who now had become Governor of the State of Illinois. This opened up the Secretary of State's license facilities to intensive examination. The United States Attorney's Office indicted Governor George Ryan; a jury convicted him and in 2006 sentenced him to six and a half years in jail.

XIV.   The FBI had little idea that there had been a deal brokered between the On Leong Chinese Merchants Association and the Outfit's 26th Street crew, Frank Calabrese and his murdering boys. This deal had been brokered years before by Joe Eto to provide the Chinese some protection from the constant police raids that were destroying the pleasure of gambling in their authentically constructed pagoda building, placed in the center of Chinatown in Chicago.

The On Leong had to pay street tax to the 26th Street crew and an additional fee to keep the police off their backs. That was until the FBI started investigating this arrangement. Tangled up in the web were two evil syndicate politicians, Pat Marcy and Fred Roti, both made members. The investigation was successful in convicting numerous Chinese On Leong leaders for operating an illegal gambling business and dealing in narcotics (heroin).

In 1988, the U.S. government seized the On Leong Merchants Association Building, valued at more than $3 million, but allowed the On Leong to manage and use it free of charge until it was purchased in 1993 and renamed the Pui Tak Center.

- END NOTES -

[1] Ackerman, Thomas H., FBI Careers the Ultimate Guide to Landing a Job as One of America's Finest, JIST Publishing, 2006, page 51.

[2] United States District Court data found on the internet site of same.

[3] My original notes indicated the word NOT so I got off the hook. Wringer did forge her name on over $500,000 worth of stock purchases.

[4] 4. Press Release, U.S. Attorney's Office, Northern District of Illinois, April 25, 2005, "14 Defendants Indicted for Alleged Organized Crime Activities; "Chicago Outfit" Named as Rico Enterprise in Four-Decade Conspiracy Alleging 18 Mob Murders and 1 Attempted Murder. Seven defendants allegedly committed or agreed to commit murders between 1970-1986"

[5] 5 Roemer, William, R. Jr., The Enforcer Spilotro: the Chicago's Mob's Man over Las Vegas, Ivy Books, 1994, page 28.

[6] See Appendix for arrest reports of Eto's bosses.

[7] See Appendix for arrest report of Ken Eto.

[8] "Chicago Tribune", "Mob Generation Gap Endangers Tony Accardo and His Pals", 5/1/1977.

[9] United States Criminal Code, Title 18, Section 1955, Interstate Gambling.

[10] "A Short Chronology of Japanese American History", adapted from Japanese American History: An A-to-Z Reference from 1868 to the Present, Edited by Brian Niiya, New York: Facts-on-File, 1993.

[11] Internment Centers were Manzanar and Tule Lake, California; Amache, Colorado; Minidoka, Idaho; Topza, Utah; Heart Mountain, Wyoming; Rohwer and Jerome, Arkansas; and Gils River and Poston, Arizona.

[12] Hill Street Blues, National Broadcasting Company (NBC) weekly television series about police that aired from 1981-1987. Described as a "haven of controlled chaos in a crime infested racially torn ghetto located in an industrial city".

[13] Later I would learn that just having your gun displayed with arrestees around could be dangerous. I was out with Tom for dinner on a Saturday night when he got a call of a police shooting. Tom was retired and working for the CPD as the Chief Investigator for OPS and as such went to all of the police involved shootings, I mean all of them. I was there so I went with him to Area 1 where a prisoner in custody of the detective had taken the dick's gun discharged it once and then swallowed the barrel and blew his brains out. The other detectives responding also shot him after the prisoner had K5'd himself. Tom told me that the CPD didn't have a policy for not having your weapon on when in the presence of a prisoner or an arrestee. It seemed a prisoner at Area 4, years earlier and Area 4 had a policy that an officer was to not have their weapon in their possession when handling a prisoner who was not cuffed or secured. Tom was not sure why Area 4's experience and rules weren't shared by the rest of the CPD.

[14] Idaho Title 18-3127. Crimes and Punishments, Chapter 31, "Receiving or Possessing Fraudulently Obtained Goods or Services," False Pretenses, Cheats and Misrepresentations.

[15] Idaho Title 18-3127. Crimes and Punishments, Chapter 31, "False Pretenses, Cheats and Misrepresentations." Punishment will be a fine and up to a year in jail for up to $1,000. Punishment will be a fine and up to five years in jail, or both for up to $50,000.

[16] United States Federal Criminal Code, Title 18, Section 1952.

[17] United States Federal Criminal Code, Title 18, Section 1955.

[18] United States Federal Criminal Code, Title 18, Section 371.

[19] Over the years, there have been countless times when people have said that to me. I have never known what to reply. It would have been snotty to say, "Well, do I look like an FBI agent should look? How would you imagine a female FBI agent should look? Do I look okay?" I can only imagine the self-conscious feelings of my fellow female agents, who may be a little overweight or fit less into the all-American girl standard of acceptable looks. I once had an instructor tell me that I should discourage a Hispanic female agent from looking too ethnic by keeping her hair long.

[20] Black P Stone Nation, a.k.a. Black Panther Party, a communist political and black activist party founded by street gangs with a violent proclivity. In 1969 alone, four members/leaders were killed by Chicago Police. They were Larry Roberson, Spurgeio Winters, Fred Hampton, and Mark Clark. Cleaver, Eldridge, Soul on Fire, Word Books, 1978.

[21] Chicago Tribune, John O'Brien, "U.S. probes cop-hood ties," November 28, 1974.

[22] Chicago Tribune, "Doing a number on the Mob," April 21, 1974.

[23] Fixer attorneys were used for their ability to bribe Cook County Judges, not their legal abilities.

[24] Cooley, Robert with Hillel Levin, When Corruption Was King, Carroll & Graf Publishers, New York, New York, pages 160, 279

[25] "Making your bones" is a term used by the mobsters to mean, doing your first ordered killing, beating or score. To become a member of the Outfit you had to do at least one ordered hit.

[26] "KSB 210" was the radio room at the FBI office, 219 S. Dearborn. It is staffed 24 hours a day and must have been jumpin' that night.

[27] Larry Bradi was the son of former north side crew member Lawrence "Larry the Hood" Buonaguidi. The old man had died and left behind a son who had become a Chicago cop and was so inept that he was fired from that job. He now dealt kilos of cocaine in the bars of Rush Street. He got away with it because his father was a made guy. Who knows with whom he was sharing a cut of the profit? I had information, but no proof yet that Bradi loaned Eto money for his *bolita* business.

[28] My comment. From interviews with Ken Eto.

[29] My comment. From interviews with Ken Eto.

[30] My comment. From interviews with Ken Eto.

[31] My comment. From interviews with Ken Eto.

[32] My comment. From interviews with Ken Eto.

[33] My comment. From interviews with Ken Eto.

[34] My comment. From interviews with Ken Eto.

[35] My comment. From interviews with Ken Eto.

[36] My comment. From interviews with Ken Eto.

[37] My comment. From interviews with Ken Eto.

[38] My comment. From interviews with Ken Eto.

[39] My comment. Cline later became Superintendent of the Chicago Police Department from 2003 -2007.

[40] My comment.From interviews with Ken Eto.

[41] See United States Department of Justice document – Letter of Immunity – Ken Eto. From the estate of Ken Eto.

[42] My comment. From interviews with Ken Eto.

[43] My comment. From interviews with Ken Eto.

[44] My comment. From interviews with Ken Eto.

[45] My comment. From interviews with Ken Eto.

[46] My comment. From interviews with Ken Eto.

[47] "Administratively pure," in Bureau terms, meant he always followed the rules and regulations to the exact word and felt more at ease in the office than on the street with the thugs.

[48] Allen Dorfman had been convicted of defrauding the Teamsters' pension fund through his company, Amalgamated Insurance. He was the money man, representing the Chicago syndicate's control of the Teamsters' Union. Dorfman used Teamster funds to provide loans to Las Vegas casinos, but he never repaid the Teamsters. This theft of funds forced the casinos to provide a certain portion of the profit, or so-called "skim," to the Chicago Outfit. A large sum.

[49] Dr. George Block, Chief of Surgery at University of Chicago Hospitals, former President of the American College of Surgeons, was also the doctor that eventually did save Tom's life.

[50] The Tylenol murders occurred in 1992, when seven people in the Chicago area died after taking Extra Strength Tylenol capsules that had been laced with cyanide. This was the first incident where the cause of death was deliberate product tampering.

[51] He was talking about Joe Doyle, but I loved that he didn't pronounce his name correctly.

[52] This is infamously known in organized crime circles as the "walk and talk" so that it is impossible to have fixed listening devices. If the conversation is ever found to be recorded, then one of the participants is the "rat" wearing the wire.

[53] This was when all the sweat, work, and headaches of making this case paid off!

[54] Robert Cooley with Hillel Levin, When Corruption was King ,Carroll & Graf, New York, New York, 2004.

[55] Chicago Tribune, "Big drive is readied against the mob," Roger Worthington and Marianne Taylor, February 16, 1983.

[56] Joseph 'Joe Cargo' Valachi (September 22, 1903 – April 3, 1971) was the first Mafia member to publicly acknowledge the existence of the Mafia. He is also the person who made Cosa Nostra (meaning "this thing of ours") a household name.

In October 1963, Valachi (a "soldier" in New York City's powerful Vito Genovese crime family, whose primary "job" within the family was that of a driver) had testified before Senator John L. McClellan's congressional committee on organized crime that the Mafia did exist. Although the low-ranking Valachi's disclosures never led directly to the prosecution of many Mafia leaders, he was able to provide many details of its history, operations, and rituals, aiding in the solution of several uncleared murders, as well as naming many members and the major crime families. The effect of his testimony, which was also broadcast on radio and television and published in newspapers, was devastating for the Mob. After Valachi's testimony, the Mob was no longer invisible to the public eye.

Vito Genovese had apparently ordered Valachi killed (offering $100,000 to anyone who did so) because the powerful Mob boss believed Valachi had betrayed him to the authorities in exchange for a lighter prison sentence, thus violating the strict Mafia oath of Omertà (silence) which traditionally was punishable by death.

[57] William Hanhardt was Chicago's Deputy Superintendent of Police, and Chief of Detectives on February 10, 1980. As protocol, he would have had a report of Eto's shooting on his desk the next morning, if he hadn't been called at home by the "Acting Street Deputy" that very night.

[58] Known as the RICO statute, this was clearly the strongest law passed by the U.S. Congress to enable law enforcement to go after the mob. Prosecutors could charge crimes well after the statute of limitation had expired, to use violations of state laws and to sentence violators from 20 years to life in prison.

[59] Time Magazine, "Big, Bad and Becoming", The Mafia, May 16, 1977.

[60] Bureau talk for turning a person's loyalty from one organization to another; in this case from the Mafia to the FBI.

[61] Personal papers of Eto estate.

[62] Chicago Tribune, "Eto," Henry Wood, July 5, 1983, "…Jasper Campise had been jailed for 2 1/2 months for contempt of court in 1966 when he refused to testify before a Cook County grand jury investigating the murder of a mob associate in the 800 block of North Avenue in Chicago. Dominick Galiano was leaving what police described as a high-stakes poker game when he was shot in the back. Campise and another man were taken into custody when they were caught by police running away from the scene."

[63] Nick DeJohn came from a long line of Mob murder victims. The most recent was his brother, John DeJohn, who had been gunned down because he had been selling cocaine to the whores on Rush Street and it had been bad for business; yet here he was representing one of the men who had been part of the group that had done it.

[64] Journal of American Medical Association, "Fatal Car Trunk Entrapment Involving Children-United States, Feb. 1987-1998. (internet)

[65] Chicago Tribune, "Mob killed 2 out of fear, cops say," John O'Brien and Ronald Koziol, July 17, 1983.

[66] Ibid.

[67] The time of death can be calculated by the growth of maggots on a dead body. The more mature the maggot is, the longer the body has been decaying. As the examiners from D.C. were able to tell us, Jasper and John did die on the afternoon of July 12.

[68] Joe used this word frequently. It is a Yiddish word meaning just talking to pass the time, not about anything of great importance, but of many topics.

[69] Every single law enforcement agency had an inferiority complex when it came to dealing with the FBI. You could say hello to someone and they would immediately be on the defensive and think you wanted to put them down or play at being superior. When I became a manager, I would tell agents all the time, "You may be the one and only FBI Special Agent a person ever meets in his life. Make sure you leave that individual with the best possible impression. Make them proud they pay your salary."

[70] The building in which FACES was located was owned by Eto. Solano took over his contract, and the property, 936 North Rush Street, was transferred into the name of Vincent Solano, Jr., an attorney.

[71] The word "crap" was about the most swearing you ever got out of Marc.

[72] Chicago Sun-Times, August 9, 1983, "Mobster's Van Found," photo by Richard Derk.

[73] A court-authorized wiretap, which is difficult to get, a nightmare to manage, and a boring, tedious job to work. Such as the one on George, the jeweler, whose wiretap got me assigned to an organized crime squad to begin with?

[74] Wire rooms were where the monitoring agents sat and waited for incoming or outgoing calls and decided whether to tape them or not. These were usually small rooms manned seven days a week, 24 hours a day, and within a week they turned into smelly, litter-strewn pigsties.

[75] Jasper Campise used to hold card games there and extend juice loans, and Ken Eto picked up Gattuso and Campise from an American Legion Hall. I thought these locations were for the socialization of former military members. Jasper Campise has no record of serving in the Armed Forces. According to www.legion.org, its preamble states the American Legion was chartered by Congress in 1919 as a patriotic veteran organization. Its eligibility requirements are that the person served in one of the seven wars/conflicts listed on the website.

[76] Transcript of Ken Eto, Northwest Hospital, February 10, 1980, courtesy of Eto estate.

[77] Chicago Tribune, January 23, 2005, Rick Jervis and Liam Ford, with Ray Gibson and Art Barum, contributors, "Grand jury lifting veil on unsolved mob hits."

[78] Reveal that the witness had received compensation for his "services."

[79] The rapid approval by FBI headquarters made me upset that I hadn't doubled the amount I requested and then negotiated with D.C. for a lower sum if I had to.

[80] Deceased is marked only when the individual was deceased in 1983.

[81] Lefty Rosenthal was put in charge of the Stardust Casino skim on the recommendation of Chicago's gambling genius, Dominic Angelini. Lefty, while in Las Vegas in the early 1970s, kept an eye on Allen Glick, who was fronting for the Outfit at the Stardust and the Hacienda. Glick had gone to college with one of Frank Balistrieri's sons, who recommended him. Before Glick knew it, he had been made owner of the Stardust Casino and was given a $62.75 million loan from the Teamsters' Union Pension Fund.
Roemer, William, "Man Against the Mob," Ivy Books, New York, New York, 1989, p. 129.

[82] Chicago Sun Times, April 27, 2005, "Secret weapon in war on mob," Mark Brown.

[83] U.S. Department of Justice, United States Attorney, Northern District of Illinois, Press Release, April 25, 2005, "14 Defendants Indicted for Alleged Organized Crime Activities; 'Chicago Outfit' Named as RICO Enterprise in Four-Decade Conspiracy Alleging 18 Mob Murders and 1 Attempted Murder."

[84] U.S. Department of Justice, United States Attorney, Northern District of Illinois, Press Release, April 25, 2005, "14 Defendants Indicted for Alleged Organized Crime Activities; 'Chicago Outfit' Named as RICO Enterprise in Four-Decade Conspiracy Alleging 18 Mob Murders and 1 Attempted Murder."

[85] Chicago Tribune, April 29, 2002, "Former Outfit hit man wishes Hanhardt his best", John Kass.

Made in the USA
Monee, IL
21 September 2021

77660983R20154